ASPECTS OF EARLY EGYPT

ASPECTS OF EARLY EGYPT

EDITED BY

JEFFREY SPENCER

BRITISH MUSEUM PRESS

© 1996 The Trustees of the British Museum

Published in 1996 by British Museum Press
A division of The British Museum Company Ltd
46 Bloomsbury Street, London, WC1B 3QQ

Printed in Great Britain by Henry Ling, The Dorset Press

A catalogue for this book is available from the British Library

ISBN 0-7141-0999-1

Front cover: The ivory label of King Den from Abydos,
British Museum EA 55586

CONTENTS

PREFACE

This volume publishes the papers presented at the international colloquium on Early Egypt, held at the British Museum in July 1993, together with additional contributions on the same theme. The colloquium formed part of the celebrations for the opening of the new 'Raymond and Beverly Sackler Gallery of Early Egypt'. A substantial quantity of recent research is presented, based primarily on the interpretation of material from excavations. Some of this fieldwork is relatively recent and it allows new discoveries to be brought into discussion; in other cases the finds of early excavators have been re-evaluated to produce fresh conclusions. The evidence has been used in various ways to illustrate different aspects of the early culture of Egypt, including chronological division, funerary practices, the evolution of towns and cult centres, together with trade and administration. A range of modern methods has been applied to the treatment of the evidence, incorporating statistics and detailed techniques of chemical analysis, allowing new insight into this fascinating period of Egyptian culture.

In order to avoid considerable duplication, the bibliographic references for all the articles have been amalgamated into a unified bibliography at the end of the volume, an editorial decision which I trust will not unduly offend contributors. Assistance in the preparation of the text and plates has been received from Vivian Davies, Claire Thorn, Janet Peckham and Pat Terry, and the task of seeing the publication through the press has been ably accomplished by Joanna Champness of the British Museum Company.

Very special thanks are due to the Raymond and Beverly Sackler Foundation for making the new gallery possible, and for a generous grant towards the costs of this publication.

Jeffrey Spencer
Assistant Keeper
Department of Egyptian Antiquities
British Museum

AUTHORS' ADDRESSES

Barbara Adams, The Petrie Museum of Egyptian Archaeology, University College London, Gower Street, London, WC1E 6BT, U.K.

Renée Friedman, Department of Near Eastern Studies, University of California at Berkeley, USA.

Stan Hendrickx, Sint-Jansstraat 44, B-3118 Werchter, Belgium.

Karla Kroeper, Staatliche Museen zu Berlin, Preussischer Kulturbesitz, Ägyptisches Museum und Papyrussammlung Schloßstrasse 70, D-14059 Berlin, Germany.

Beatrix Midant-Reynes, Centre d'Anthropologie des Sociétés rurales, UMR 150 du CNRS, 56 rue du Taur, 31000 Toulouse, France.

Naomi Porat, The Israel Geological Survey, 30 Malkhe Street, Jerusalem 95501, Israel.

Stephan J. Seidlmayer, Freie Universität Berlin, Fachbereich Altertumswissenschaften, Ägyptologisches Seminar, Altensteinstrasse 33, 14195 Berlin, Germany.

Margaret Serpico, Department of Egyptology, University College London, Gower Street, London, WC1E 6BT, U.K.

Edwin C. M. van den Brink, Chovevei Tzion Street, 52, 63346 Tel Aviv, Israel.

Elite Graves at Hierakonpolis

Barbara Adams

To the south of the Predynastic Town on the desert edge on the west bank of the Nile at Hierakonpolis there is a pillaged Gerzean cemetery which was excavated in 1899 by F.W. Green (Quibell & Green 1902), just north of the dune wadi and a complex of deflated cobblestone structures (see map in Friedman, this volume, fig.1). He found 150 tombs, all robbed, of which at least five were the larger rectangular type like those found in the separate 'royal' T cemetery at Naqada (Adams 1974b). One of these graves, no.100 (4.5 x 2.0 x 1.5m), dated to Naqada IId by its contents, became renowned as the 'Decorated Tomb' (Case & Payne 1962; Payne 1973; Kemp 1973). It is the only tomb of the Gerzean period known anywhere that had painted decoration on the wall and the half partition. Recently C14 analysis was undertaken on some shells from Tomb 100 which gave the rather early result for the Gerzean of 3685 BC (Burleigh 1983). The decoration of men and animals and what have been identified as river boats was painted in red, white, green and black on a yellow plastered ground. By this time, the decorated marl and crushed calcium carbonate tempered (hard orange) ware pottery with applied plum-red paint designs had gained favour, and the motifs of cabined boats with plant flag devices on the concave decks are paralleled by those in this scene. There is a median red zone on the five white boats with two huts on the centre, and a naos (*sḥ nṯr*, divine booth) at the left end beneath palm fronds. Only one of the five white boats has a group of human beings in association with it, including a figure seated beneath a canopy with other men wearing loin cloths with outstretched arms, perhaps in an act of worship. The sixth black boat, the high stern profile of which would seem to make it unnavigable, has a treble arched, reed funerary tent (*wrmt*) on its deck. The men depicted around the platforms in the rest of the scene are shown taming animals and fighting amongst themselves; one even holds a pear-shaped macehead above a row of bound captives, a precursor to the often repeated scene of the king smiting his enemies in later reliefs. Unfortunately the site of this tomb has not been relocated, the cemetery itself (Locality 33) now being partially under cultivation, so the sadly faded mud plaster fragments now in the Cairo Museum are the only relics of this unique discovery, which has been described as the tomb of one of the legendary kings of Upper Egypt.

On the northern side of the Wadi Abul Suffian, near its mouth, is an imposing structure built of mud-brick which is known as the Fort. Its interior wall is 5m thick and its remaining height is 11m. Because of inscribed fragments of granite found near the niched bastion gateway in the internal wall by Ambrose Lansing of the Metropolitan Museum in 1934 (Lansing 1935), it is usually associated with King Khasekhemwy of the Second Dynasty (ca.2650 BC), and possibly has affinities with the Shuneh structures at Abydos (O'Connor 1989, 1992). Underneath, both within and around this double-walled rectangular edifice (approx. 670m x 570m), is a cemetery (Locality 27) with an area of 68,432 m², which was in use from the Predynastic to the Early Dynastic period. The level of this cemetery is about 1.5m below the foundations of the Fort walls and it has been partially excavated four times. The cemetery enclosed by the Fort was dug in 1905 by John Garstang of Liverpool University [188 graves] (Garstang 1907; Adams 1987); a small area north east of the Fort by H. de Morgan in 1907 [8 graves] (de Morgan 1912; Needler 1984); the area on the south, or wadi side, near the gateway by the aforementioned Lansing [100 graves] in 1934 (Diana Craig Patch in prep.); test excavations within the Fort by Fairservis in 1978 and 1981 [9 graves] (unpublished MSS), and nearby by Hoffman in 1980 [1 grave] (Hoffman (ed.) 1982a). What has been revealed is a cemetery which spreads from near the wadi on the south in the Gerzean (Naqada II) period then under the Fort to the north and beyond in the Protodynastic and Early Dynastic periods. New analyses (Kemp 1963; Adams 1987) of the unpublished work of the early excavators seem to indicate that this was not a cemetery with an elite section, although the one grave uncovered there in 1980 revealed a large Protodynastic pottery coffin and a lid decorated with an incised bovid and a bird (Trad 1992). It is more likely to have been the cemetery which served the general population of the growing town of Nekhen, all buried in fairly shallow graves in a crouched position with a quantity of pottery and not much in the way of exotic funerary goods. The richest Gerzean (Naqada IId1-d2) grave in the Fort cemetery in terms of the quantity of pots was that of a child (no.66), who was also buried with a copper bracelet and fish-hook, a slate palette in the form of a falcon and a bone comb surmounted with an archaic falcon (Nekhen) device.

Between 1979-85, the Hierakonpolis expedition, under the direction of the late Michael Hoffman, undertook excavations in the large cemetery, Locality 6, in the great wadi, or Wadi Abul Suffian, over 2 km from the desert edge. The Locality 6 cemetery (fig.1) is on the west side of the great wadi, flanked by steep sandstone hills to its east and west, occupying a relatively flat terrace of Late Pleistocene silts. The site extends up wadi (southwest) for about 200m and averages about 35m wide (7000m²); surface survey indicates that it contains at least 200 graves. At the down wadi (northeastern) end there are traces of a Predynastic (Naqada I-II) settlement in the form of a concentration of stone and midden, and a small cobblestone structure. This area may relate to the settlement complex of Localities 11 and 14 located on the pediplain of Pleistocene silts across the great wadi to the east, or more likely to similar graveyards (Localities 12 and 13), which are situated on the low hills opposite the north end of the Locality 6 cemetery and much affected by erosion from feeder wadis.

The Locality 6 cemetery had been found and summarily investigated by Green and Garstang, and then gone over by Lansing in 1934; photographs of Tomb 2 were taken by Harry Burton and remain in the Metropolitan Museum's archive. Apart from this cursory archaeological work, there have been at least two phases of pillaging in the cemetery, one of them in the Late or Ptolemaic period, and the other in more recent times (an Arabic coin dating to 1835 was found in the backdirt near Tomb 2), possibly at the end of the last century after the New Kingdom tombs in the nearby Burg el-Hamman were made known by Bouriant (1885) and Renouf (1887), or at the beginning of this century after the work of Green and Garstang, who was certainly concerned that his work had exposed the area to risk (Adams 1995).

At the up wadi, southwest end a large rectangular tomb, no.2 (L: 6.5 W: 2.1 D: 4.15m) was located by previous investigators and re-cleared by the expedition in 1979 (Hoffman (ed.) 1982a: 48-50, pl.I.7). When the loose wind-blown sand which filled the tomb to 1.3m of its mouth was cleared, a three chambered structure was revealed that had been cut through 65cm of silts and wadi gravels 3.50m into the soft basal cross-bedded sandstone and shale which form the basement complex in the Hierakonpolis region. The rectangular hole in the rock is surrounded at the top by a rock-cut step 20cm high, apparently designed to carry the roofing cross timbers (fig.2). The open pit extended down 2.10m into the rock, the walls battering outward at a 4-5° angle. The lower courses of this chamber, where they cut through the rotten shale, were originally covered with a thin coating (1cm) of mud-plaster, a trace of which remained in the area of the north corner. At the western end of this chamber was a rough hewn portcullis of cherty limestone (H: 1.40 W: 0.90 Th: 0.20m). Another almost identical portcullis was found at the eastern corner of the roughly rectangular hole cut 1.75m into the floor at the southeastern end of the main chamber. These portcullises were perhaps meant to close off a second subterranean 'chamber' tunnelled into the soft shale underlying a resistant stratum of sandstone on the east side. This third chamber (1.75m N-S and 1.50m E-S) is angled toward magnetic north and its height dwindles from 1.60m to 0.50m at the far end. This may signify that it was unfinished, or that a second stratum of resistant sandstone under the shale caused building problems. Its roof was partly plastered with mud up to 2cm thick. A roughly shaped sandstone ledge or bench was left extending from the lowest sandstone stratum in the second chamber to the back of this side chamber where the stonecutters left a knob of sandstone (L: 45.0 W: 25.0 H: 20.0cm).

Pottery sherd gleanings including crushed calcium carbonate (hard orange) wares (some comma painted) taken from Tomb 2 in 1979 suggest a Protodynastic (Naqada III) date, but there was an equal admixture of Predynastic black-topped red and straw-tempered pottery and one nearly intact Ptolemaic ribbed vessel (Adams 1982). In 1980 Hoffman determined to elucidate the date of Tomb 2 by controlled excavation of the area north-east and south of the stone-cut structures (Lupton 1981). He had noted a grouping of bovid burials south of Tomb 2, and clearance of the surface around the tomb established the existence of a rain and foot hardened surface into which all the tombs had been cut. In 1980 further clearance to the north and west of Tomb 2 uncovered what appeared to be a line of seven postmoulds

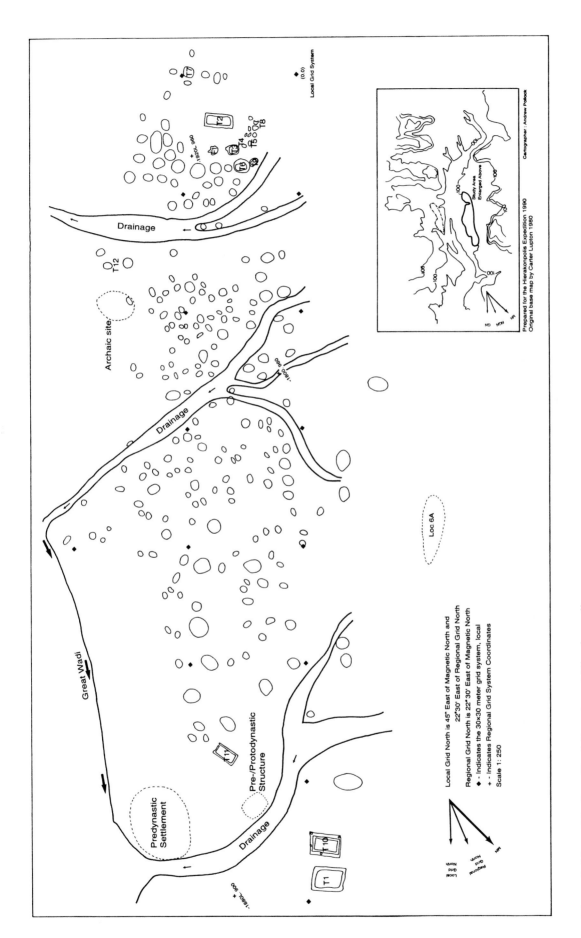

Figure 1 Map of the Locality 6 Cemetery at Hierakonpolis

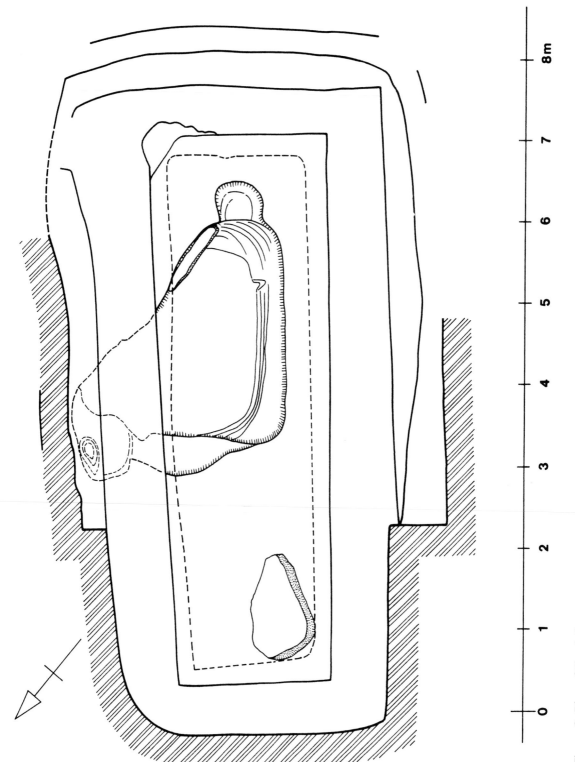

Figure 2 Plan of Tomb 2

cut into the old ground surface (D: 20 to 50cm) at a distance apart varying from 0.60 to 1.30m extending for 6.5m. The last two holes on the southwest side give the line a distinct curve until they are cut into by a disturbance caused by two irregularly shaped pits lying side by side, each with a maximum length of 1.50m with a width of 0.90m and a depth of 0.50m (originally designated as Tomb 8). The northern hole contained the remnants of a small post against one side; neither of the depressions contained any artifacts. Under the old looters' backdirt pile on the east of Tomb 2 there is a large, roughly circular depression (Feature 1 - D: 1.0 D: 0.20-0.40m), which had the remains of two small wooden posts around the perimeter and contained a cache of marine shells. It also contained small pieces of ostrich shell with an incised design, further fragments of which were found in the northwest backdirt and from the fill in Tomb 3. This type of decorated ostrich eggshell water container is known in Nubian contexts (Reisner & Firth *passim*).

The clearance of the old backdirt piles about 6.5m north of Tomb 2 revealed the roughly square depression of a grave which was excavated in 1980 (Lupton 1982: 50-52). This large rectangular grave (Tomb 3) was cut through the silts and wadi gravels until it bottomed out on the sandstone bedrock at about 1.80m below the original surface. At its base it measures 2.50m long by 1.80m wide. Both sherd gleanings from its surface and pottery from the backdirt indicated that the contents of the grave might prove to be early Predynastic. Very little in the grave was *in situ* except for matting linked by twine attached to wooden strips with resin indicating the remains of biers or trays originally laid beneath the burial on its floor. One of the boxes made of matting and wood on the floor had notched arrow shafts of reed (*Phragmites australis*), painted red and buff, laid in it. Other fragments of basket and wood were associated with a transverse chert arrowhead. A black and white porphyry disc mace head was also found partially covered by a few semi-articulated goat bones lying on a mat of *Cyperus alopecroides* on Tamarix wood on the floor (Hoffman (ed.) 1982a: pl.I.8). Other fragments of twigs (*Ficus sycamorus*), leather bound around fibres, wood (*Tamarix*) and matting of interwoven fibre (*Desmostachya bipinnata*) and rushes on linen bound with fibre (*Halfa*) were found in the fill of the tomb, as were scraps of linen. These denote the original presence of a box or basket around the burial as well the presence of container baskets, which are indicated by coiled centres made of palm fibres and date-palm fibre leaflet (*Phoenix dactylifera*) bindings (Hadidi 1982).

Human bone had been found in the backdirt piles but there were only fragments remaining in the fill of the tomb, enough to suggest two individuals, the skull of one, a young man, was partially reconstructed. Excavation of the fill produced numerous pottery sherds which could be wholly or partially reconstructed into nine black-topped red ware [Predynastic Corpus (Petrie 1921) types: B21d, B22a (Hoffman (ed.) 1982: fig.I.14-15), B74a, B78d] and eight straw-tempered vessels [R81N (Hoffman (ed.) 1982: fig.I.16), R85c4, R86D], supplemented by pots from the backdirt pile which probably came from this tomb. One of the reconstructed pots from Tomb 3 is a straw-tempered, brown coated, vertically burnished globular jar with a flat base (Hoffman (ed.) 1982: fig.I.17; Adams & Friedman 1992: fig.10a) with shape parallels among Nubian types (Reisner & Firth 1910). Nearby, but probably also from Tomb 3, was a fragmentary, globular black pottery jar (Adams & Friedman 1992: fig.10c), which is similar to type 5b from Maadi (Rizkana and Seeher 1987), and fragments of an originally lug handled basalt vase were found in the fill and near the tomb. Tomb 3 can be dated to SD 38-40, or Naqada Ic-IIa in Kaiser's Stufen system (Kaiser 1957), i.e. late Amratian early Gerzean. It should be noted that there was only one polished red sherd (C-class) with a white filled incised design in association with Tomb 3 and none from the other excavated tombs nearby. This type of pottery has been found however on the surface of the Locality 6 cemetery and also on the surface of the unexcavated Locality 12 cemetery to the east. This decorated and relatively rare early Predynastic pottery would no doubt have been a target for the looting undertaken in modern times when the distinctive wares became acquirable objects.

Just west of Tomb 3 was a small, oval pit (pl.5a: Tomb 4) about 0.90m long and 0.70m deep which contained a bundled, human male skeleton, with the femurs under the skull (Hoffman (ed.) 1982a: 53-4). The long bones have 'butchering' marks on the surface, possibly indicating deliberate defleshing of the body and the ribs; the vertebrae and the small bones of the hands and feet were poorly represented. Scraps of linen found in the shallow grave suggest that the major bones were wrapped in bandages. No artifacts were found in this secondary burial.

Next to Tomb 4 on the west, another similar pit (L: 1.20 W: 0.75 D: 0.40m) was excavated which contained a multiple dog burial (Tomb 5). No complete skulls were found in the grave, but several had been discovered in the backdirt pile from Tomb 2. The teeth indicate the presence of at least five or six individuals and there were also scraps of linen in the grave.

Just to the north of Tomb 3 was a large crater in the line of tombs north and east of Tomb 2. Excavation of this revealed a grave (Tomb 6) which was rectangular in shape at the base (L: 2.90 W: 1.60) and, unlike Tomb 3, did not extend to the sandstone bedrock but ended in a thin layer of gravelly wadi conglomerate 1.5m from the original surface (Hoffman (ed.) 1982a: 52-3). Again, organic fragments were abundant throughout the fill including pieces of twigs, ropes and basketry and there were numerous small patches of hair, perhaps from the skin which covered the tomb's occupant. A fragment of porphyry disc mace head and 15 transverse, snapped chert arrowheads were found in this tomb, but only two of the reed arrow shafts like those noted in Tomb 3. Human bones were scattered throughout the fill indicating the remains of three individuals, one of them immature. Given the admixture of joining sherds between this grave and Tomb 3, perhaps the maxillary fragment and the femur of this juvenile belong with the similar remains from that Tomb. The contents of Tomb 6 were mostly found in the fill at the bottom of the grave and 10 black-topped red ware and straw-tempered pots were reconstructed and typed [R81N, R86D, R83, B25f, B25h, B77a]. Around the circumference of one of the R81 straw-tempered jars three designs are incised: an animal, and two potmarks in the form of standards and another potmark is incised into the base of a red polished vessel. The ceramic contents of this tomb date it to Naqada Ic-IIa, contemporary with Tomb 3.

A third grave, Tomb 9 (L: 2.00 W: 1.10 D: 1.25m) in a line to the west of Tomb 6 was also excavated in 1980 (Hoffman (ed.) 1982a: 53). This contained sherds of a black-topped red ware vessel [B53c/B68D] and straw-tempered sherds which reconstructed with others from Tomb 6. Apart from these sherd gleanings, there were a couple of fragmentary human long bones in Tomb 9.

It was obvious that all the datable tombs located to the north and west of Tomb 2 were late Amratian/early Gerzean in date, and lines of contemporary tombs were traced on the east almost to a point in line with the central axis of Tomb 2, but not excavated. It seemed that these Predynastic tombs did not extend much further southwest on the other side of Tomb 2, so a bovid burial was selected for excavation on that side in 1980 (Hoffman (ed.) 1982a: 55-6, pl.I.19). Tomb 7 was almost square (2.2m), only 0.75m deep and lined with stone slabs. It produced abundant Bos bones comprising a large (probably male) adult, a smaller (probably female) adult, a juvenile and possibly another, smaller individual, all buried intact (i.e. not defleshed). Under a layer of Halfa grass matting the in situ ribs, scapula and vertebral column of one individual lay in the centre of the grave, partly overlying the forefeet of a second individual. Several of the ribs were encased in a dark organic substance and the excavator, Carter Lupton, suggested that the animal's abdominal cavity had been packed in a early attempt at mummification.

Another animal grave (Tomb 12) about 13m northeast of Tomb 2 was excavated and analysed by the zooarchaeologist, John McArdle, when the expedition returned to Locality 6 in 1982. In this case the 2m long grave contained the bodies of four baboons, including two skulls. Two baboon skulls had been found in the backdirt on the east side of Tomb 2 in 1980 (McArdle 1982). There were ten small sherds in the fill of the tomb and one Palaeolithic flint blade. All the pottery scraps from Tomb 12 are Predynastic and include straw-tempered body sherds, polished red sherds and one white cross-lined ware rim sherd.

Hoffman (1983, 1989) argued that the animal graves in this southwestern part of the wadi cemetery (cattle, baboons, dogs) and random finds of an equid (E. asinus), hippopotamus, elephant and crocodile bones constituted a Protodynastic animal cemetery in association with Tomb 2. He also suggested that the layout of the cemetery at that time represented a microcosm of Upper and Lower Egypt with the stone tomb at the upstream end, surrounded by the abundance of fauna from the south, and the mud-brick lined tombs with their reed fences, like the marshes of Lower Egypt in the north, at the downstream end, signifying the unification that was just then (3200-3050 BC) coming about. Obviously, although extremely provocative, this was a speculative interpretation formulated to explain the complex chronological interrelationships posed by the limited excavation of the cemetery and the apparent hiatus in use from the middle Gerzean to the Protodynastic. Normally, as can be seen in the

Fort cemetery, which grew to the northeast, and at other sites, Predynastic cemeteries grow horizontally over time, usually in one direction, although smaller graves have a tendency to cluster around larger, elite tombs. It is certain that Tombs 3, 6 and 9 date to the Naqada I-II transition period and that they signify the expansion and establishment of hierarchial structures at the end of the Amratian at Hierakonpolis. Tomb 4 is possibly a re-burial, or a sacrifice. It should be noted that the Predynastic graves do cluster on the east side of Tomb 2, which, if it is Protodynastic, would have pre-dated its construction by four or five hundred years, but it does not seem stylistically possible to date this large structure to the early Gerzean. It is highly likely that Tomb 7, the Bos burial to its west is Protodynastic, but in the absence of any artifacts, this can not be proved. Further to the northeast, Tomb 12, the stone-cut baboon grave with a few sherds *in situ*, would seem to date to Naqada I-II and therefore be contemporary with the tombs on the east side of Tomb 2. Even if Tomb 2 is not contemporary with the Predynastic graves nearby, it seems certain that the area was used for sacrifice and animal, as well as human, burial for sometime.

At the east end of the cemetery Hoffman excavated a large rectangular tomb, no.1 (L: 6.5 W: 3.5 D: 2.5m) in 1979 (Hoffman (ed.) 1982a: 43-7, pls.I.3-7), which is lined with triple-course mud brick walls. The floor showed barely visible remains of wooden planks and at each end were five postholes cut 50cm into the sandstone bedrock averaging 28cm in diameter. These posts originally supported the roof which was level with the surface of the ground, as was indicated by mud plaster found in situ in the corner of the tomb. An orange coated, streak-burnished bowl [Protodynastic Corpus (Petrie 1953) type 14q] containing finger scraped mud plaster was thrown out of the tomb by looters. On the surface surrounding the tomb there was a picket fence approximately 13.75m and 9.50m wide pierced by a gate in its northeast wall (cf. Dreyer 1991) and supported at the corners by more substantial, squared posts. Inside the fence perimeter were larger postmoulds and rotted posts approximately 30cm in diameter that supported a superstructure over the tomb. Hoffman noted that the several posts and a large rock in the centre line of Tomb 1 align with a rock-cut basin and postsocket on top of a cliff about 25m to the northwest. Beneath a rock overhang under this basin there are various incised graffiti, most of which appear to be New Kingdom in date, but there is an early device with the figure of a bull which may relate to Tomb 1. Hoffman speculated that this tomb might have belonged to Scorpion.

Tomb 1 had been looted in two phases, as was apparent from excavation of the backdirt pile. The ancient looting, represented by the lowest part of the pile, contained whole pots, whilst the upper portion of the backdirt was thoroughly sorted and contained nothing but the occasional sherd. No objects of personal ornamentation were found in the grave and the only sign of the original burial was a small, adult human femur. Analysis and identification of the whole pots and some reconstructed vessels from Tomb 1 has been undertaken by the author since excavation. The types include examples of black-topped and brown burnished hard orange (crushed calcium carbonate tempered) ware 'hes' jars [Proto.74v], a type which is linked to Narmer at Naqada and Djer at Abydos and was also found as full size and model examples in the Main Deposit in Nekhen (Adams and Friedman 1992: pls.4-5). Other pottery types include deep bowls [Proto. 3b, 3h, 3n], streak-burnished plates and dishes, [Proto. 12p, 14e, 14m, 14q, 31f]; large majurs [Proto. 40]; very large cylinder jars [cf. Proto. 50L]; storage vessels [Proto. 65h,k, 66b,f, 68f-t] and pedestal stands with circular cut-outs, [cf. Proto. 100T and 100P/R]; of special note are the nine straw-tempered 'granary' vessels, [Proto. 70o-p]. After further field study in 1992, it can be suggested that the very large straw-tempered vessel rims which were identified as cylinders (maximum reconstructed diameter 97.0cm) could have been combined with the large majurs (maximum reconstructed rim diameter 52.0cm) to form round-based vases which rested on stands decorated with impressed or cut-out triangles, a type which is modelled as a composite in faience in the votive deposits in the temples at Hierakonpolis, Abydos and Elephantine (Petrie 1903: pl.XI, 236, 244; Adams 1974a: cat. no. 163; Spencer 1980: cat. nos. 526, 527; Dreyer 1986: tafel 41). The assemblage from Tomb 1 can be dated to SD 77-80, or Naqada IIIb1-b2 in Kaiser's system, although it fits more comfortably into the Naqada IIIb (-IIIC1) phase defined by Hendrickx (this volume: pp.36ff.) and perhaps pre-dates Narmer. The one Carbon-14 date taken from the tomb gave a result of 2980 ± 141 BC (Damon correction in Hassan 1984a), which averages to approximately 3050 BC.

Tomb 10, which is adjacent to Tomb 1, was excavated in 1982 and is slightly smaller (L: 4.70 W:

1.90m). It is also surrounded by a wooden superstructure and lined with triple course mud-brick walls, which are much deflated towards the centre (fig.3). Niches were found above the mud brick walls for the insertion of roofing beams (figs.4-5). There is a stepped section across the base of the tomb to the west and three postholes to support the roof at each end (pl.1a). As well as being looted in ancient times, this tomb was thoroughly cleared in the early part of this century and it appears that the contents might have been sieved then. Fortunately, the sieving missed a fragment of mud sealing which was found by the excavator, Carter Lupton, on the mud-brick lining in the southwest corner. The sealing has the same sign group which appears on large 'Weinkruge' storage vessels from the Delta, Abu Roash, Saqqara and Abydos, dated to the time of Den of the First Dynasty (van den Brink 1992b: fig.1). The limited pottery sample from Tomb 10 includes black-topped 'hes' jars [Proto.74v], straw-tempered jars [Predynastic Corpus L30p]; cut-out pedestal stands [cf. L86B, (Adams & Friedman 1992: fig.11b)]; streak-burnished dishes [Proto. 12t], rim sherds of medium hard orange jars [possible Proto. 90-92) and some Predynastic sherds. The most notable ceramic piece is a triangle impressed and fenestrated straw-tempered pottery stand (Adams & Friedman 1992: fig.12), which is similar to one found in the pit in the ceremonial complex at Locality 29A, which also contained part of a black-topped orange 'hes' jar (Adams & Friedman 1992: fig.8). Certain straw-tempered sherds recovered from the fill of Tomb 10 comprised a pottery coffin which has been partially reconstructed to a length of 90.0cm, width 41.5cm and height of 22.0cm, which is certainly large enough to have contained a crouched adult burial.

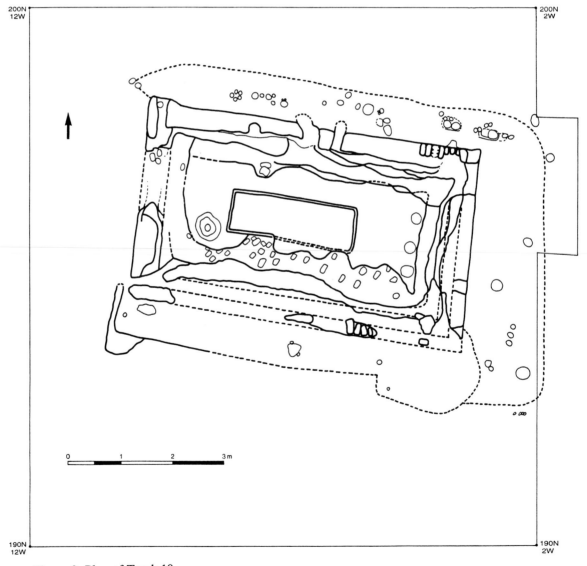

Figure 3 Plan of Tomb 10

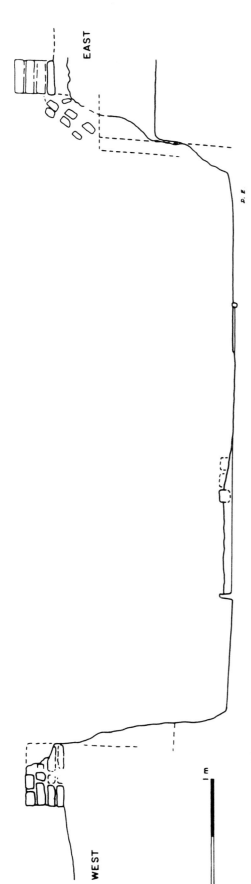

Figure 4 Tomb 10: Section East-West

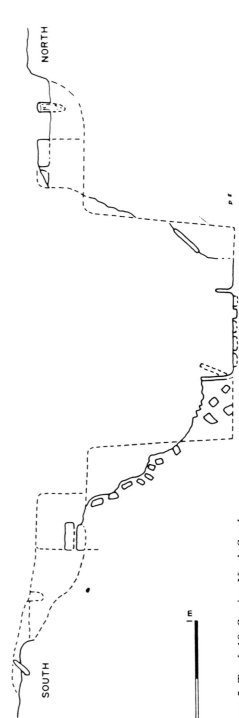

Figure 5 Tomb 10: Section North-South

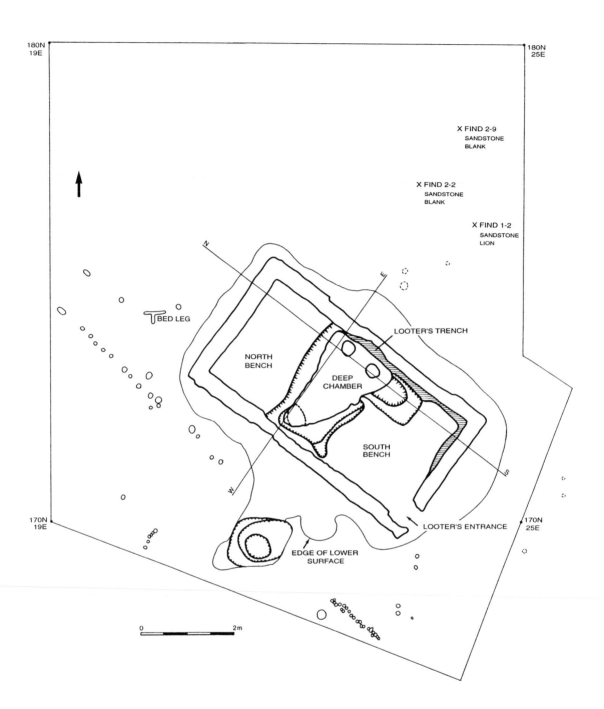

Figure 6 Plan of Tomb 11

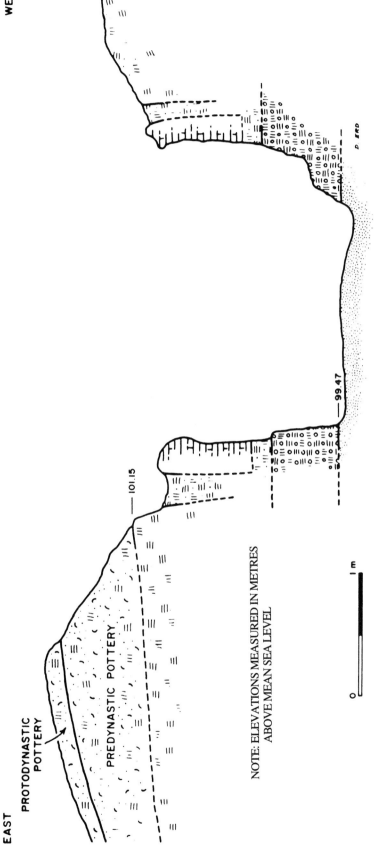

WEST

EAST

PROTODYNASTIC
POTTERY

PREDYNASTIC POTTERY

101.15

99.47

D. ERD

NOTE: ELEVATIONS MEASURED IN METRES
ABOVE MEAN SEA LEVEL

1 m

0

Figure 7 Tomb 11: Section East-West

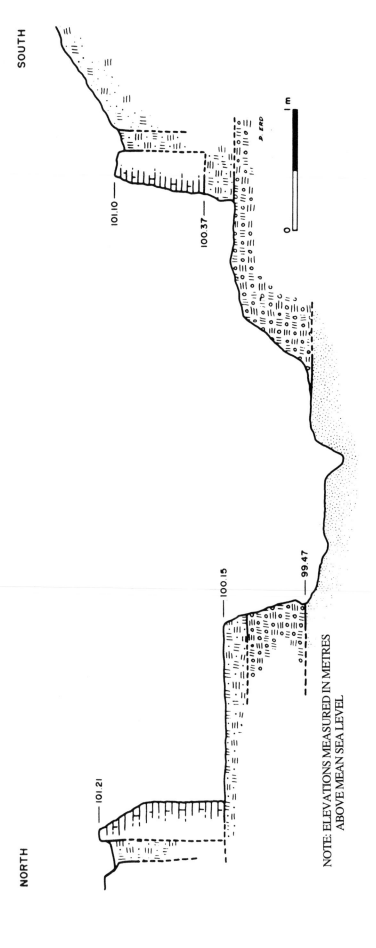

SOUTH

NORTH

101.21

100.15

99.47

100.37

101.10

D. ERD

NOTE: ELEVATIONS MEASURED IN METRES
ABOVE MEAN SEA LEVEL

Figure 8 Tomb 11: Section North-South

Tomb 11, which is situated southeast of Tombs 1 and 10, survived the despoiling somewhat better and two seasons of excavation in 1982 and 1985 produced a wide range of artifacts from within and around the tomb. The 1982 season resulted in the clearance of the tomb and revealed a line of post moulds on the southwest side (pl.1b). The second season of excavation in 1985-6 cleared a low mound on the north and east and exposed several postmoulds (fig.6). Hoffman suggested that the mound had originally covered the tomb and a wood and reed superstructure was erected on top of it. The tomb itself (L: 5.0 W: 2.40m) was again lined with triple course mud-brick walls and had a deep, irregular, central 'chamber' cut down to the sandstone bedrock with north and south benches left in the soft silts at each end (fig.7). It had been robbed in several phases. The last looting through a robber's trench on the northeast side left a backdirt pile which contained sherds of Protodynastic and Dynastic pottery, as well as wood fragments, an iron nail, brass knobs and modern wool (fig.8). Beneath the first layer of this backdirt pile the mound contained Predynastic pottery, including a whole late Gerzean straw-tempered 'cornet' [R74, SD 66] and a white cross-lined sherd. There is also what was probably the first, ancient looter's trench cut into the southwest corner of the mud-brick lining, but there was no particular pile of backdirt associated with it and the trench only contained a few flints and shells. A deep, circular depression nearby might be a looter's trial pit or an offering cache.

Outside the tomb in the backdirt on the north side a fine wooden bed with carved bull's leg feet (Hoffman 1983) had been thrown by the tomb robbers; this pile of fragments was extricated and the reconstruction of the side piece with lashing holes suggests an original length of 70cm. In the 1986 season small sandstone carvings of birds, animal-shaped blanks, some with base sockets suitable for carrying on poles, and a lion (Adams 1992: 71-77, figs.2-3) came from around the tomb on the north-east side, as did a leopard's claw, which may have fallen from a priest's skin robe at the graveside when the burial ceremonies took place. In this case it seems that the tomb was not sieved in modern times so that the smaller objects retrieved from the backdirt piles and the fill of the tomb were also rich: gold, silver, turquoise, garnet, carnelian, copper, faience and silver beads; copper tool fragments; obsidian and crystal blades; flint blades and flint and carnelian microliths; calcite gaming pieces and plaques; hippopotamus ivory carvings, including bulls' feet from boxes and a harpoon; lapis lazuli fly and shell amulets; small stone boat models; a fine basalt cup and part of a squat faience vase. The number of imported materials again testify to the procurement of luxury items beyond the local and national frontiers. Obsidian could have come by the sea route from Abyssinia, via the Wadi Hammamat, or through Nubia, where the gold was no doubt obtained in the mining region of the Wadi Alaqi. The lapis lazuli and silver, both non-native in Egypt, would have come from further afield, from sources in Afghanistan and Western Asia respectively (Adams & Friedman 1992).

There were also two anthropomorphic artifacts. The first is a pottery sculpture on a straw-tempered Nile silt vessel of hand-supported, bulbous breasts beneath a crude ledge handle copying a Palestinian type (Adams & Friedman 1992: fig.16). The only other anthropomorphic representation which came from the fill of Tomb 11 is a pottery figurine, broken below the hips (Adams & Friedman 1992: fig.18). The figure has a bird-like head with a double bagged head-dress and wears a penis sheath curled back to the waist with its hands tied behind its back in the classic prisoner mode, reminiscent of figures from the Main Deposit in the temple at Nekhen (Quibell 1900: pls.XI-XII). In addition to these figures and the sandstone animals from the tomb surround there were also other pottery and stone figures of animals including cattle and pigs from the tomb fill. The fragments of a pottery coffin from the tomb were reconstructed to form a box which is 37.0cm long, 23cm high and 22cm wide with a possible 'door' cut into one end. This would not be big enough to contain even a crouched adult body, but might have contained a child, a possibility which is also suggested by the size of the bed and the nature of some of the other objects from the tomb and the fact that there seems to have been a tradition for the provision of rich contents in the graves of certain children, according to social status. This tradition seems to have been continued in Lower Egypt (Kroeper 1992: 140).

During three short study seasons since 1986 it has proved possible to reconstruct much of the pottery scattered in and around Tomb 11 in order to establish the types and fit them into the relative dating sequence. Pottery types from Tomb 11 include: wavy line cylinder jar [Predynastic Corpus W60g]; net painted cylinder jars [W62 and Proto. 46D2]; a large comma painted jar [D26d]; conical jar [Proto. 54g]; straw-tempered bowls [R26A]; straw-tempered jars [L36a and n]; hard orange jars

[Proto. 63b]; *hes* jars [Proto. 74v], which also occur with a brown coated and polished surface, and numerous fragments of straw-tempered cylinders decorated with impressed and cut-out triangles.

There are some particularly interesting examples among the reconstructed pots. The fullest reconstruction of the black-topped *hes* jar type (Adams & Friedman 1992: fig.14) shows that it does not have the later exaggerated 'waist', and therefore may be slightly earlier than the Narmer/Djer type associated with Tombs 1 and 10, the Main Deposit and Locality 29A. The thin walled, tall, late forms of wavy handled jars [Proto. 44f], have a somewhat sandy, hard orange body coated with a vertically burnished cream slip (Adams & Friedman 1992: figs.13a-b). These two fine jars were extremely difficult to restore from the many fragments into which the tomb robbers had smashed them. Their exaggerated length and delicacy suggests that they were never meant for use, but most probably produced especially for the grave. Eliezer Oren reported finding jars of a similar shape with vertical burnishing, some without wavy handles, in his survey in north Sinai and petrographic analysis has shown that they were locally made, but were of hybrid Egyptian/Canaanite manufacture (Oren 1989; Oren and Yekutieli 1992). Two examples of these hybrid Early Bronze Age I jars have recently been identified in the Petrie Museum and British Museum collections by Yuval Yekutieli of Ben-Gurion University (Yekutieli in press).

Fragments of a small jug stood out easily from the initial sherd mass from Tomb 11, but unfortunately the pot could not be completely restored (Adams & Friedman 1992: fig.15). There is a thickening adjacent to the hole in the body wall, particularly below it, which indicates that a handle was once attached there and it probably ended at the rim or neck, which is also broken. From the suggested reconstruction, the nearest parallels that can be located in the Palestinian repertoire seem to be the two juglets from the Proto-Urban (=EBI) burial caves at Azor (Ben-Tor 1975). A Canaanite example of this type was found in the royal L-cemetery at Qustol in Nubia (Williams 1980, 1986: 371, fig.182, pl.25). The fabric of the Hierakonpolis example is the compact pink colour of Hk. ware type 5A (i.e crushed calcium carbonate tempered Nile silt), but the surface is covered with an unusual red wash and there are external manufacturing marks above the base. Although not a Palestinian pot, it is almost certainly a copy of one. The assemblage of pottery from Tomb 11 covers SD 74-81 and cannot be fitted exactly into Kaiser's Naqada III Stufen divisions, but has closer correspondence to Hendrickx's Naqada IIIA1-IIIA2 (-IIIB).

Tomb 2 has been compared with the larger tombs in Cemetery L at Qustol in Nubia (Williams 1986: 176), particularly with Tomb L2 (L: 6.35 W: 1.26m), which also has a side chamber. There are larger tombs (L23 and L24) with side chambers at Qustol, although none of them are rock-cut, and a bovid burial (3.0 x 1.30 x 1.60m) with Egyptian [Proto. 63] jars was associated with Tomb L23 (9.25 x 2m). Cache pits and circular burial pits associated with the large tombs at Qustol, also found in many other Terminal A-group cemeteries, complete the parallel. The pottery from these tombs, particularly the fenestrated vessels and the storage jars, would seem to be contemporary with that from the Protodynastic tombs in Locality 6. A trench grave (2.25 x 1.05 x 1.52m) with a side chamber beneath the floor on the east side closed by inclined slabs was excavated near the Fort at Hierakonpolis by Henri de Morgan in 1908 (de Morgan 1909: 27, fig.130). This grave (Burial 8) contained a Terminal A-Group painted bowl (Needler 1984: 54, 111, cat.no. 97) with Egyptian Naqada III vessels. A few trench tombs with side chambers closed by stone slabs, sometimes, but not always, used for the burial, of Naqada III date have been excavated within the dynastic enclosure at El Kab (Hendrickx 1984, 1994). In an unpublished manuscript of the introduction to his planned site report series written in 1989, Hoffman had realised that his analogy of an Upper Egyptian (southern) and Lower Egyptian (northern) cemetery layout at Locality 6 during Naqada III had to be taken further. The southern complex of Tomb 2 actually connects further south with northern Lower Nubia and is symbolic of the pivotal role played by Hierakonpolis in south-north contacts (Smith 1991: 108-110).

Pottery analysis of the two thoroughly robbed, aligned tombs (1 and 10) at the north end of the Locality 6 cemetery indicates that they both date to the Protodynastic period (Hendrickx' IIIb), and that Tomb 1 is possibly slightly later than Tomb 10 (SD 73-81). Tomb 1 may be the last grave in the cemetery, both geographically and chronologically. These tombs were pre-dated by Tomb 11, which is further southeast into the cemetery. So, together with the evidence from the cluster of Tombs 3-9 (and 12) from the other, southwest end of the cemetery (ignoring Tomb 2 for the moment), it can be suggested that there was a horizontal expansion to the north through time. This, together with the discovery of one or two Naqada IIcd pottery types near these élite Protodynastic tombs and the discovery of fine bifacial and rippled flints (for instance Friedman and Adams 1992: 68) over the surface, would suggest that the Locality 6 cemetery might not have had the period of abandonment between the early Naqada II and late Naqada III periods which was Hoffman's suggestion based on the data available to him in 1982. It is possible that other élite tombs of the classic Naqada IIbcd (SD 45-63) and early Naqada III (SD 63-76) await discovery in the centre and northwest of the Locality 6 cemetery, south of Tomb 11, where the early rulers of the Hierakonpolis kingdom of Upper Egypt were probably buried over a period of five hundred years. Narmer, the last of the pre-unification kings, is traditionally credited with the final push north into Lower Egypt.

The Ceremonial Centre at Hierakonpolis Locality HK29A

Renée Friedman

The primary objective of the 1985-86 campaign at Hierakonpolis was to fill in the last major chrono-logical gap in the regional Predynastic - Early Dynastic settlement sequence by excavating a Gerzean (Naqada II) period habitation area. In an area which played such a critical role in the development of the Egyptian state and kingship the importance of attaining a complete sequence of regional Predynastic cultural developments was obvious. To this end, excavations under the direction of the late Dr. Michael Allen Hoffman were undertaken at a portion of the site designated as Locality HK29A. To our great surprise, we uncovered what appears to be a large ceremonial complex in the midst of Gerzean settle-ment remains; as such, it is the earliest ceremonial or cultic establishment known from Egypt and provides valuable insights into the size and scope of early religious architecture, previously recon-structed only from ambiguous two-dimensional representations.

The excavated area at Locality HK29A is located on a slight elevation of Sahaba silts some 200m southwest of the present edge of the cultivation, grid east or river south of the mouth of Wadi Abul Suffian, the so-called 'Great Wadi' (fig. 1). This locality was chosen to fulfil our initial goals for a number of reasons. Most importantly, HK29A is part of a larger settlement nucleus which includes HK29, the site of the semi-subterranean, wattle and daub house of late Amratian (Naqada IIa) date located 150-180m farther into the desert (see Hoffman 1980, 1982c). This settlement covers an area of about 44,634m^2 and represents one of the largest clusters of habitation remains within the vast ex-panse of domestic debris which Quibell and Green (1902) called 'The Predynastic Town'.

Systematic sampling of the surface indicated that this cluster represents the remains of one contigu-ous but laterally shifting settlement. The temporal shift in habitation eastward towards the river from HK29 to HK29A is clearly demonstrated by the spatial distribution of artifacts (Harlan 1985: 48-77; 1992). This distinction is so clear that the zone of transition between these horizontally stratified areas can be pinpointed at approximately 375m from the edge of the modern cultivation (Hoffman 1987:14; Harlan 1985: 61-2, 67). Thus, by digging a later component of the same site, we hoped to study diachronically the same community as it changed over a period of about 200 years (Hoffman 1985). The exact location of the 1985 excavation at HK29A was chosen on the basis of chronological indica-tors such as fragments of Decorated ware visible on the surface, and because of the relatively moder-ate density of artifacts in an area that is often covered with an incredibly profuse array of cultural material. Harlan (1985:62) noted that in one 1x1m square the surface population of potsherds reached over 500 fragments! Ridges of moderate accumulations of artefacts and *in situ* mud-bricks suggested a site with the best possibilities of preservation and minimal disturbance.

At the end of the initial season of excavation in 1985, we thought we had been successful in our primary goal of uncovering a domestic structure. Architectural remains in the 5x5m test sounding (fig. 2: the southeastern quadrant of square 150L50) included part of a prepared mud-plastered floor which extended to a low mud-brick wall. Parallel to this wall was a large trench, made to support a fence wall composed of posts and reeds, which appeared to be associated with a much denuded area of modified Sahaba silts, which were assumed to be the remains of animal pens (Hoffman 1985).

Resuming work the following season (Nov. 1985-Feb. 1986), we found the physical extent of these architectural features to be far greater than expected. Both the paved area and the large wall trench continued until monumental or at least non-domestic proportions had been attained. Following the clearance of over 600m^2, the site can now be characterised as a multi-phase architectural complex dominated by a large oval mud-plastered floor over 32m long and 13m wide (pl.2a and fig. 2). This paved area is bounded by a mud-brick wall (Wall 1) and a composite wall composed of mud-brick and stone (Wall 2) on its north and southeastern perimeter respectively. Surrounding the complex on the north is a large trench over 35m long (Wall Trench 1), built to support a wooden-post wall, which originally was pierced by a portal flanked by two large posts (Gate). Directly across from this gateway are four large post-holes and smaller wall trenches, which form the remnants of the main structure, presumably a temple or shrine (Structure III). In addition, pits, post-holes and traces of walls of various sizes are also encountered. All these elements are portions of distinctive structures, whose architectural and chronological interrelationships are not entirely clear owing to wind deflation and the reuse of the site in antiquity.

The focal point of the excavations, if not of the complex, is the parabolic-shaped open-air courtyard paved by a succession of four carefully smoothed, Nile mud, floors. These floors have been labelled from earliest to latest 'a-d' with an additional area of localised patching in the southwest called floor 'e'. Separating these pavings are relatively sterile layers of fill, composed of ground-up Sahaba silts or silty sand mixed with chaff. The interrelationship of these floors to the architectural elements, coupled with the information derived from the approximately 280,000 horizontally stratified potsherds, indicates at least three phases of construction or renovation followed by alternating periods of abandonment and reuse for ceremonial or other purposes. The following discussion of the site's history is taken from Hoffman (1987: 48-64), the field report of Elias (1986), and personal observation during all three seasons of excavation at HK29A (1985, 1986, 1989). All coordinates in the following discussion are oriented to the site grid. Grid north is approximately perpendicular to the local course of the Nile.

About the extent and nature of the earliest floor 'a', we know little. This surface, only a light smoothing of the underlying Sahaba silts, predates the majority of the surrounding structures. Associated with it are a number of post-holes outlining Structure VI, which is located just south of Wall Trench 1. Floor 'a' has been identified only in the corridor between Wall Trench 1 and Wall 1. It is possible that floor 'a' extended across the courtyard to Features 5 and 6, large, apparently subterranean structures, but as the overlying floors were not removed, the full extent of floor 'a' is not yet known.

The overlying floors 'b' and 'c' are closely related. During these phases (if not earlier) Wall Trench 1 was dug along the northern and eastern side of the courtyard. This trench, over 35m long and up to 44cm deep, was built to support a substantial wall of wooden posts and reeds, which on the basis of modern examples might have been 2-3m in height (Barakat and Hoffman 1987: 40-41). Well preserved wooden posts with sharpened ends were recovered from this trench. The action of insects, however, left only the fragile silica skeleton of the wood, and as a result the posts disintegrated upon exposure to light. Near the northwestern end of Wall Trench 1, two large post-holes mark a doorway facing the Nile. To the west of this gate, the further continuation of this zeriba-type wall could only be traced for another 2-3m as the area is very denuded. Thus, the complete extent of this wall trench, as well as the entire complex, remains undetermined.

At the eastern, curved, end of the floor, Wall Trench 1 bifurcates. One branch continues beyond the end of the floor in a much diminished size. Nevertheless, it features a lining of mud bricks specially fashioned to support a series of wooden posts, which may form the façade of a building (Structure IVa). This building is part of a series of structures located along the northern side of the wall trench, which may have served as store rooms, workshops and other dependencies of the complex. Architectural remains here take the form of post-holes and shallow cuttings into the Sahaba silts. One room within this series of ancillary buildings, however, has a plastered floor of its own.

The other branch of Wall Trench 1 curves around the eastern end of the floor. This area is unfortunately badly damaged and neither the full extent of the wall trench nor the nature of the structures at this raised end of the complex could be ascertained. Another series of isolated post-holes here suggests that a much less substantial wall enclosed the courtyard and continued around its southern perimeter. Although the association is no longer preserved, this wall may have run up to what may be considered the main structure at this phase: a mat and pole structure represented by a series of five medium-sized post-holes, some 35-50cm in diameter, oriented on an axis with the entrance to the complex.

The paved area itself follows the grade of the underlying silts and slopes up rather steeply at a 9° angle toward the east. At this up-hill end, a large post-hole (Feature 16; fig. 3), 80cm deep in its final form, was sunk into the floor. This pit contains two large stones, one roughly battered and pecked into shape, apparently intended to support a tall solitary pole, perhaps the cultic emblem. The original post-hole was dug into native Sahaba silts but, as time passed and the floor level was raised, the borders of

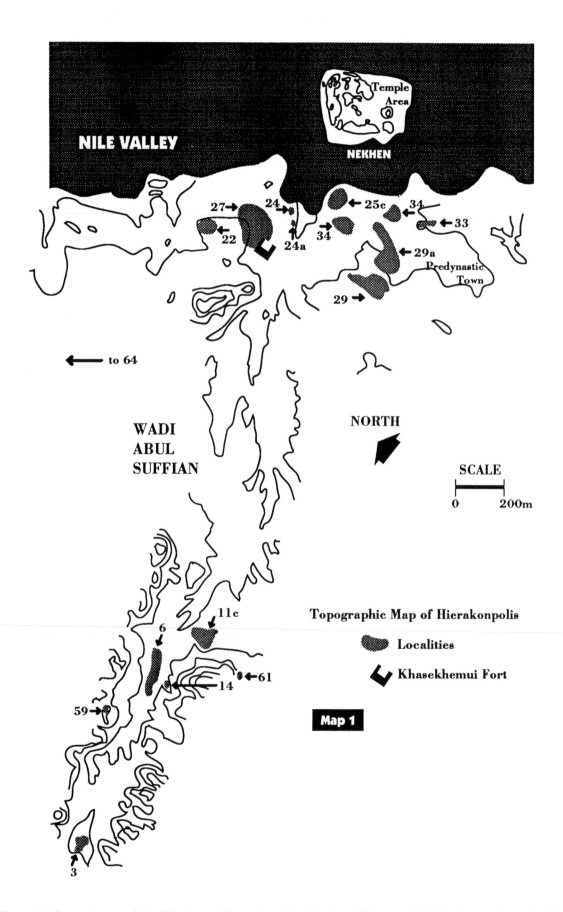

Figure 1   General map of the Hierakonpolis region (after Harlan 1992: map 1). Numbers refer to locality designations used by the Hierakonpolis Expedition to denote internal distinctions within the 144km^2 concession boundaries (see Hoffman 1982b)

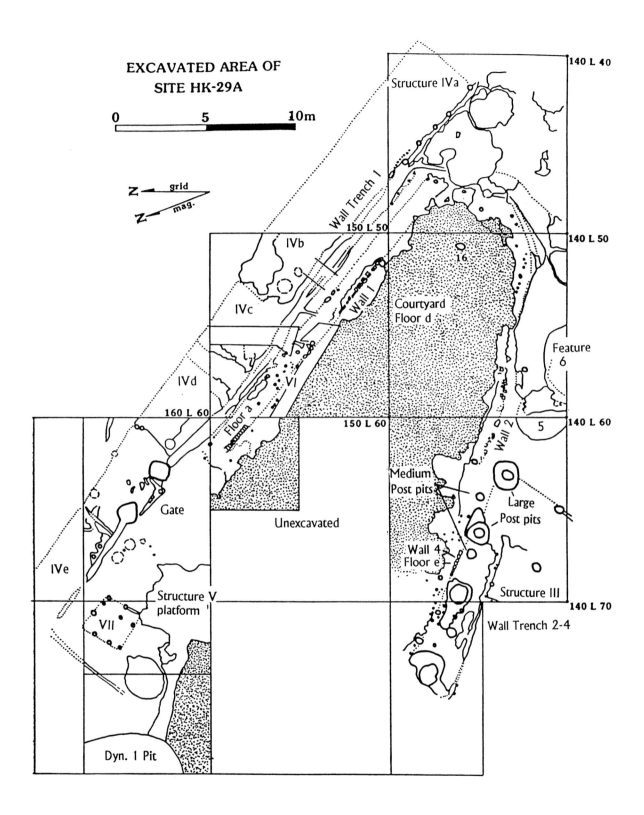

EXCAVATED AREA OF SITE HK-29A

0 5 10m

Z — grid
Z — mag.

Structure IVa
140 L 40

Wall Trench 1

150 L 50
140 L 50

IVb

IVc

Wall 1

Courtyard Floor d

16

Feature 6

IVd

VI

Floor a

160 L 60
150 L 60
140 L 60

Wall 2

5

Medium Post pits

Large Post pits

Wall 4 Floor e

Gate

IVe

Unexcavated

Structure III

Structure V platform

140 L 70

VII

Wall Trench 2-4

Dyn. 1 Pit

Figure 2 The excavated area at HK29A (after Hoffman 1987: fig.9). Roman numerals indicate Structures. Arabic numerals indicate Features. Grid squares measure 10x10 metres

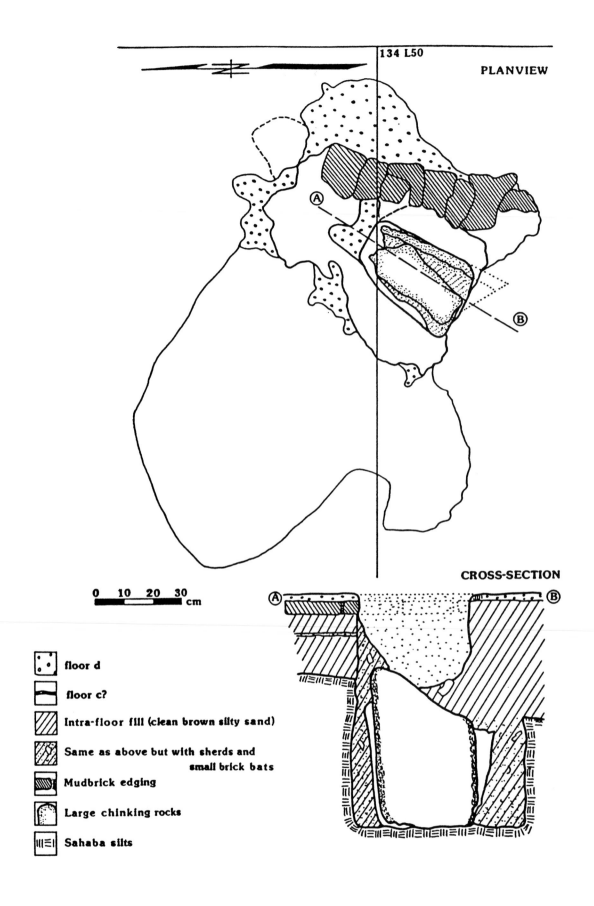

134 L50

PLANVIEW

CROSS-SECTION

0   10   20   30
cm

floor d

floor c?

Intra-floor fill (clean brown silty sand)

Same as above but with sherds and
small brick bats

Mudbrick edging

Large chinking rocks

Sahaba silts

Figure 3 Feature 16: post-hole near the apex of the courtyard (after Hoffman 1987: fig. 11)

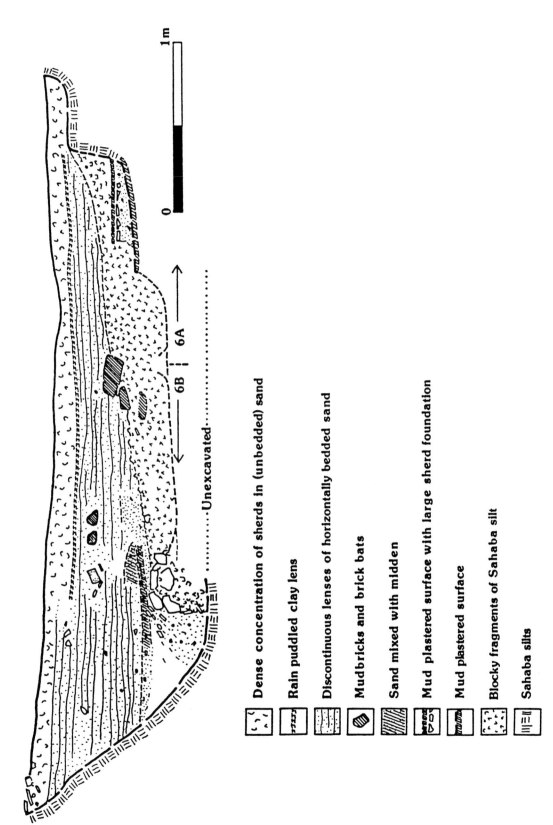

Dense concentration of sherds in (unbedded) sand

Rain puddled clay lens

Discontinuous lenses of horizontally bedded sand

Mudbricks and brick bats

Sand mixed with midden

Mud plastered surface with large sherd foundation

Mud plastered surface

Blocky fragments of Sahaba silt

Sahaba silts

Figure 4 Feature 6: large pit of unknown function (Hoffman 1987: fig. 10)

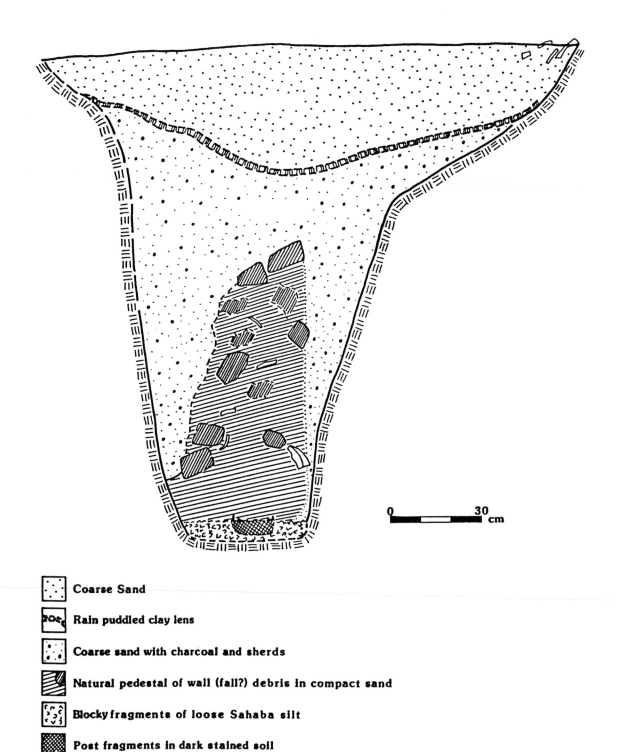

Coarse Sand

Rain puddled clay lens

Coarse sand with charcoal and sherds

Natural pedestal of wall (fall?) debris in compact sand

Blocky fragments of loose Sahaba silt

Post fragments in dark stained soil

Sahaba silts

Figure 5 Cross-section of one of the large post-holes forming the facade of Structure III
(Hoffman 1987: fig. 12)

the post-hole were modified. At some point, perhaps related to plastering of floor 'd', mud-brick edging was provided to add further stability for the pole and its standard.

In association with this or the earlier phase of the complex, two very large, irregularly shaped pits (Features 5 and 6) were cut into the silts beyond the southern periphery of the courtyard. These features contained a variety of debris including fragments of glossy slag and may have been used for storage or industrial purposes. Incorporated into a fairly elaborate peripheral flooring, these pits appear to have had a complicated occupational history of their own, perhaps paralleling that of the entire complex. Feature 6 was remodelled several times (see fig. 4). The original pit, 6A, was initially lined with mud but later resurfaced with a mud-plaster floor placed upon a foundation of carefully laid potsherds. At some point the floor of 6A was deliberately cut and this pit was expanded into a large subterranean chamber, 4m across (Feature 6B). The internal floors have not yet been excavated. Thus, the initial date of this feature is unknown. The pottery from this feature, however, is some of the earliest found at the site and may be provisionally dated to Naqada IIb.

The last plastering of the extensive courtyard is floor 'd'. It is not only the best understood, but also preserves the footprints of a child and his dog scampering across the still wet mud-plastered surface. A number of modifications to the architectural plan of the complex appears to correlate with this repaving. In clear association with floor 'd' is a mud-brick wall (Wall 1) which runs parallel to Wall Trench 1 at a distance of 1.2m to the south. The plaster of floor 'd' runs up to and laps against the southern face of this mud-brick wall to form a concave coping. The wall survives to a height of 38-40cm in three courses of brick preserved only sporadically along its length. The brick size of 26-28x14x6.5-7cm is well within size limits for contemporary Pre- and Protodynastic architecture (cf. Spencer 1979: 5). At the extreme western end, however, the bricks are somewhat larger, measuring 30x17x7cm, and create a thickening that may correspond to the wall's termination along the eastern flank of the compound's entrance-way. The bricks are, for the most part, tempered with sand or midden. Some, found only in the fallen debris, were impressed on their long, narrow sides with either parallel rows of depressions or two to three large depressions, created by the insertion of several of the brick maker's fingers. The decorated face was always carefully wet-smoothed and sometimes peaked. The opposite face was often caked with gravel, flint chips and mortar. These bricks no doubt capped the wall and the depressions in them may have been decorative or made to facilitate the display of objects on or above the wall, as discussed below.

The purpose of Wall 1 is unclear. Hoffman (1987: 51) described Wall 1 as a curtain wall, but he also suggested a casemate construction with an internal filling of sherds and debris.[1] The evidence for the northern casing wall along the edge of Wall Trench 1, however, is weak. If it were a casemate wall, the height could have been substantial and as a result the post wall in the Wall Trench would be superfluous. Alternatively, Wall 1 may have been built to hide the mounds of debris heaped up against the perimeter wall and found in the fill of Wall Trench 1. It is from this debris that the best evidence for the dating and function of the complex was recovered. It is also possible that Wall 1 existed in concert with the post wall in Wall Trench 1 to create a screened corridor running from the courtyard's entrance to the elevated eastern apex of the floor.

On the southeastern side of the floor another wall (Wall 2) composed of mud-bricks and naturally exfoliated sandstone slabs cemented with straw-tempered mortar sits upon floor 'd'. The super-position above floor 'd', as well as the smaller size of the bricks (23x11x4.5cm) from which it is constructed suggests that this wall is part of yet another phase in the reappointing of the complex. Unfortunately, the relationship of this composite wall to other features along the southern perimeter of the court is unclear. Although it is not apparent from the plan, when discovered, the line of this poorly preserved wall appeared to be sinusoidal or serpentine. Sinusoidal walls occur with some frequency only in the Middle Kingdom in religious and occasionally also in urban contexts. Their function is unclear, but appears to be associated with creating a magical line demarcating a sacred precinct. From a structural point of view, however, their undulating line makes them strong and economical revetment walls (Sliwa 1992).[2]

Evidence for further remodelling of the complex is attested by the construction of a structure fronted by four extremely large post-pits (Structure III) on the southern side of the court (pl.2b). This structure replaced, at a slightly different orientation, the main building composed of the medium post-holes of the earlier phases. These new post-pits, 1.50m in diameter and 1.60-1.70m deep (fig. 5), must have been dug to support extremely tall pillars. In fact, remnants of wood and bark found at the bottom of one of these post-pits have tentatively been identified as cedar. Originally, these posts formed the monumental façade of a structure about 13m across which was internally subdivided into three compartments as attested by shallow wall trenches (Wall Trenches 2-4) and various post-holes. This building phase, however, is associated with floor 'e', a limited area of localised patching no doubt necessitated by the installation of the tall posts (pl.5b). The low segment of wall (Wall 4) composed of a single course of squarish tile-like mud-bricks (20x18x5cm) bedded in fine mortar sitting upon floor 'e' appears to have served as a threshold or sockle for this building. A provisional reconstruction of the appearance of this structure is provided in fig. 11a, but see below for further discussion.

At the northwestern end of the floor, the evidence for the various architectural units has been severely disturbed and deflated and is therefore difficult to interpret. Just west of the gateway, a series of post-holes outlines a square building (Structure VII) which is considered to be a pavilion of some type. Its relationship to a floor, broken away in this area, is unclear. It is perhaps associated with the large area of melted and toppled mud-bricks (Structure V) resting upon floor 'd', which may be the remnants of a platform. Among the sherds sealed beneath the brick fall were fragments of Petrie's Decorated ware depicting a boat, datable to Naqada IId, which provide an important *terminus post quem* for this particular addition to the complex.

The ceramic evidence for dating suggests that a relatively short period of time is involved with regard to floors 'b-d', although few datable sherds were found within the inter-floor fillings. It seems that during the main phase of its use, the courtyard was kept quite clean. Nevertheless, a chronologically and typologically consistent Naqada IIc ceramic assemblage was found along the curving perimeter of the court to the north, east and south. In particular, the heavy accumulation of sherds, bone, and other cultural material found within Wall Trench 1 provides the best evidence for the dating and purpose of the complex. It was assumed that the majority of this debris was created during ceremonial activities and was swept from the floor and heaped up against or thrown over the walls shortly after the events. However, the consistency of the ceramic finds and the number of brick-bats suggest that this debris represents a major clearance undertaken in conjunction with one of the various renovations.

The non-domestic nature of the lithic, ground stone, faunal and the ceramic assemblage recovered in the accumulated debris clearly indicates that the ceremonial function of the HK29A complex need not be determined on the basis of the monumental architectural features alone. The study of the mammalian fauna shows that unlike other sites in the low desert at Hierakonpolis, cattle and caprines (sheep/goat) were of nearly equal importance. Of these, a substantial number were young animals with unfused epiphyses. The skeletal data indicate that several caprines were, in fact, new-borns. This is clearly not an effective use of the food supply and bespeaks unusual circumstances (McArdle 1987, 1992). Butchery was done at the site. This is made clear not only by the recovery of all portions of the skeleton,[3] but also by the high percentage (80%) of the lithic artefacts which are debitage from the manufacture and sharpening of bifacial tools and a few fragments of bifacially-flaked knives were also found (fig. 6a -c) (Holmes 1987, 1992).

Among the aquatic fauna there was a definite preference for the Nile perch (*Lates niloticus*) and *Tilapia*, fish that are today most favoured for their taste and in antiquity were the most frequently depicted of all the Nile species. The reconstructed size of many of the Nile perch specimens, up to 2m in length, illustrates that they were not part of any ordinary catch. In order to land perch of this size, not only specific knowledge of their reclusive habits but also specialised fishing techniques were required.[4] Catches of such size could not have been frequent and transport must have been difficult. One exceptional specimen recovered in modern times from Lake Nasser measuring 2m in length weighed 175kg (Brewer and Friedman 1989: 74-79). The presence of substantial amounts of turtle and crocodile bone also reinforces the impression that large and dangerous aquatic fauna were being caught specifically for use in the complex (Brewer 1987).

Aside from the debris from the manufacture or sharpening of bifacial tools, the lithic assemblage reveals a very activity-specific bent. The remaining portion of the lithic assemblage is composed predominately of microdrill bladelets probably used in the production of beads (fig. 6d-f). Crescent drills for the manufacture of stone vessels are also noted (Holmes 1987, 1992a). Beads of carnelian,

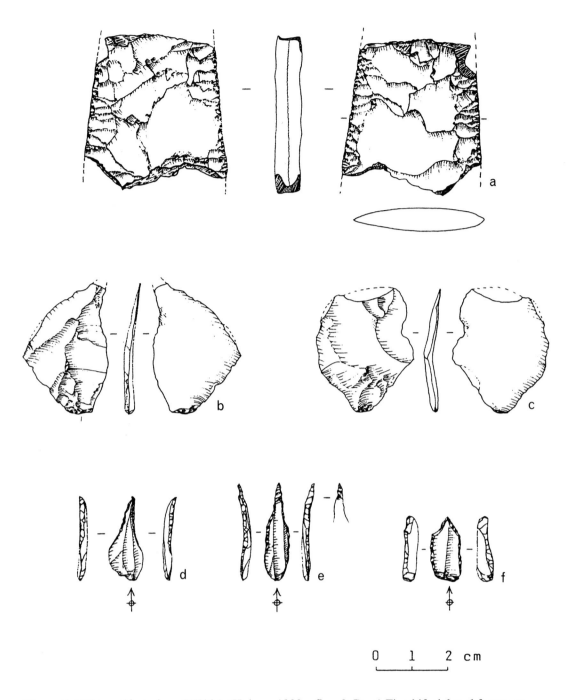

Figure 6 Lithic artifacts from HK29A (Holmes 1992a: figs. 2-5): a) Fine bifacial tool fragment
b-c) Biface thinning debitage; d-f) Microdrills

Figure 7 Small hawk head of burned steatite (Hoffman 1987: fig. 43)

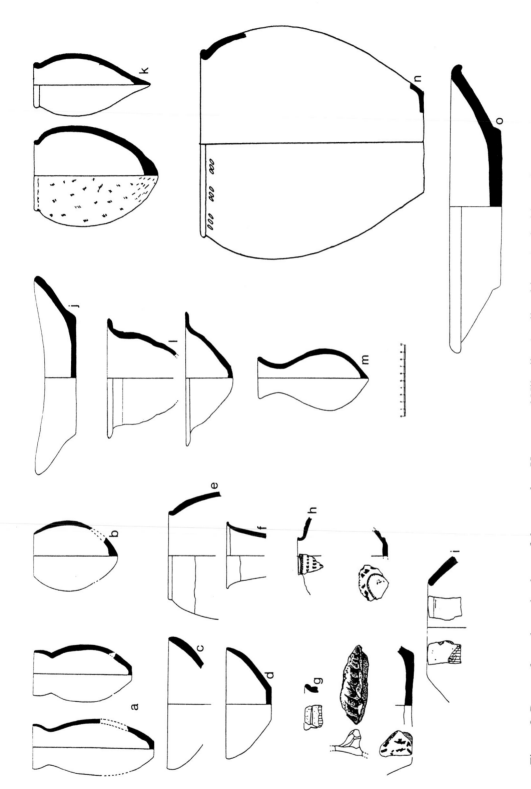

Figure 8 Pottery from the main phase of the complex. Untempered Nile silt: a) collared jar coated with a red wash; b) black polished ovoid jar; c) bowl with red slip and polish on both surfaces; d) bowl with a red polished slip on the interior only; e) black-topped jar; f) black-topped beaker. Exotic pottery: g) fragments of Palestinian pottery, calcite-tempered; h) punctate impressed jar, straw-tempered; i) shale-tempered hole-mouth jar, possibly from the Eastern Desert. Straw-tempered Nile silt: j) elliptical platter; k) rimmed jars; l) hat-shaped bowls; m) bottle; n) large storage jar; o) large basin

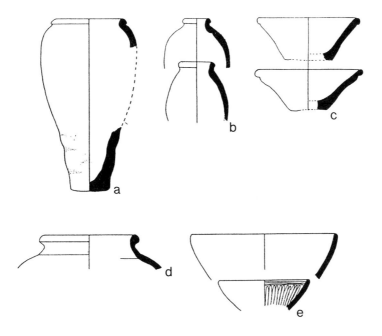

Figure 9 Pottery from the "floor deposit": a) straw-tempered jar; b) straw- or sand-tempered small jars; c) straw-tempered ledge-rim bowls; d) marl jar, coated with brown wash; e) marl bowls, slipped and polished on the interior only

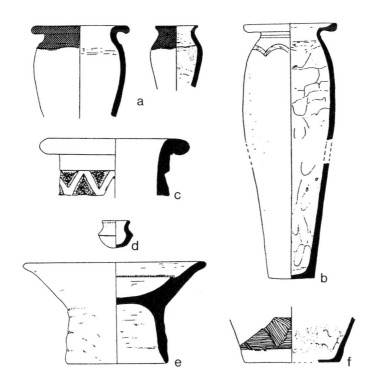

Figure 10 Pottery from the Dynasty 1 pit: a) black-topped jars; b) marl jar; c) marl jar-stand with cut-out design; c) small jar, possibly imported from the Delta; e) straw-tempered incense burner; f) jar base with combed designs, imported from Palestine

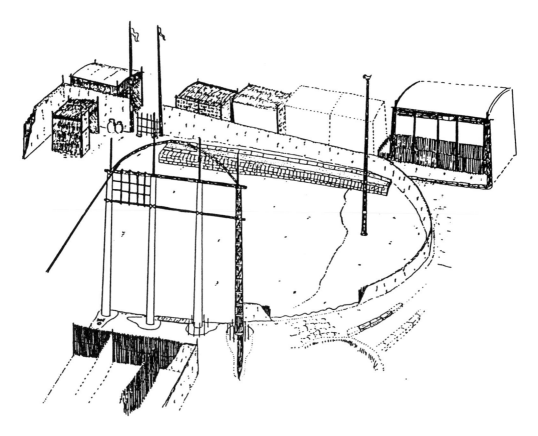

Figure 11a A provisional reconstruction of the HK29A complex by M.A. Hoffman (1987: fig.9)

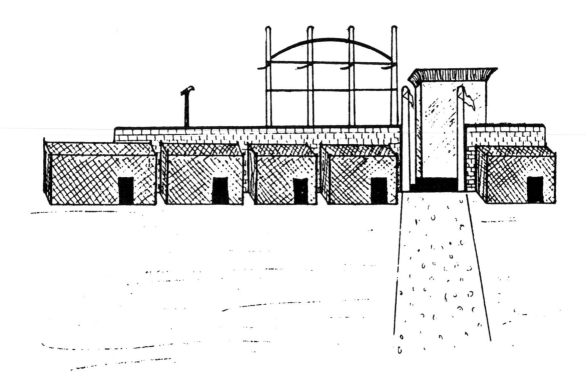

Figure 11b Reconstruction of the complex as approached from the Nile
(adapted from an original by M. Genato)

agate, obsidian, and quartz crystal, as well as several fragments of fine stone vessels in a variety of hard stone were recovered. The association of craftsmen with temples is certainly a regular part of the Dynastic economy (Kemp 1972) and suggests a function for the subsidiary buildings on the northern perimeter of the complex. Of specifically cultic or votive offerings, such as seen in the contents of the Main Deposit at Nekhen and other Archaic period town temples (see Adams 1974; Dreyer 1986), there is little evidence. A small bivalve shell of ivory, a hawk head of glazed steatite (fig. 7) and several fragments of clay figurines are all that remain (Hoffman 1987: 213-217). It is possible that a specific favissa containing the votive offerings remains to be uncovered or, more likely, that the cultic objects were moved to the temple in the alluvium at Nekhen after the site was abandoned.

Pottery contemporary with the main use of the site also shows certain aspects that have no counterpart in the domestic assemblages. Although fine polished wares, the equivalent of Petrie's B and P wares, make up less than 10% of the ceramic material found within Wall Trench 1, two distinctive shapes dominate the collection (fig. 8a-b). The most common shape is a collared jar coated with a bright red wash that is never polished. Parallel and spiralling rill marks on the broad collar and the interior of the body provide the earliest clear evidence of the use of the slow wheel to form an entire vessel. The second most common vessel is a small ovoid pot coated with a finely polished black slip. Together these shapes make up over 45% of the rim, base and body sherd collection. Without parallel or rare elsewhere in Egypt, and unknown from any other locality at Hierakonpolis, these distinctive vessels clearly served some cult function.[5] The black polished jars bear a strong resemblance to later *nw* pots, in which the gods were offered a variety of beverages (see Balcz 1934: fig. 103), and the collared jar is remarkably similar to the vessel depicted atop the jar stand on the Narmer macehead (see fig. 12). The distinction between the matte red and lustrous black surfaces may also have been invested with symbolic significance.

The presence of Nubian pottery, calcite-tempered pottery imported from Palestine, incised and impressed pottery possibly from Lower Egypt and shale-tempered ceramics perhaps from the Eastern Desert (fig. 8g-i) also suggests that the complex contained vessels not generally dispersed throughout the population (see Adams and Friedman 1992).

Among the straw-tempered Rough wares, elliptical bowls, perhaps to be considered offering platters, dominate the collection (fig. 8j). These platters are followed in frequency by modelled rim jars of various sizes (fig. 8k).[6] The contrasting frequency of Rough ware shapes in the collection from the eastern apex of the complex suggests that storage or manufacturing activities took place there, as indicated by a higher number of jar, large storage jar and large basin rims (fig. 8k,n,o).[7] For the purposes of dating, fossil indicators such as Wavy handled and Decorated wares are conspicuous by their relative rarity. Only two well-formed wavy handles and five fragments decorated with spirals were recovered. These and other chronological indicators suggest a Naqada IIc date for the main phase of ritual activity and a slightly later date of Naqada IId for the final additions on the west side of the courtyard (Friedman 1987, 1989, Adams and Friedman 1992; Hoffman 1987: 186-195).

Following the last construction phase, the complex appears to have been abandoned for a period of time. The mud-brick walls began to melt and the silts and brick-bats from this melt are found intercalated with lenses of windblown sand. The only clearly anthropogenic deposit over the floor —all other deposits are water or wind borne— is the so-called 'floor deposit', which is represented by a very distinctive ceramic assemblage that is clearly later than that found filling Wall Trench 1 and associated areas. The ceramics, datable to Naqada IIIa, were found within organically rich charcoal-laden silts located about 5cm above the surface of floor 'd' and include crude oval platters made of friable straw and grit-tempered silt, high-shouldered jars, and ledge-rimmed bowls (fig. 9). Although this assemblage may represent the last ceremonial activity conducted in this courtyard, this occupation appears to have taken place after the complex had fallen into disrepair as the large, fresh, sherds of this occupation occur in conjunction with, but are nowhere sealed beneath, the melted mud-bricks of the perimeter walls (Elias 1986: 4).

Following this episode, some 40cm of sand containing charcoal, ash, light lithic material and small abraded sherds accumulated over the floor (Hamroush 1987). Nevertheless, the site was not forgotten. Continued activity in the complex was revealed by renewed excavations in 1989 in the northwestern section of the court, where a large pit cutting into floor 'd' was found. This pit contained pottery of

Dynasty 1 (Aha-Djer) date including potstands with cut-out designs, *hes* vases, incense burners, and pottery imported from the Delta and EBII Palestine (fig. 10). Many of these vessels have direct parallels in the Main Deposit and the large tombs at HK6 (see Adams, this volume). It is, however, difficult to make a direct association between the activities which resulted in this pit and the courtyard complex unless one assumes that the sand covering the floor area had already attained a depth that effectively hid the rubbish below. It is also possible that some of this sand was intentionally placed over the courtyard to create a sand mound similar to those reported from within the temple and palace enclosures at Nekhen (Quibell and Green 1902; Fairservis 1986: 12-13; fig.7,21-22) and Khasekhemwy's funerary enclosure at Abydos (O'Connor 1992: 84-89). As further evidence of Early Dynastic activity is attested by surface finds north of the complex and extends into the cultivation, the area must have continued to have significance at a time when the low desert had been abandoned to mortuary activities exclusively.

Either prior to or shortly after this event, the complex was intentionally deconstructed. The fill of the large post-holes clearly indicates that these rare wooden features were not allowed to rot in place (fig. 5) and there is further evidence to suggest that other wooden features (wall posts, poles, etc.) and cultic items were removed to the new complex being built in the sacred precinct at Nekhen. Unfortunately, none of the pottery found within the post-holes provides a clear date for this demolition.

The material remains of the ceremonial centre at HK29A admit of several reconstructions, the provisional interpretation by Hoffman illustrated in fig. 11a being just one of them. This sketch is based on the belief that most of the architectural elements had been in use simultaneously, and that the resurfacing of the court did not involve major changes in the appearance of the complex. I wish to make only two corrections to this proffered reconstruction, both concerning the badly disturbed western portion of the site. First, the melted mud-brick platform or building (Structure V) has not been included, as its original appearance is unclear, but its presence should not be forgotten. Secondly, the 1989 excavations showed that the courtyard continued further west than indicated and the evidence for a rectilinear northwestern corner is ambiguous.

Archaeological evidence for Predynastic cultic establishments has hitherto been limited to the recovery of ceramics and other objects of that age beneath temples of later date which are only assumed to be remnants of an earlier religious site (e.g., Coptos: Petrie 1896, Williams 1988; Abydos: Petrie 1902; Nekhen: Quibell and Green 1902: 4-5; Armant: Mond and Myers 1940: 75-76). The mud-plastered floors and low walls found beneath the small Dynastic temple at Badari, although considered domestic remains, are the only contemporary architectural counterparts to the complex at Hierakonpolis (Brunton 1927: 18-21, pl.xxiii; Brunton and Caton-Thompson 1928: 44-45, pl. lviii). Thus, for the original appearance of the structures at HK29A, there are few contemporary parallels to which one can refer. The schematic renderings of mat and pole or wattle and daub structures found on Predynastic Decorated vessels and cylinder seals are not especially enlightening (e.g. Payne 1993: 76, fig.600; Williams 1986: 152-3, pl.84; Kaiser 1990: pl.68.3-5, 12-14; Porta 1989: pl. v-x). They attest only to the existence of cultic structures composed of a series of upright posts and lattice work surrounded by fences and ornamented with poles bearing standards. The details they illustrate, however, provide useful explanations for some of the features of the cultic establishment at HK29A. For example, representations of fences topped with the impaled animal heads (mainly cattle) may explain the head to torso discrepancy among the faunal remains at HK29A (see note 3).

A Decorated jar significantly from the nearby Fort cemetery at Hierakonpolis depicts a structure before which stands an object which has been interpreted as an *imy-wt* standard. This *imy-wt* is composed of a pole to which have been tied the internal organs of a flayed bird (Logan 1990). The huge amounts of animal bone and the numerous biface sharpening fragments prove that some area, probably the floor at HK29A, was a butchery site. If the organs were then displayed and wrapped around a pole, perhaps the one at the apex of the floor,[8] it would be no surprise that the court was repaved with some frequency. The depiction of the structure before which this standard was place, is unfortunately too schematic to be of much use for the reconstruction of main structure at HK29A, but does suggest a structure composed of tall vertical poles with a matt or wickerwork curtain wall, similar to that known from other contemporary depictions.[9]

Many of these Naqada II depictions have been viewed in association with a royal cycle of events by

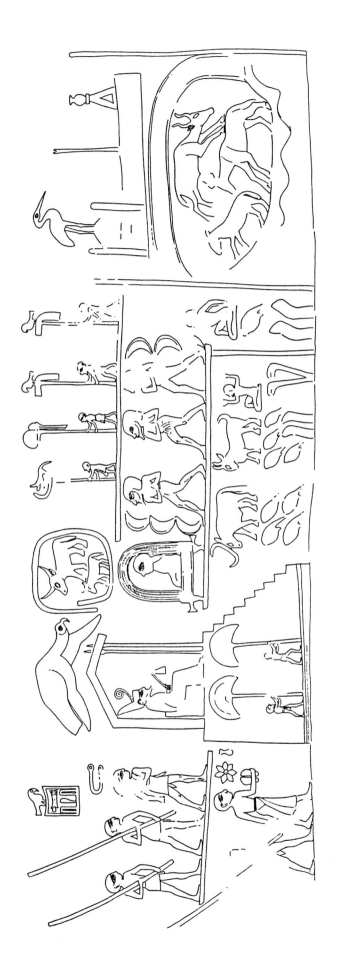

Figure 12 The Narmer macehead (Ashmolean E.3631; courtesy of the Ashmolean Museum)

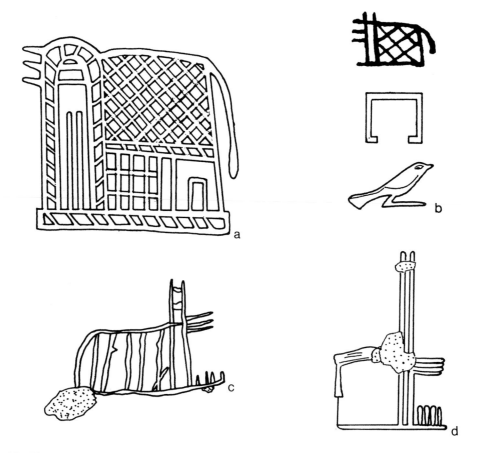

Figure 13 The prototypical Upper Egyptian shrines and the *pr wr*: a) Shrine on a sealing from the time of Hor-Aha (after Emery 1939:fig.47); b) Developed form of the shrine on a wooden seal (BM 49018); c) Graffito at El Kab (from author's photograph); d) The *pr wr* on the false door in the Southern Tomb at Saqqara (after Lauer 1962a: pl.xxv and fig. 54)

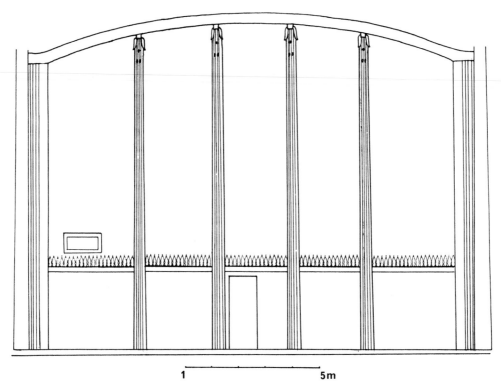

1   5 m

Figure 14 Theoretical reconstruction of the House of the South at Saqqara (after Lauer 1962a: pl. 25b)

Williams and Logan (1987), specifically the ceremony surrounding the appearance of the king. Considering the importance of such an event in historic times, Kemp (1989: 57) suggests 'we should anticipate that each age sought a dramatic setting for this great moment, built around certain basic elements; a large open space, an elevated place where the king could be seen within a formal framing, and a token palace where robing and resting could comfortably and privately take place.' Considering the relationship Hierakonpolis had with kingship in Egyptian tradition, it is not inappropriate to seek these elements in the HK29A complex (i.e., a large courtyard and an elevated platform with a small pavilion near by). And, indeed, the similarities between the material remains at HK29A and the complex in which Narmer makes a ceremonial appearance on his macehead found only 600 metres away at Nekhen have not escaped notice (Hoffman 1987: 220; Elias 1986).

The salient points of the Narmer macehead's depiction of the ceremonial appearance of the king for the reconstruction of the complex at HK29A are the stepped and canopied throne dais from which Narmer views the festivities (cf. Structure V) and the small building surrounded by a low courtyard wall (fig. 12). Within the court stands a pole supporting an image now lost and a jar on a potstand. In the scene immediately below, horned animals cavort within a walled oval courtyard, perhaps the court shown immediately above it.[10] The thick wall on one side, carved as a raised band, and the sinusoidal wall on the other are strikingly similar to arrangement at HK29A.[11] Given the continued activity at HK29A into Dynasty 1, it is tempting to suggest that the structure the Narmer macehead is not just similar to, but actually is a representation of this ceremonial complex.

It is, however, difficult to reconcile the shrine and the heron perched above it with this dramatic interpretation.[12] Similar round-topped structures within courtyards depicted on Early Dynastic dockets, all apparently dedicated to Lower Egyptian deities, have been identified with *Pr-nu-* or *Pr-nzr-* type shrines, the archetypal or ideal form of the Lower Egyptian temple In contrast, Early Dynastic representations, almost exclusively on seals and sealings, of what is considered to be the prototype of the Upper Egyptian counterpart, the *Pr-wr*-type shrine, portray a vaulted structure composed of posts and lattice work shaped in the silhouette of a crouching animal complete with tail and horns (fig. 13a) (*inter alia* Arnold 1982; Jequier 1906; Kaplony 1963: 14, ill. 137-174; Lauer 1962: 167f; Porta 1989:77-88; Ricke 1944: 27-38; Vandier 1955: 556-568, Weill 1961: 69-99).

The earliest depictions of the *pr-wr* type structure from the reigns of Narmer and Aha (Emery 1939:99; Quibell 1905: pl.15) have much to offer for the reconstruction of the main structure at the Hierakonpolis complex. They illustrate a high arched entrance apparently supported by four columns (each one sporting a projecting horn-like attachment) and a small door at the back (fig. 13a). Several examples depict the structure on a diagonally hatched rectangular or oval base which may represent a base wall or sockle (Ricke 1944:29) perhaps exemplified by Wall 4 at HK29A. In later representations, many of these details are omitted; the structure becomes more rectilinear and the corner post of the facade projects increasingly further beyond the height of the roof (fig. 13b and c notably from a graffito at El Kab) until it attains its final and named form depicted on the southern false door in the Southern Tomb of the Djoser complex at Saqqara (fig. 13d).

This architectural distinction between the typical shrines of Lower Egypt typified by a rounded roof and Upper Egypt designated by a vaulted structure with a façade composed a tall posts was maintained in the row of dummy shrines lining the jubilee court at the Step Pyramid and all subsequent jubilee depictions. Nevertheless, at Saqqara the stone renditions of what have been considered the actual *pr wr*, the shrine of the white crown and its protectress Nekhbet, and the *pr nu*, the shrine of the Wadjet of the red crown, differ only in minor details. The façades of both the House of the South (fig. 14) and House of the North consist of four slender engaged fluted columns, indicating that the originals were of wood, supporting a slightly curved roof. At the top of these columns are pendant leaf-shaped capitals with brackets and holes for affixing the characteristic horns or other insignia. Mat screens topped by a khekher frieze fill the spaces between the pillars and a slightly off-centre doorway provides access to the interior.

It is in these stone buildings that the main structure at HK29A finds its closest parallel. In the reconstruction by Lauer (1936: 154-77, pl.73,81; 1962: pl.25), the entire façade of the House of the South is approximately 20m wide. The columns are 11.5-12m high and separated by a distance of about 3-4m, dimensions which are remarkably close to the post structure at HK29A. While the height proposed by Lauer may be somewhat inflated, the depth of the post-pits at HK29A and the provisional identification of their contents as logs of cedar, a tree which can grow to 40m high (Germer 1986:1357f.), suggest that Lauer's reconstruction may not be far from the truth.[13] The similarity in scale also suggests that the structure at HK29A or something like it was the mat and pole original which the Saqqara monuments sought to reproduce.

Although shrines to the crown goddesses were set up at the Residence in Memphis in the Early Dynastic period (Kaplony 1963), the original home of the *pr wr* is considered to be at Hierakonpolis (Arnold 1982b:934; Kaplony 1963:6 but also see Gardiner 1944: 27 note 3). It is thus possible that the complex at HK29A is the *pr wr*.

The appearance of early temples in Egypt has been the topic of much recent discussion. The small one and two room mud-brick sanctuaries of the Satet temple at Elephantine, Medamud and other Early Dynastic-Old Kingdom town sites stand in opposition to the wooden post and lattice work structures expected from the contemporary representations (Dreyer 1986: 11-18; Kaiser et al. 1988: 140-1; Kemp 1989: 65-91, but see O'Connor 1992). Kemp (1989: 91-101) has explained this distinction as a reflection of two separate architectural traditions. One is a tradition of temporary structures composed of wooden frames and mats which was later to determine the form of Egyptian stone architecture. The other is a rectilinear style based on the use of mud-brick which seems to appear only with the beginning of the historic period.

The mixed media of the building materials employed in the HK29A complex, however, demonstrate that these traditions need not be as separate as they appear. Walls and other features of mud-brick were gradually introduced into the complex but did not entirely replace the wooden elements. Further, the scale of the complex at HK29A and its numerous renovations indicate that the buildings in the mat and pole tradition need not have been of a temporary nature. The prototypes for traditional Egyptian stone architecture may well have been archaic mat and pole structures that stood for several centuries but subsequently disappeared without a trace in places less conducive to their preservation than the low desert at Hierakonpolis.

In a variety of ways, the imposing, non-funerary, and not necessarily temporary, wood-frame and mat-work structures of Predynastic cultic or ceremonial establishments exemplified by the discoveries at HK29A must have exerted an immediate and profound influence on the architecture (non-mortuary and mortuary) of the succeeding periods (e.g. see O'Connor 1992: 84-89 and Adams 1995: 72-3 for similarities with the temple at Nekhen). The number of elements which find their earliest appearance at HK29A (e.g., extensive use of mud-brick, possibly sinusoidal walls, and temple workshops) illustrates the debt Dynastic Egypt owes to its Predynastic antecedents. As the only example of a full-sized original, and perhaps the original *pr wr*, the ceremonial complex at HK29A is of obvious importance to our growing understanding of the fundamental stages of Egyptian civilization and architecture.

Notes:

1 If Wall 1 were a casemate wall, the inter-wall filling has disappeared or been transferred into Wall Trench 1, perhaps by brick robbers, ancient or modern. This seems unlikely, although a Turkish pipe fragment and a fragment of blue painted New Kingdom pottery were found on the surface mixed with debris filling this wall trench.

2. Sliwa (1992) has observed that sinusoidal walls of the Middle Kingdom occur in three principal forms: 1) carefully constructed sinusoidal walls enclosing funerary complexes and urban developments; 2) low and less carefully executed auxiliary walls on a sinusoidal line that serve as permanent or temporary retaining walls against loose material; 3) low, regularly laid symbolic walls without any actual structural purpose.

Although Sliwa concluded that the function of most sinusoidal walls is symbolic or magical, it is worth noting that sinusoidal walls result in a 100% increase in resistance to sand pressure when compared to straight walls of similar thickness, but require only 20% more bricks to construct. Although there is no evidence to suggest the need for a revetment wall during the main phases of the complex at HK29A, the great quantity of sand found covering the courtyard may, in part, be a result of the last remodelling phase with which this wall may possibly be associated.

3. Although no single anatomical region predominated, McArdle (1992) noted a discrepancy between the number of post-cranial elements from young animals and their cranial remains (both caprines and cattle). This discrepancy may be explained by the existence of some ritual practice at the site which involved either the collection and/or use of the skulls of more mature individual or the consumption of the headless carcasses of younger animals. The use of the skulls of mature cattle as decorative elements in temples and tombs in this early period is well documented by representational and actual evidence.

4. Nile perch prefer deep, well oxygenated waters. Once they attain a size of 40cm in length they become very reclusive and live in sheltered areas such as rock crevices. For the symbolic significance of the Nile perch and Tilapia see Brewer and Friedman 1989:7-9, 79.

5. The collared jars are without exact parallel, although Petrie's Corpus P48 is close. Within Wall Trench 1, 33% of all untempered Nile silt body sherds were coated with its distinctive red wash (n=640). The 113 rim and 41 base fragments together make up 27.8% of the diagnostic sherds in this assemblage. Parallels for the black jar are provided by Petrie's Corpus F91d and Brunton 1948:pl.xi.F25 from Matmar. The rim and base fragments of these vessels make up 17.9% of the diagnostic sherds (n=67 rims; n=32 bases). The remainder of the assemblage is mainly composed of bowls with fully polished or half-polished red slipped surfaces (fig. 8c-d). Black-topped jars and beakers make up a negligible percentage of the collection (fig. 8e-f).

6. Platters make up 34% (n=1122) of the identifiable straw-tempered rims in Wall Trench 1; rimmed jars 30.5% (n=1006). These shapes are followed in frequency by 'hat-shaped' bowls (fig. 8l), making up 16.2% (n=574) and bottles (fig. 8m), comprising 3.4% (n=120) of the assemblage of straw-tempered rims.

7. Rimmed jars make up 62% of the identifiable rims at the eastern end of the wall trench. Elliptical platters comprise only 14.4% of the collection, large storage jars or pithoi and basins 2.3% and 5.6% respectively.

8. A wide range of objects were elevated on polls, any number of which could have graced the courtyard at HK29A. A new addition to the list of possible poll toppers is provided by a recently cleaned ivory from the Main Deposit at Nekhen. This ivory mace handle depicts the large commemorative maceheads, also found at Nekhen, elevated on poles and surrounded by a procession of animals (see Whitehouse 1992).

9. For an idiosyncratic interpretation (but one not necessarily incompatible with the architectural remains at HK29A) of the evidence for the appearance of early temples from the Painted Tomb at Hierakonpolis and Decorated 'Boat Pots', see Monnet-Saleh 1983, 1987.

10. Millet (1990:54-57) interprets this scene in a different fashion. Instead of a courtyard, he views the lines surrounding the animals as landscape details. He concludes that this scene of wild cows pasturing in the desert near a water course was included on the macehead only to impart the information that the location of the festivities was at Buto. However, see Petrie 1901:pl.IIIa for a bull most certainly within an enclosure wall.

11. The resemblance of the elliptical shaped courtyard to the oval writing of the name of Nekhen (Gardiner 1957: Sign O47) has not escaped notice. Sethe (1917:57) long ago considered the sign to represent an offering court with two wall spurs. The round form of the writing is securely attested from the reign of Den (Kaplony 1963: note 623). Although the oval variant of the sign may be seen on a Protodynastic painted bowl from Qustul (Williams 1986:155, pl 86) and in a personal name on a cylinder seal from Abydos (BM 528136; Kaplony 1963:552, but see Spencer 1980: no. 417), it does not seem to appear again until Dynasty IV in the writing of the nome emblem on a series of hieratic ostraca from Helwan. Significantly, these mummy dockets are for ladies from the Hierakonpolis nome who held positions in the *Pr wr* (Fischer 1960: 187-190, fig. 7). The hieroglyphic writing of the oval sign is not found until Dynasty VI (Davies 1902:ii.6; Sethe 1933:123:12;132:5). Nevertheless, archaic sealings from the time of Djer-Den depicting a series of three or four wide or narrow ovals without internal slashes have been read as Nekhen by Kaplony (1963:104-107). What relation these early hieroglyphs may have to the architectural remains at Hierakonpolis is as speculative as their proposed readings (see also Wilson 1955:234-235).

12. The heron perched on a round-topped shrine is symbolic of the town of *Db'wty*, or Buto (Altenmüller 1974: 1098-1099; Dreyer 1992: pl. 6.3).

13. Reconstruction of the wooden original by Ricke (1944:96-99, pl. iv) makes the structure about half the size; 6-7m high and about 10m wide. Williams' (1988: 49-50) reconstruction of the Predynastic temple of Min at Coptos using the proportions of the Min colossi, although highly speculative, is of great interest. He suggests that the maximum height of the temple façade would have been 8-10m, its width 8-14m, with a courtyard fronting it of about 16-30m in length. Although the complex at HK29A does not have the axial alignment Williams reconstructs for Coptos, the upper-end proportions are remarkably close.

The Relative Chronology of the Naqada Culture[1]

Problems and Possibilities

Stan Hendrickx

1. Introduction.

Terminology regarding the relative chronological periods within the predynastic and early dynastic culture of Egypt is nowadays frequently used in a manner suggesting complete reliability. Nevertheless, several fundamental problems concerning the relative chronology of the Naqada culture still exist. It has already been stressed by several authors that no generally accepted terminology exists for Egypt's late prehistory and early history (e.g. Mortensen 1991: fig. 1; Tutundzic 1992). For instance, the terms Semainean (Petrie 1920: 46-50), Protodynastic (Scharff 1931: 16-30; Kantor 1965; Baumgartel 1970a), Naqada III (Kaiser 1957; 1990: Abb. 1) or Terminal Predynastic (Hassan 1988) can be used, and are actually used, for more or less the same period. Besides tradition and personal preferences, the main reason for this confusion seems to be that the terms are in most cases ill-defined, both archaeologically as well as chronologically. Since the relative chronology of the Naqada culture has not been dealt with in a systematic way during the last few decades, and since meanwhile the available information has increased considerably, it seems absolutely necessary to re-examine the subject.

2. Sequence Dating.

The original study goes back to the early years of the century, when W.M.F. Petrie worked out his Sequence Dating (Petrie 1899; Petrie & Mace 1901: 4-12; Petrie 1920: 3-4), the first attempt at what is now known as seriation. The Sequence Dating is based on the gravegoods from the cemeteries excavated by Petrie and his assistants at Naqada, Ballas (Petrie & Quibell 1896) and Diospolis Parva (Petrie & Mace 1901). As a first step, the pottery was arranged in a corpus of 'predynastic' pottery, consisting of nine classes of pottery and over 700 types (Petrie 1921, see also below, pp.44-46). Next, all objects from each grave were noted on a slip of card. Finally, the cards were arranged in a relative chronological order based on the resemblance of types. In this stage of the work, Petrie used only nine hundred relatively intact graves containing five or more different pottery types, out of over four thousand excavated graves. The chronological order was defined by two main principles. First, an earlier and a later phase were distinguished through the observation that the classes of White Cross-lined pottery on one hand, and Decorated and Wavy Handled pottery on the other hand, never or almost never occurred together. Secondly, it was accepted that there had been a degradation of the form of the Wavy Handled types, going from globular to cylindrical shapes. When all grave cards had been arranged in order, Petrie divided the cards into fifty equal groups, each of them consisting of 18 graves, numbering them as Sequence Dates from thirty to eighty. By choosing to start at SD 30 he left space for earlier cultures, which he thought were still to be discovered. Finally the fifty SD's were divided into three groups which he considered to be archaeologically, culturally and chronologically different. The 'cultures' were named Amratian (SD 30-37), Gerzean (SD 38-60) and Semainean (SD 60-75), after some important predynastic cemetery sites.

The Sequence Dates were continued with a second typological corpus, for the 'protodynastic' pottery (Petrie 1953). This is almost exclusively based on material from the extensive cemeteries at Tarkhan (Petrie, Wainwright & Gardiner 1913, Petrie 1914). This time the number of types reached 885 (see below, pp.46-47) and no classes of pottery were distinguished. The 'protodynastic' corpus partly overlaps with the most recent types of the 'predynastic' corpus, as a result of which the Sequence Dates for the 'protodynastic' corpus start from SD 76 and continue to SD 86, which should mark the beginning of the Third Dynasty. However, the SD's 83-86 remained almost completely theoretical because of the lack of Second Dynasty material. The distinction between the individual Sequence Dates is not carried out in the same manner as for the predynastic corpus, but the transition to a new Sequence Date is based on typological breaks which Petrie defined mainly through the development of the Wavy Handled types. Finally, Petrie connected the Sequence Dating with the historically dated pottery types and other objects from the royal tombs of the earliest dynasties at Abydos (Petrie, Wainwright & Gardiner 1913: 3).

Although the development of the Sequence Dates certainly represents one of the major intellectual achievements in the study of predynastic Egypt (cf. Kendall 1963), a number of methodological shortcuts and possible errors were afterwards pointed out by several authors, among whom Legge (1913), Scharff (1926: 71-4), Kantor (1944), Baumgartel (1955: 2, 1970a: 4-5) and Kaiser (1956b) are the most important. Among the methodological problems several points may be noted.

It is obvious that Petrie makes no clear distinction between typology and chronology. He postulates the evolution of the Wavy Handled class without sufficient evidence for the earlier stages of its evolution (Kaiser 1956b: 93-5). Also, the criteria used for the definition of the pottery classes (Petrie 1921) are heterogeneous. The basic criterion may be either the fabric (Rough class), the method of firing and/or finishing (Black-Top and Polished Red), the decoration (White Cross Lined and Decorated), the shape (Fancy), a morphological detail (Wavy Handled) or the relative chronology (Late). This last class causes a special problem because of the lack of consistency in pottery fabric (cf. Patch 1991: 171). Furthermore, the definition of the individual types within these classes is not bound by strict rules (cf. Petrie 1921: 5). Also, the types are not distinguished in the same way for each of the pottery classes. All these factors will cause problems for any type of seriation, including the one devised by Petrie. When subsequent use is made of this kind of typological corpus for typing objects in the grave registers of excavations not carried out by Petrie himself, it is only to be expected that errors are bound to arise.

Petrie period	Cal BC (1)	years	Petrie SD's	number SD	years/SD
Semainean	3300-3050	250	63-76	14	17.86
Gerzean	3650-3300	350	38-62	25	14.00
Amratian	3900-3650	250	31-37	7	35.71

(1). After Hassan (1988): 138.

Tab. 1. Absolute chronological implications of Petrie's Sequence Dates.

As already stated, the system was developed using only nine hundred graves containing five or more pottery types. Since it is now obvious that the average number of objects in a grave increased through time (cf. Seidlmayer 1988), it is generally accepted that this causes the earlier periods to be under-represented by Petrie (e.g. Petrie 1920: 4; Kaiser 1956b: 92). However, if we test this idea with the currently accepted absolute chronology, a rather puzzling image appears (table 1). The importance of the final phase of the predynastic period, as defined by Petrie, seems not over-represented, although it remains a fact that the earliest phase is under-represented. This is most probably the result of the numerically dominating role of the Main Cemetery at Naqada when Petrie developed his the Sequence Dates. Indeed, at this cemetery the number of graves belonging to the Naqada III period is restricted (cf. Payne 1992: fig. 1-2).

The SD's for the 'predynastic' and the 'protodynastic' corpus were not defined in the same way. This implies of course that their eventual chronological value cannot be compared. Also, the protodynastic SD's were defined by means of typological differences, which were *a priori* accepted to have chronological value. Furthermore, Petrie treats cemeteries from different sites as an entity. He accepts the cultural uniformity of the predynastic culture as guaranteed, leaving no place for local variation. This is characteristic of the time when Petrie was working; far more attention was paid to cultural diffusion than to local growth and evolution.

Finally, the definition of the original Sequence Dates was made in a manner to minimize the chronological dispersion of each type of pottery. This results in a compromise between the competing claims of all pottery types for closer proximity. This perfect balance, however, is purely artificial, since, whenever new graves are added to the system, the range of Sequence Dates for a number of types will have to be expanded and the accuracy suggested by the Sequence Dating becomes purely hypothetical. Also, it is not at all clear in what manner Petrie added new types to the already existing corpus. Probably new types were dated according to characteristic types (e.g. Wavy Handled) in the company of which they were found and no longer according to grave groups (Mortensen 1991: 16). Of course, when adding new data to the system, the original point that each SD represented the archaeological material from 18 graves was also lost. Obviously, the fact that each SD was originally based on an equal number of graves never implied that every SD represented a similar period of time. This was realised by Petrie himself (Petrie 1920: 4) and always remained an inconvenience of the system, since one automatically tends to consider the SD's as chronological units.

However, the most striking omission of Petrie's way of working remains the fact that he never took the horizontal distribution of the graves into consideration. This despite the fact that he noticed, for instance, that none of the cemeteries from Diospolis Parva covered the whole range of the Sequence Dates but that, on the contrary, 'early' and 'late' cemeteries could be distinguished (Petrie and Mace 1901: 31-2). Strangely enough, Petrie does not mention spatial distribution within the cemeteries of Naqada, Ballas or Diospolis Parva, although it is hardly imaginable that he did not notice anything at all. On the occasion of later excavations by former assistants of Petrie, the existence of groups of chronologically related graves, and therefore the differences in the spatial distribution of objects, was noticed several times at different sites (e.g Randall-McIver and Mace 1902: 3; Ayrton and Loat 1911: 2; Peet 1914: 18; Brunton and Caton-Thompson 1928: 50-1) but no attempts were made to use these observations for chronological purposes.

3. *Stufen* chronology

Although Sequence Dating was rightly criticised, the general principles of the development of the Naqada culture, as established by Petrie, were never fundamentally contradicted, neither are they today. Nevertheless, it has long been obvious that the original Sequence Dating cannot be maintained, since it gives a misleading idea of great accuracy, while in reality the system will become increasingly imprecise as new data are incorporated. Therefore, Sequence Dating is nowadays generally replaced by W. Kaiser's *Stufen* chronology (Kaiser 1957). Unfortunately, the study of Kaiser was only published in an abridged version as an article of nine pages accompanied by eleven plates, and this already 38 years ago. Because of the limitations of space within the publication, Kaiser was unable to include details on his analytical method. Recently Kaiser mentioned in an article the extension of his *Stufen* chronology into the First Dynasty (Kaiser 1990: Abb. 1, see also p. 42), but the manner in which this was done still remains unpublished.

In his original study, Kaiser starts from the horizontal distribution of pottery classes and types of objects within the cemetery 1400-1500 at Armant (Mond and Myers 1937). Although this cemetery was published to a very high standard for the time, the identification of the objects cannot be controlled, since the original objects are no longer available and only types which were not yet represented in the corpus were drawn. Three spatial zones were distinguished by the relative percentages of Black-Topped, Rough and Late Wares, each of them dominating one zone. These zones are considered to be chronological stages, which can be regarded as the three main stages of the development of the Naqada culture. Within these three periods, eleven subperiods, called *Stufen*, were recognised according to the clustering of types of objects, chiefly pottery. Thus the distinctions between the individual *Stufen*, and therefore also between the three main periods, are made up primarily on the basis of object type and not by the representation of wares. Since the Armant cemetery contains only 149 graves and more than half of the pottery types occurred only once, the grouping of limited numbers of related types was unavoidable (Kaiser 1957: 77, n.67), although this is not free from risk (see below). Of course, this method can be criticised from the methodological point of view, since it more or less postulates the chronological implications of the spatial distribution, but this does not seem to be a major practical problem within Egyptian cemeteries.

When compared to the Sequence Dating, Kaiser's system has the advantage of including not only the information from the typological apparatus, but also from the spatial distribution of the objects. Furthermore, it does not give an impression of extreme accuracy, but by defining periods, it escapes largely, although not completely, the problem of becoming increasingly meaningless as new data are added.

However, this does not mean that the system is free from problems. Although Kaiser included data from a number of cemeteries besides the one at Armant, essentially it remains true that data from only a single cemetery has been used for the description of the Naqada culture throughout Upper Egypt. Nevertheless, Kaiser is well aware of the possibilities for regional differentiation, and has noticed regional phenomena, at Mahasna for example (Kaiser 1957: 74). The problem caused by using the cemetery of Armant becomes even more complicated since the earliest phase of the Naqada culture is not present there, and also the most recent phases are very sparsely documented or absent. Therefore, the definition of the *Stufen* Ia and Ib is based on mere hypothesis, although examples from cemeteries other than Armant are given. The description of *Stufe* IIIb, though less hypothetical than *Stufen* Ia and Ib, is also based on information from other cemeteries. In most cases it was not possible to study the spatial development of these cemeteries and therefore Kaiser's description of *Stufen* Ia-b and IIIb depends largely on the theoretical evolution of pottery types as already accepted by Petrie.

An initial point of debate is whether or not Kaiser's division of the Naqada culture into three phases is valid. If so, it should be questioned whether the limits of the three main periods of the Naqada culture are based on facts which are sufficiently obvious. As far as the distinction of three periods is concerned, there seems to be no problem on first inspection. Several cemeteries belonging to the Naqada culture bear evidence for the presence of three groups of graves, dominated respectively by the presence of Black-Topped, Rough and Late pottery. However, these three classes are identified in different manners (see above, pp.44-5), although Black-Topped stands primarily for a Nile Silt fabric, mainly Nile Silt A; Rough stands for a straw-tempered Nile Silt fabric while Late stands mainly (cf. below) for a Marl fabric (for all fabrics, cf. Nordström 1986). Most of the other pottery classes and a number of their individual types can be attributed to one of these three fabrics. It would be more logical to study the spatial distribution of the three fabrics and not only of the pottery classes defined by Petrie. Kaiser noted the problem and describes the relation between the fabrics and the pottery classes, but continues to work by Petrie's pottery classes (Kaiser 1957: 76, note 8).

The transition from *Stufe* I to *Stufe* II at the Armant cemetery raises certain questions (table 2a-b, cf. Friedman 1981: 70-1). According to Kaiser's general principles, *Stufe* I should be dominated by Black-Topped pottery, which is indeed the case, and *Stufe* II by Rough pottery. This rule, however, fails to apply for *Stufe* IIa, when Black-Topped pottery remains dominant. Comparing Nile Silt A pottery with straw-tempered Nile Silt pottery, the dominance of the second fabric (52 % <> 39 %) remains limited even for *Stufe* IIb. The differences between *Stufe* IIa and IIb, when the dominant class of pottery changes from Black-Topped to Rough, as well as between *Stufe* IIb and IIc, with the introduction of Wavy Handled and a number of new Decorated types, are much more important than the difference between *Stufe* Ic and IIa (cf. table 2a-b). Another point of importance in this discussion, is that the Rough pottery does not appear out of the blue at a certain moment in the evolution of the Naqada culture. It is more than obvious from settlement excavation that the Rough ware makes up the large majority of pottery from the beginning of the Naqada culture (e.g. Brunton 1937; Hendrickx & Midant-Reynes 1988: 8; Friedman 1994), but the Rough ware finds its way only slowly to the cemeteries. Since the Rough pottery already existed at a period prior to its regular appearance in graves, its absence or presence is not sufficient reason for distinguishing two main periods in the Naqada culture. However, Kaiser's distinction between *Stufe* I and *Stufe* II does not depend only on the representation of the wares. Of great importance is the appearance in *Stufe* IIa of a number of pottery types, especially small bag-shaped Rough types (R 65 b, R 66 a, R 69 r, R 93 c), which were not yet present during *Stufe* Ic. Nevertheless, if a distinction between a first and a second period within the development of the Naqada culture is to be made, it seems more logical to draw the line between *Stufe* IIa and IIb or perhaps even between *Stufe* IIb and IIc.

	IC	IIA	IIB	IIC	IID1	IID2	IIIA1	IIIA2
B	28	38	32	15	4	5	-	-
C	1	-	-	-	-	-	-	-
N	-	1	-	-	-	-	-	-
F	1	-	-	-	1	-	-	-
P	9	8	21	20	16	16	7	5
D	-	-	8	9	2	2	1	1
R	-	19	70	82	36	39	10	13
L	-	-	4	5	2	1	9	51
W	-	-	-	9	4	10	3	1
st.v.	-	-	-	1	-	-	-	-
pal.	8	4	-	1	4	-	-	1
flint	5	-	-	1	-	2	-	-
total	52	70	135	143	69	75	30	72

Tab. 2a. Armant Cemetery 1400-1500. Number of objects, after Kaiser 1957.

	IC	IIA	IIB	IIC	IID1	IID2	IIIA1	IIIA1
B	53,8	54,3	23,7	10,5	5,8	6,7	-	-
C	1,9	-	-	-	-	-	-	-
N	-	1,4	-	-	-	-	-	-
F	1,9	-	-	-	1,4	-	-	-
P	17,3	11,4	15,6	14,0	23,2	21,3	23,3	6,9
D	-	-	5,9	6,3	2,9	2,7	3,3	1,4
R	-	27,1	51,9	57,3	52,2	52,0	33,3	18,1
L	-	-	3,0	3,5	2,9	1,3	30,0	70,8
W	-	-	-	6,3	5,8	13,3	10,0	1,4
st.v.	-	-	-	0,7	-	-	-	-
pal.	15,4	5,7	-	0,7	5,8	-	-	1,4
flint	9,6	-	-	0,7	-	2,7	-	-
total	100,0	99,9	100,1	100,0	100,0	100,0	99,9	100,0

Tab. 2b. Armant Cemetery 1400-1500. Percentage of pottery classes for each *Stufe*, after Kaiser 1957.

The transition from *Stufe* II to *Stufe* III is also not without problems. The difference between them is made up by the Late class which takes over from the Rough class as the numerically most important group. However, Kaiser's view of the spatial distribution of the Rough and Late pottery at Armant (Kaiser 1957: tf. 15 B-C) does not take into account the fact that an important number of the Late types are in reality made in the Rough fabric (especially the types belonging to the L 30 series), although he is well aware of the problem (Kaiser 1957: 76, note 9). Counting these with the Rough class gives a completely different picture. The Late types reach 50% of the pottery types in only one, small, grave (1592), where two out of four pots belong to the Late class, the other two being Rough types. On the other hand, for all of the graves in the southern section of the cemetery, the Rough types make up 50 % or in most cases far more of the pottery. Thus, at Armant there is no part of the cemetery which is dominated by Marl clay pottery. However, this does not mean that groups of graves dominated by Marl clay pottery do not occur during the Naqada culture. On the contrary, large groups of graves, at Elkab for instance, (Hendrickx 1994) and Hierakonpolis (Adams 1987) and even entire cemeteries such as those of Tarkhan (Petrie, Wainwright & Gardiner 1913, Petrie 1914), Tura (Junker 1912) and Abu Roash (Klasens 1957-61) are completely dominated by Marl clay pottery. Only the transition in dominance from 'Rough' to 'Late' pottery should be placed later.

Besides these problems concerning the main structure of the *Stufen* chronology, a few problems related to particular *Stufen* have to be mentioned. At first, the distinction between *Stufe* Ia and Ib is apparently based on the contents of a number of graves from sites for which no cemetery plan is published (Abydos, el-Amrah and Mahasna, cf. Kaiser 1957: 73-4). Fifteen graves, containing 37 objects, are attributed to *Stufe* Ia and 27 graves containing 66 objects, to *Stufe* Ib. Although there is a difference between the group of objects attributed to each of the *Stufen*, it must also be noticed that several types (B 22 b, B 22 f, B 26 b, P 1 a, P 17) occur for both *Stufen*. This, together with the limited number of data and the fact that the spatial distribution of the objects cannot be controlled, seems to indicate that the *Stufen* Ia and Ib should better be considered as an entity, as long as no further evidence is available.

Another problem is caused by the relationship between Kaiser's *Stufen* IId2 and IIIa1, which share the same Wavy Handled types and differ mainly through the presence or absence of Black-Topped types, and through their Decorated types. Also of importance are the transitions from R 84-86 to L 30 b,c and from P 40 g1 and P 40 e1 to P 40 q and P 46 b/Arm, as well as the appearance of restricted bowls (P 24 q). However, when looking at the important Decorated types which Kaiser (1957: tf. 23) gives as typical for *Stufe* IId2, it appears that there is not a single grave where one of these Decorated types is present together with a Black-Topped type and a Wavy Handle jar typical for *Stufe* IId2.[2] Among the other significant types, several of them occur only occasionally,[3] while the frequently occurring types R 84-86 and L 30 b,c are related to each other and belong to a group of types into which Petrie apparently allowed important variations (cf. p.45). It is therefore to be feared that the attribution of a vessel to one of these types by excavators other than Petrie may have been rather arbitrary. Also the spatial distribution at Armant Cemetery 1400-1500 easily allows a different clustering of graves, by which the group defined by Kaiser as *Stufe* IId2 no longer exists. Finally, since the Wavy Handled types, from the moment of their first appearance during *Stufe* IIc until their disappearing at the end of the First Dynasty, always seem to display the fastest evolution of shape, it would be very strange if this would not also have been the case during *Stufe* IId2-IIIa1. For all these reasons the archaeological description of the *Stufen* IId2 and IIIa1 cannot be maintained in the way it was defined by Kaiser.

The reason for the confusion between the *Stufen* IId2 and IIIa1 probably originates from Kaiser's analysis of the Armant cemetery. The distinction between the *Stufen* IIIa1 and IIIa2 causes a particular problem. First it should be noticed that on the spatial distribution map where the graves belonging to each *Stufe* are shown (Kaiser 1957: tf. 20 C), the symbols indicating respectively *Stufe* IIIa1 and IIIa2 have erroneously been interchanged. This would not be a real problem if it did not suggest that it is the latter *Stufe*, at the extreme southern limit of the cemetery, which is represented by only three graves (1558, 1559, 1594; and one more isolated grave, 1578, in the northern part of the cemetery, which however has not one type in common with the other three graves). Looking at the spatial distribution with this correction in mind, it is *Stufe* IIIa1 which is represented by just three graves, the two richest of them containing Wavy Handled types (W 41) which are closely related to those occurring further north (cf. Kaiser 1957: tf. 16 B) in the groups of graves attributed by Kaiser to *Stufe* IId2. As already mentioned, straw-tempered Nile Silt pottery is dominant for the entire southern part of the cemetery, just as it is for Kaiser's *Stufe* IId2 graves. Therefore, it seems appropriate to omit the four graves from *Stufe* IIIa1 as a separate group.

Next we have to turn to the *Stufen* IIIb-IIIc3, which are not represented at Armant cemetery 1400-1500. *Stufe* IIIb was already defined in Kaiser's original publication, the more recent period however was originally described in another way. Starting with architectural information, inscriptions and archaeological material, Kaiser distinguishes three periods, called *Horizonten* (Kaiser 1964: 92-6; Kaiser & Dreyer 1982: 260-9).[4] The definition of the *Horizonten* does not rely on spatial distribution and is therefore of a different order from the *Stufen* chronology. With regard to the pottery, the *Horizonten* are described as follows (Kaiser & Dreyer 1982: 264):

Horizont A (before Irj-Hor): W 80 and similar 'protodynastic' types; large jars 74 b, 75 q-v.

Horizont B (Irj-Hor - Narmer): cylindrical jars with and without incised wavy decoration, but the second group increases in number ('protodynastic' type 50); large jars as for previous group with additional types 76 and 75 a-o.

Horizont C (starting with Hor-Aha): cylindrical jars without incised decoration; large jars mainly belonging to type 76 or 75 a-o.

From the archaeological description of the *Horizonten* it immediately becomes clear that *Horizont* A can be identified with *Stufe* IIIb. The difference between the *Horizonten* B and C is less obvious. The information from which Kaiser starts is very limited since he deals only with graves in which *serekh* marks have been found. However, this is not the main problem. The distinction between *Horizont* B and *Horizont* C is particularly difficult to make since there are no types of objects which are characteristic for each individual *Horizont*, and the difference can only be made through the frequency of the same types. Also, the diagnostic types with 'Wellendekor' (proto- dynastic 74 b, 75 q-v) occur only very exceptionally. At Tarkhan only 8 examples are present among 5138 pots.[5]

Recently Kaiser extended the *Stufen* chronology up to the end of the Second Dynasty (Kaiser 1990: Abb. 1). *Stufe* IIIb was divided into two subphases and three *Stufen*, IIIc1, IIIc2 and IIIc3, were added. With the late types of the Wavy Handled class as main characteristics, the chronological stages distinguished by Kaiser are summarised in table 7.[6]

The distinction Kaiser makes between *Stufe* IIIb1 and IIIb2 does not seem justified, since at Tarkhan, for instance, there are 226 graves in which one of the types occurs which should be characteristic for *Stufe* IIIb2 (48 s,t or 49 d,l), whilst in 116 of these graves (i.e over 50 %) types belonging to the 46 and 47 series (*Stufe* IIIb1) are also present. Furthermore, the spatial distribution of the two groups of types shows no obvious patterning (see also p.59) and the very obvious spatial distribution of the Turah cemetery does not support the idea of a chronological difference between the above-mentioned types. This view might be supported by the observation that the difference between the types belonging to the 47 series and types 48 s,t / 49 d,l is not a difference in the shape of the vessels, nor even in the shape or importance of the decoration, but only in the technique by which the decoration was applied. Therefore, and also by virtue of the fact that *Stufe* IIIb2 covers a very limited period of time according to Kaiser (cf. Kaiser 1990: Abb. 1), it is preferable to make no distinction between the *Stufen* IIIb1 and IIIb2.

Kaiser's *Stufe* IIIc1 consists of types which are partly characteristic of *Stufe* IIIb2 and partly of *Stufe* IIIc2. The existence of these kinds of 'transitional periods' within the evolution of the Naqada culture can of course not be denied, but it should be questioned whether it is necessary to distinguish a period for which there are no characteristic and unique types of objects. This is especially true since the archaeological description of the *Stufen* is often used for dating individual graves or even objects. It therefore seems better to distinguish fewer periods, and admittedly have eventually a slightly less detailed idea of the chronological evolution of a cemetery, whilst on the other hand archaeologically distinct chronological phases will offer far better points of comparison.

Finally we should pay attention once more to Kaiser's 1957 article. In this study, the description of the *Stufen* is illustrated by plates on which the most important and characteristic types of objects for each *Stufe* are drawn (Kaiser 1957: tf. 21-4). These plates have been reproduced or referred to in a large number of studies dealing with the Naqada period. However, the relationship between these plates and the study of the Armant material is not obvious at all. The plates present 244 types of pottery. Of these only 119 – less than half – are represented at Armant. The other 125 types come from graves found in other cemeteries which were allocated by Kaiser to a particular *Stufe*, but this is not based on the horizontal stratigraphy of these cemeteries. Among these 125 are the large majority of White Cross-lined, Decorated and Wavy Handled types, which are often used as diagnostic when the relative chronology of the Naqada culture is discussed, or when attempts are made to compare fresh data with the *Stufen* chronology. For the types represented at Armant, 37 out of 112, i.e. 32,8 %, are given by Kaiser as characteristic for more than one *Stufe*, while the figure is only 13 out of 125, i.e. 10,4 %, for the pottery types not represented at Armant. Furthermore, in a number of cases, the assignment of pottery types to a certain *Stufe* does not correspond between the plates and the results of the Armant study. This is true for 34 [7] out of 112 types represented at Armant, among them three out of the five Wavy Handled types. It is therefore obvious that the plates shown by Kaiser have to be regarded with great prudence and certainly cannot be considered as absolute guidelines, as occurs too often in the literature, since this was not Kaiser's intention, and the plates are only to be considered as an idealised outline of the development of the *Stufen*.

4. The present information available for cemeteries belonging to the Naqada culture in Upper and Lower Egypt.

Since Kaiser's study in 1957, an important quantity of data on predynastic and early dynastic cemeteries has become available. Several cemeteries, already excavated in Upper Egypt during the first two decades of this century, have since been published.[8] E.J. Baumgartel published, after long and painstaking work, the corpus of objects from the Naqada cemeteries (Baumgartel 1970b, corrections and supplements Payne 1987, Hendrickx 1986), which however will always remain incomplete since a large number of objects, mainly Rough types, remained in the field. The publication by B. Adams of Garstang's excavation at the Fort Cemetery of Hierakonpolis (Adams 1987), and of the other cemeteries at Hierakonpolis explored by Quibell and Green (Adams 1974a), is most important since no cemetery from this major site had been published previously. More information concerning Hierakonpolis and a number of other sites between Esna and Gebel es-Silsila comes from the work of H. de Morgan in this area during the beginning of the century, also published relatively recently (Needler 1984, Cleyet-Merle & Vallet 1982). The edition by Dunham of Lythgoe's notes on cemetery 7000 at Naga ed Deir (Lythgoe & Dunham 1965) is of course valuable, but does not allow a detailed identification of the gravegoods. This however, is supplied by Friedman (1981), while the human remains have been published by Podzorski (1990). Dunham was also responsible for the publication of an early dynastic cemetery at Zawiyet el-Aryan, excavated by Fisher and Reisner in 1910 (Dunham 1978).

Important information comes from excavations which had already taken place during the decade before World War II, but especially since the end of the fifties.[9] Between 1957 and 1959 A. Klasens excavated, on behalf of the Leiden Museum, several early dynastic cemeteries at Abu Roash (Klasens 1957-1961). More recent are the excavations in 1965-8 at el Sheikh Ibada where a small early dynastic cemetery was discovered (Zimmerman 1974) and in 1966-7 by the Egyptian Antiquities Organisation, under the direction of A. el-Sayed, of a predynastic cemetery at Salmany, near Abydos (el-Sayed 1979). The surprisingly rich results of the excavations of the *Deutsches Archäologisches Institut* (DAI) at Umm el Qaab, which started in 1977 and are directed by G. Dreyer (e.g. Kaiser & Grossman 1979; Kaiser & Dreyer 1982; Dreyer 1990, 1992a, 1993) are of course of the utmost importance for the connection between the Naqada culture and the historical period. A Naqada III cemetery of limited extent was excavated by the author at Elkab between 1977 and 1980, on behalf of the *Comité de Fouilles Belges en Égypte* (Hendrickx 1994). Across the Nile, at Hierakonpolis, a number of cemeteries were investigated by the Hierakonpolis Project under the direction of the late M. Hoffman (1982a). Finally, for Upper Egypt, there are the excavations of the *Institut Français d'Archéologie Orientale*, directed by B. Midant-Reynes at Adaïma (Midant-Reynes et al. 1990; 1991; 1992; 1993b; 1994). In the Memphite area, a few early dynastic graves from North Abu Roash were published by Hawas (1980), while the apparently far more important cemetery from the same age at Abusir has only recently been found (Radwan 1991; Boessneck, von den Driesch & Eissa 1992; Leclant & Clerc 1992).

In recent years, a considerable number of excavations have shed new light on the relation of the Naqada culture between Upper and Lower Egypt.[10] Besides the very important Munich excavations at Minshat Abu Omar in the Eastern Delta, which started in 1978 and are under the direction of D. Wildung and K. Kroeper (e.g. Kroeper & Wildung 1985; 1994; Kroeper 1988; 1992), one has also to mention the limited number of graves found at Tell Ibrahim Awad (van den Brink 1988b: 77-114; 1992c: 50-1), Beni Amir and Tell el-Masha'la (Krzyzaniak 1989, el-Hagg Ragab 1992), Ezbet Hassan Dawud (el-Hangary 1992) and a number of other sites (cf. Krzyzaniak 1989). Important new information has also become available for Nubia,[11] but this falls beyond the scope of the present article.

5. Problems related to the published data [12]

Nevertheless, despite the importance of all this new information, it is obvious that the old excavations still represent the majority of the data available. There are two fundamental problems for re-studying these excavations. The first one is that, in many cases, no map of the cemetery, or only an incomplete one, has been published and it therefore becomes impossible to study the spatial distribution of objects or archaeological characteristics. The second is that the cemeteries were, in the best cases, published by grave registers which referred to typological systems. The great majority of the original objects are neither described nor drawn. The objects themselves are no longer available for study in their totality, and they will never be accessible again since only a (limited) number of them have found their way into museums, and even then in many cases the details of their provenance has been lost. An important number of vessels which were less attractive for the museums were left in the field. Therefore, one inevitably has to rely on the published grave registers and the typological systems to which they refer (cf. Seidlmayer 1990: 2-4).

Three typological systems, the 'predynastic' (Petrie 1921), the 'protodynastic' (Petrie 1953) and the 'archaic' (Emery 1938-58, Klasens 1957-61), have to be discussed, although more have been used (Reisner 1908: 90-9; Reisner & Firth 1910: 314-22; Junker 1912: 31-44; Junker 1919: 48-79, Scharff 1926: 16-35). All three of them are descriptive typologies, to which types could always be added.

The 'predynastic' typology was first developed by Petrie for his excavations at Naqada and Ballas (Petrie & Quibell 1896). At that time he distinguished about 300 pottery types. However, after excavations at other sites by himself and others, the number of types was augmented to 1718 when the 'predynastic' corpus was published (Petrie 1921). Finally, after additions by other excavators, a total of almost 3000 types was reached.[13] The real significance of this enormous number of types is very difficult to evaluate, since Petrie never described the criteria used for distinguishing a type from a related one. He only stresses on several occasions that 'needless multiplications' should be avoided (e.g. Petrie 1921: 5). As a result, it is to be expected that the definition of types, and therefore the addition of new types to the corpus, was not applied uniformly by all excavators. It is most obvious that Brunton, when publishing his excavations at Badari (Brunton & Caton-Thompson 1928), Mustagedda (Brunton 1937) and Matmar (Brunton 1948), recognised new types more readily than Petrie did some decades earlier (see also Kaiser 1957: 76, note 10).[14]

Out of about 3000 distinguished types, only 1553 were used for the publication of the cemeteries.[15] The great difference between these numbers came about for various reasons. One of the most important is that pots with decoration, or other particular characteristics, were readily made into separate types, but a large number of them had been purchased rather than excavated, and therefore did not feature in an excavation report. The fragmentary grave register of the Naqada cemeteries is another reason why a number of published types are not represented.

The relation between the number of types and the number of examples known for each type, shows important differences between the pottery classes distinguished by Petrie (table 3). The numerically well-represented classes (Black-Topped, Polished Red, Wavy Handled, Rough, Late) also show the highest ratio per type, between 4 and 7 examples, while the numerically less dominant classes (White Cross-lined, Fancy, Black Incised, Decorated) are represented by 1 to 2 examples per type only. This indicates that the typologies of the classes of decorated pottery, or pottery with particular shapes, are to be regarded as an almost complete corpus rather than a typological system. Whenever the individual excavation reports are examined, even stronger differences appear. It is obvious, for instance, that Petrie distinguishes far fewer Rough types, and therefore will have a far larger number of examples for each of these types, than Brunton does. An obvious example are the subtypes distinguished by Brunton for the very frequently occurring large, pointed jar R 81 (Brunton 1927: pl. XLII), which were apparently considered as one uniform type by Petrie.

frequency		# types	# examples	% examples	% types
1		740	740	10,35	47,65
2		222	444	6,21	14,29
3		139	417	5,83	8,95
4		91	364	5,09	5,86
5		55	275	3,84	3,54
6		45	270	3,77	2,90
7		37	259	3,62	2,38
8		32	256	3,58	2,06
9		23	207	2,89	1,48
10		13	130	1,82	0,84
11-15		57	730	10,21	3,67
16-20		31	561	7,84	2,00
21-25		26	607	8,49	1,67
26-30		8	224	3,13	0,52
31-40		14	468	6,54	0,90
41-50		11	492	6,88	0,71
51-60	(1)	5	265	3,70	0,32
61-70	(2)	2	125	1,75	0,13
82	(3)	1	82	1,15	0,06
237	(4)	1	237	3,31	0,06
total		1553	7153	100,00	100,00

Tab. 3. Frequencies for Petrie's "predynastic" typology (cf. note 16).

(1): B 57 b; R 24 a; R 85 h; W 19; W 43 b.
(2): P 22 a; R 22 a.
(3): R 84.
(4): R 81.

The number of examples known for one type may differ greatly (table 3). Types of which only one example is known represent 47 % of the types but only 10 % of the examples. Some 89 % of the types occur less than 10 times, representing 45 % of the pottery. The 11 % of the types which occur 10 or more times represent 55 % of the pottery. The unique 'types' are less exceptional than the figures suggest since they are part of series of related types (cf. Seidlmayer 1990: 9).

Finally, some practical problems should be noted for the 'predynastic' typology. First, confusion exists in the numbering of the types because Petrie renumbered previously published types when integrating them into his corpus. A number of these alterations were mentioned by Petrie (1921: pl. LX), but others were not (Hendrickx 1989, II: 33-5; Patch 1991: 177-8). Secondly, if the pottery from new excavations is to be identified with the Petrie typology for comparison with the old excavation reports, this is not only hampered by the fact that the 3000 types are scattered over a number of publications, but also by the small scale and abbreviated details of the drawings. Also, it would be useful to investigate the accuracy of the drawings, a task which should be possible since a large amount of the drawn pottery is presently in the Petrie Museum of Egyptian Archaeology.

The 'protodynastic' typology was first developed for the cemeteries of Tarkhan (Petrie, Wainwright & Gardiner 1913; Petrie 1914). The original typology of Tarkhan consists of 527 types, which had been augmented to 885 by the time the 'protodynastic' corpus was posthumously published (Petrie 1953), on which occasion a number of the original type identifications from Tarkhan were changed. The additional types are almost exclusively from the royal tombs at Umm el Qaab.[16] The additions by other excavators, representing a further 234 types, were not included,[17] which brings the total to 1119 types. Out of these, 743 were used for the publication of cemeteries.[18] The number of examples known for each of the types (table 4) shows different characteristics when compared to the 'predynastic'

frequency		# types	# examples	% examples	% types
1		301	301	5,76	40,51
2		136	272	5,20	18,30
3		67	201	3,85	9,02
4		35	140	2,68	4,71
5		41	205	3,92	5,52
6		27	162	3,10	3,63
7		17	119	2,28	2,29
8		19	152	2,91	2,56
9		7	63	1,21	0,94
10		4	40	0,77	0,54
11-15		27	328	6,28	3,63
16-20		15	263	5,03	2,02
21-25		11	260	4,97	1,48
26-30		6	168	3,21	0,81
31-40		8	269	5,15	1,08
41-50		3	137	2,62	0,40
51-60	(1)	6	320	6,12	0,81
61-70	(2)	1	67	1,28	0,13
71-80	(3)	2	155	2,97	0,27
81-90	(4)	1	84	1,61	0,13
91-100	(5)	1	94	1,80	0,13
101-150	(6)	2	223	4,27	0,27
151-200	(7)	5	865	16,55	0,67
339	(8)	1	339	6,49	0,13
total		743	5227	100,00	100,00

Tab. 4. Frequencies for Petrie's "protodynastic" typology (cf. note 19).

(1): 46 p; 47 h; 48 s; 49 g; 63 g; 66 j.
(2): 59 p.
(3): 47 p; 60 j.
(4): 60 m.
(5): 46 k.
(6): 49 l; 60 g.
(7): 46 d; 46 f; 46 m; 49 d; 60 d.
(8): 46 h.

typology. Types for which only one example is known represent 40 % of the types but not even 6 % of the pottery. A total of 87,5 % of the types is represented by less than 10 examples, making up 31 % of the pottery. The 12,5 % of the types which occur 10 or more times represent 69 % of the pottery.

The 'protodynastic' typology (Petrie 1953) distinguishes no classes of pottery, since, according to Petrie, only the Late and the Wavy Handled classes continued into the early dynastic period. However, it has already been seen that the Late class is not homogeneous with regard to the ceramic fabric. This, of course, causes confusion between the well-made pottery in Marl clay and the Rough pottery, mostly made from straw-tempered Nile Silt. Since the published drawings are small and similar types are known to occur in both ceramic fabrics, in a limited number of cases it cannot be decided to which category a particular vessel belongs.

A particular problem is raised by the confusion which is apparent within the group of cylindrical jars, which are the descendants of the Wavy Handled class. Petrie uses the shape of the wavy handle decoration itself as the main criterion for distinguishing types (Petrie, Wainwright & Gardiner 1913: pl. XLIX), while the differences in shape of the vessels are considered to be only of secondary importance. This results, for instance, in important differences in shape between certain vessels which are all attributed to type 46 d (Petrie 1914: pl. XXVIII). As for the published drawings, the same problems occur as in the 'predynastic' corpus.

The 'archaic' typology was developed by W.B. Emery for the publication of the finds from the large mastabas at Saqqara (Emery 1938-58). This typology has been developed in a more structured manner than the 'predynastic' and 'protodynastic' typologies. On the other hand, an indisputable disadvantage is that Emery limited the number of types by allowing a considerable degree of variation within one type. Unfortunately, this cannot be checked, since the original objects are not available for study, and because Emery, in his 1949, 1953 and 1958 publications, uses a set of standard drawings which are always repeated for illustrating his finds. Comparison with Emery 1938, before these standard drawings were used, makes it clear that important differences occur between vessels attributed to the same type (e.g. types A 3 and A 4). As a result, it is not clear if there is any real value in the standardisation of the gravegoods suggested by Emery's publications.

The 'archaic' typology was enlarged by A. Klasens the on occasion of his excavations at Abu Roash (Klasens 1957-61). Klasens adds an important number of types to the already existing list, despite the fact that the number of objects was far smaller than those found by Emery at Saqqara. This is one more indication of the variation Emery allowed within the types. When considering the relation between the number of types and the number of objects for the cemeteries at Abu Roash alone (table 5), it is remarkable that 42 % of the types occur once but this represents only 5 % of the pottery, whilst 81 % of the types occur less than 10 times, representing 25 % of the pottery. The 19 % of the types which occur 10 or more times represent 75 % of the pottery. The drawings of the objects published by Klasens, although reproduced on a small scale, are of far better quality than those of Petrie's typologies. Also, Klasens publishes a large number of examples for each type, which helps considerably in understanding the principles by which the typology was established.

Besides pottery, an important number of other types of gravegoods have been found, among which are stone vessels, palettes, beads, etc. However, the types are represented in such small numbers that they offer only limited possibilities for comparison between graves. There is one exception, namely the stone vessels from Abu Roash published according to the principles used for the 'archaic' typology (Klasens 1957-61). Although 89 % of the types occur less than 10 times, this represents only 50 % of the vessels. Thus, the remaining 11 % of the types must also represent half of the number of vessels.

6. Status quaestionis of research on the relative chronology of the Naqada culture since Kaiser 1957.

Only a few studies, the most extensive of them as yet unpublished, have tried to check, correct or amend Kaiser's *Stufen* chronology. For the time being, they can be divided into two groups: those who are using computer-based multivariate seriation and those who are primarily relying on the study of spatial distribution. For a study mentioned by Vertesalji (1988), no information is available.

frequency		# types	# examples	% examples	% types
1		121	121	5,41	41,87
2		31	62	2,77	10,73
3		27	81	3,62	9,34
4		19	76	3,40	6,57
5		15	75	3,35	5,19
6		7	42	1,88	2,42
7		8	56	2,50	2,77
8		3	24	1,07	1,04
9		3	27	1,21	1,04
10		9	90	4,02	3,11
11-15		8	103	4,60	2,77
16-20		10	182	8,13	3,46
21-25		5	111	4,96	1,73
26-30		5	139	6,21	1,73
31-40		9	308	13,76	3,11
41-50		2	96	4,29	0,69
51-60	(1)	1	56	2,50	0,35
61-70	(2)	1	62	2,77	0,35
71-80		0	0	0,00	0,00
81-90	(3)	3	256	11,30	1,04
134	(4)	1	134	5,99	0,35
137	(5)	1	137	6,12	0,35

Tab. 5. Frequencies for Klasen's "archaic" typology at Abu Roach.

(1): A 3.
(2): K 2.
(3): B 8; L 7; W 7.
(4): B 10.
(5): J 1.

A study by E.M. Wilkinson (1974), dealing with seriation techniques, which are, as a test, applied to the Armant cemetery is only of historical importance.[19] Three seriations are carried out (Wilkinson 1974: 87). When compared to the spatial distribution, the results of all three seriations are completely unacceptable, even the one using Kaiser's original order as starting order.[20] Also, no archaeological evaluation of Kaiser's results is made.

More important is the article by B.J. Kemp (1982), where the seriation by multi-dimensional scaling of the graves within cemetery B at el-Amrah and the cemetery of el-Mahasna is discussed. However, it should be mentioned in advance that the seriation is not used for the evaluation of Kaiser's *Stufen* chronology, but Petrie's Sequence Dating. First, Petrie's pottery corpus was condensed to 43 types, unfortunately without mentioning which types have been amalgamated. According to the excavation report (Randall-McIver & Mace 1902), 228 pottery types are represented at el-Amrah cemetery B. Out of 90 graves for which information is available, 70 could be seriated because they contained two or more of the condensed types. After seriation, Kemp distinguishes three groups of graves (Group I-III) and two 'transitional' groups. The transitional groups represent 17 graves, i.e. 24 % of the seriated graves. If compared with Kaiser's dating of the graves at el-Amrah (Kaiser 1957: 73), Group I corresponds with *Stufe* I-IIc. The transitional group between Group I and Group II matches *Stufe* IIc (except grave 210 = IId2), while Group II, as well as the transitional group between the Groups II and III, corresponds with *Stufe* II-IId2. None of the graves from Group III is dated by Kaiser, but the objects from these graves are characteristic for his *Stufe* IIIb. The choice of el-Amrah cemetery B seems rather unfortunate, since it may well be that the entire predynastic period was covered by the cemetery, as stated by the excavators (Randall-McIver & Mace 1902: 3, see also Kemp 1982: 7-12), but only 98 graves out of about 400 have been published, and among the published graves there are none characteristic for *Stufe* IIIa1 (except grave 221) and IIIa2, as already stated by Kaiser (1957: 73). Kemp's question whether a period is missing at el-Amrah (Kemp 1982: 12) can therefore be answered positively, as far as the published data are concerned. As a consequence, it is to be expected that the separation between Kemp's Group II and Group III is very distinct.

Kemp, of course, also noticed that a number of well-known and characteristic pottery types are not represented at el-Amrah cemetery B, and therefore, a similar study was made for the cemetery at el-Mahasna, where 313 pottery types are identified in the excavation report (Ayrton & Loat 1911) and information is available for 131 graves. The pottery types are condensed to 38 types after which 98 graves could be seriated. Three groups of graves with two transitional groups are also distinguished for el-Mahasna, but this time the transition between the Groups II and III is less marked, indicating that the cemetery was in continuous use. Comparison with Kaiser's *Stufen* chronology is difficult since Kaiser dated only a restricted number of graves from Mahasna (Kaiser 1957: 74). Nevertheless, Group I seems to match with *Stufe* Ib-Ic, the transition between Groups I and II with *Stufe* IIa-IIc, and Group II with *Stufe* IIc-IId2. The transition between the Groups II and III as well as group III itself seems to be covered by *Stufe* IIIa1-IIIb, although Kaiser dated only three graves of this Group.

Apart from the 'missing' types at el-Amrah, the three Groups show strong resemblances between the two sites, as is also confirmed by the concordances with Kaiser's *Stufen* chronology. Finally Kemp discusses the validity of the three periods which are traditionally distinguished within the predynastic culture. Because of his identification of Group III at el-Amrah as early dynastic, he distinguishes only two main periods within the predynastic culture, despite the fact that the earlier part of Group III at el-Mahasna still belongs to the predynastic period.

A far more elaborate study of the relative chronology using seriation has recently been made by T.A.H. Wilkinson (1993a).[21] Eight predynastic - early dynastic cemeteries [22] were seriated using the Bonn Seriation Program. For the purpose of seriation, the types from Petrie's corpus which occurred in the eight cemeteries were condensed to 141 types. The use of a universal typology for all eight cemeteries allowed direct comparison of the seriation results. Wherever possible, horizontal stratigraphy was used to check the seriation results. In all cases, the spatial distribution confirmed the phases derived through seriation. Each individual sequence was compared against Kaiser's *Stufen* chronology. Significant differences emerged, most notably in Kaiser's demarcation of the three major Naqada culture phases. The eight individual site-based sequences were correlated using diagnostic types, to produce a 'chronological matrix' covering Lower, Middle and Upper Egypt during the predynastic - early dynastic transition.

Regarding the problems and possibilities of seriation, some general remarks have to be made. Obviously the various problems concerned with the typologies used for the publication of grave registers will have consequences for the application of seriation. As already mentioned, it is impossible to establish a new typological apparatus, more suited for computer seriation than Petrie's, since the original objects are no longer available, nor are they published in a manner allowing renewed typological work. The main problem is that the number of types is very large while the number of examples of these types is generally very low (table 3-4). Therefore, seriation seems impossible without grouping types or using only a limited number of frequently occurring types. Limiting the number of types will of course result in a tendency towards explicit differences between groups of graves. On the other hand, grouping types seems perhaps even more dangerous, considering the already discussed heterogeneity of the criteria used for distinguishing type classes as well as individual types within the Petrie typologies. More important, the variation allowed within one type seems to differ rather importantly according to the interpretation of the individual excavators. The unfortunate result of this situation is that the effect of combining types cannot be checked in an adequate way, and may well cause very different shapes and even pottery fabrics to end up as the same type. Nevertheless, if seriation is to be applied, careful grouping of Petrie's types seems to be the only possibility.

A general archaeological problem is the chronological value of seriation. In other words, the differences between the groups of related graves should be due to time and not to, for example, social differentiation or foreign influences (cf. Mortensen 1991: 15). Although, generally speaking, this is certainly an important problem for interpreting the results of seriation, the impact of non- chronologi-

Petrie 1921	Petrie 1953	Emery / Klasens	Petrie 1921	Petrie 1953	Emery / Klasens
L 10	3 m	I 1	-	65 p	C 2
L 30 c	55 l	-	-	74 g	E 23
L 30 k	55 n	-	-	74 p	D 8
L 30 m	55 n	-	-	75 a	A 4
L 30 s	55 s	-	-	75 d	A 4
L 33 m	56 f	-	-	76 a	A 6
L 34 g	56 f	-	-	76 b	A 6
L 36 a	60 d	A 3	-	76 c	A 7
L 36 a	60 m	A 3	-	76 d	A 7
L 36 b	60 b	A 3	-	76 g	A 12
L 36 n	60 g	-	-	76 l	A 8
L 37 m	65 k	C 6	-	76 m	A 8
L 38 a	59 b	B 8	-	76 n	A 8
L 38 a	59 b	B 6	-	85 d	E 2
L 46	82 c	-	-	85 e	E 2
L 58 c-d	86 d-f	-	-	85 f	E 2
W 33	44 f	E 22			
W 35	47 b2	E 22			
W 33-35	47 b5	E 22			
W 33-35	47 b9	E 22			
W 33-35	75 s	E 22			
W 51 a	43 r	-			
W 51 a	43 s	-			
W 58	46 d	-			
W 58	46 f	-			
W 58	46 h	-			
W 58	46 k	-			
W 62	46 b	F 7-8			
W 62	46 m	F 7-8			
W 62	46 p	F 7-8			
W 63	47 b	-			
W 71 a	46 j	F 9			
W 71 a	47 p	F 9			
W 71 a	48 d	F 9			
W 80	47 r	F 10			
W 80	47 t	F 10			
W 80	48 s	F 10			
W 80	49 g	F 10			
W 85	49 d	-			
W 85	49 l	-			
W 90	50 d	F 11			
W 90	50 d	(F 1)			
W 90	50 e	F 12			
W 90	50 f	F 11-12			
W 90	50 g	F 11-12			
-	50 s	(F 1)			
-	50 t	(F 1)			
-	11 b	K 7			
-	57 b	D 3			
-	59 d	B 8			
-	59 h	B 8			

Tab. 6. Table of typological concordances for characteristic pottery types.

cal elements can almost certainly be disregarded for the Naqada culture. Up to the present moment, the evidence for foreign influence on the Naqada culture of Upper Egypt is very scanty (cf. Dreyer 1992a, Holmes 1992b, Adams & Friedman 1992) and certainly cannot be considered to have an impact on the result of seriation. The only major exception is of course the Palestinian origin of the Wavy Handled pottery, but this causes no real problem since only the prototypes, which most probably arrived in Upper Egypt within a limited space of time, are to be considered as foreign influence. The morphological evolution of the Wavy Handled class took place in Egypt itself.

The impact of social differentiation upon the evolution of pottery types seems more difficult to define. However, by looking at the contents of particularly rich graves, it becomes clear that these only occasionally contain pottery of exceptional shape or function. At the same time it will be noticed that the social position of the deceased was expressed through the quantity of similar objects rather than through exceptional objects.[23] Although the existence of these kinds of objects within the graves cannot be denied, their isolated occurrence automatically guarantees that they will have no real impact on the results of seriation.

A question which is very difficult to evaluate, but which might have considerable influence on seriation, is the estimation of the period of time between the production of the pottery and the moment when they became part of the gravegoods. The pottery of the Naqada culture was not made especially for the funerary beliefs (cf. Hendrickx 1994: 50-1).[24] Different functions will cause variations in the span of time during which the vessels have been used. Also, the excavation reports never mention the conditions of use in which the pottery was found (cf. Hendrickx 1994: 50-1, 73-4).

A particular problem for seriation is raised by Petrie's distinction between the Rough and the Late class. The Late class includes a number of types which are both in shape and fabric closely related to types from the Rough class, but they are excluded from this class because of their chronological position. This should be taken into account for seriation since otherwise these types will cause marked transitions within the generated matrix. Finally, the most obvious problem for seriation is that an available source of information, i.e. the spatial distribution, is not taken in account, or only used as an element of control after the seriation has been carried out. As far as the author is aware, no attempts have yet been made to include the position of a grave into the data used for seriation.

Besides the studies using seriation for discussing the relative chronology of the Naqada culture, there is the second group which starts from the spatial distribution within the cemeteries. Once more, the problem of grouping types, already discussed with reference to seriation, will occur, although to a lesser extent.

The first study of this kind to be discussed is an unpublished master of arts thesis by R. Friedman, presented at the University of California in 1981 and concerning the spatial distribution and relative chronology at Naga ed Der cemetery 7000 (Friedman 1981). Comparison is made with Kaiser's *Stufen* chronology. Spatially distinguished groups of graves with objects characteristic for the *Stufen* Ic-IId are also represented at Naga ed Der. Although graves are present which should be placed before *Stufe* Ic, it was not possible to confirm Kaiser's difference between *Stufe* Ia and Ib. Also, a number of differences between Armant and Naga ed Der are observed, the most important being the massive presence of Black-Topped ware during *Stufe* IIb. In this respect it seems to be possible to connect the cemetery at Naga ed Der with the one at el-Mahasna (Friedman 1981: 74-5), where a similar phenomenon had already been observed by Kaiser (1957: 74).

J. C. Payne applied Kaiser's chronology to the information available for the Main Cemetery at Naqada (Payne 1990, 1992). She concludes that the same *Stufen* can be distinguished both at Armant and at Naqada and also that the differences in the archaeological description of the *Stufen* remain very limited, the most important being situated in *Stufe* IIb (Payne 1990: 81).

The graves from the cemetery at Minshat Abu Omar have been divided by Kroeper (1988, Kroeper & Wildung 1985: 92-6, see also Kaiser 1987) into four groups, some with subdivisions, according to the burial tradition and the gravegoods.[25] These groups, which vary strongly in number and whose spatial distribution shows no really obvious pattern (Kroeper & Wildung 1985: Abb. 315-21), certainly have a chronological value, but the details are not yet known, since the published report is only preliminary. Also, the relation between the relative chronology at Minshat Abu Omar, in the eastern Delta, and Upper Egypt should be a point of great caution.

Recently, the *serekh*-bearing vessels have been divided by van den Brink (this volume) into four chronological groups, starting from the *serekhs* themselves as well as the vessel types and the spatial distribution of the cemeteries in which these vessels have been found [26].

Finally, there is the author's doctoral thesis presented at Leuven University in 1989, which deals primarily with the cemeteries between Asyut and Assuan and a part of which is devoted to the problem of the relative chronology for the whole of Egypt (Hendrickx 1989: 239-46, 257-321). Although the full publication of this study will have to wait for some time, it seems nevertheless appropriate to discuss some of the results. The limited number of 'predynastic' cemeteries for which both a map and a grave register, even if incomplete, are available served as a starting point.[27] For the early dynastic period, information came from a number of 'protodynastic' and 'archaic' cemeteries in Lower Egypt. [28] As for the methodological procedure, there is not much difference from the method already developed by Kaiser. This implies that the distinction of related groups of graves is based not only on their contents but also on their spatial distribution within the cemetery. As a result, a conflict of interests will arise between the search for closer chronological proximity of all examples of one pottery type on the one hand, and the definition of spatially well-defined groups of graves on the other. Neither of these two elements can be accepted as prevailing over the other. Thus, most unfortunately, it seems impossible to establish clearly defined, 'objective' rules for the definition of archaeological complexes representing relative chronological periods within the Naqada culture. The same method, applied by Kaiser as well as by ourselves, is of course ultimately founded on the seriation principle, but depends in real terms to a considerable extent on the personal interpretation of the researcher.

By comparing the cemeteries which were analysed, it becomes clear that similar groups exist for different cemeteries. In that manner, 11 groups of graves, an equal number to Kaiser's *Stufen*, are distinguished and their relative chronological order defined through their mutual position in the cemeteries and through the evolution of the pottery classes and types of objects. However, comparing groups of related objects from geographically different cemeteries does not have to imply that they are contemporaneous in absolute chronological terms. Unfortunately, this question cannot be answered because of the limited number of C^{14} dates available for the Naqada cemeteries from Upper Egypt (cf. Hassan 1984b, 1985, Hassan & Robinson 1987). For this reason, and since related groups of archaeological objects can be distinguished at several sites, we may as well, until any proof to the contrary emerges, accept the contemporaneity of closely similar archaeological groups, meaning that the same chronological periods may well have existed for the different cemeteries. At this stage of the investigation, the data from cemeteries without published maps were integrated.

Finally, after an investigation for the possibilities of regional variability (see pp.61-3), a list of all types of objects was made, mentioning for each of them the relative chronological period(s) in which they are present and the number of occurrences. This allows an archaeological description of each of the relative chronological periods.

The general observations made by Kaiser for cemetery 1400-1500 at Armant are not fundamentally contradicted and therefore the number of relative chronological periods is equal to the number of *Stufen* distinguished by Kaiser, although in some cases important differences occur in their archaeological description (cf. *infra*). Nevertheless, though it might cause confusion, it was decided for the time being to use Kaiser's terminology but replace the word '*Stufe*' by 'Naqada' and at the same time change the letter indication into capital letters, which results in 'Naqada IA' etc.

Since my research on the relative chronology will have to be enlarged with the data from cemetery N 7000 at Naqa ed Der (cf. note 16), which seem to be characteristic for Kaiser's *Stufen* Ia/b-IId, only the Naqada III chronology will be dealt with further.

It has already been discussed that Kaiser's definition of the *Stufen* IId2-IIIa2 shows a number of problems (see pp.41-2), the most important of which is that the distinction between Kaiser's *Stufen* IId2 and IIIa1 is not reliable, since neither the spatial distribution nor the characteristic types mentioned by Kaiser allow two periods to be distinguished. Also, Kaiser's description of *Stufe* IIIa2 at Armant, is based on a very limited number of graves; it is obvious that the types of objects given by Kaiser as characteristic for *Stufe* IIIa2 (Kaiser 1957: tf. 24B) are far more numerous than can be deduced from the Armant cemetery and that they are in fact largely derived from other cemeteries, for which the spatial distribution could not be investigated.

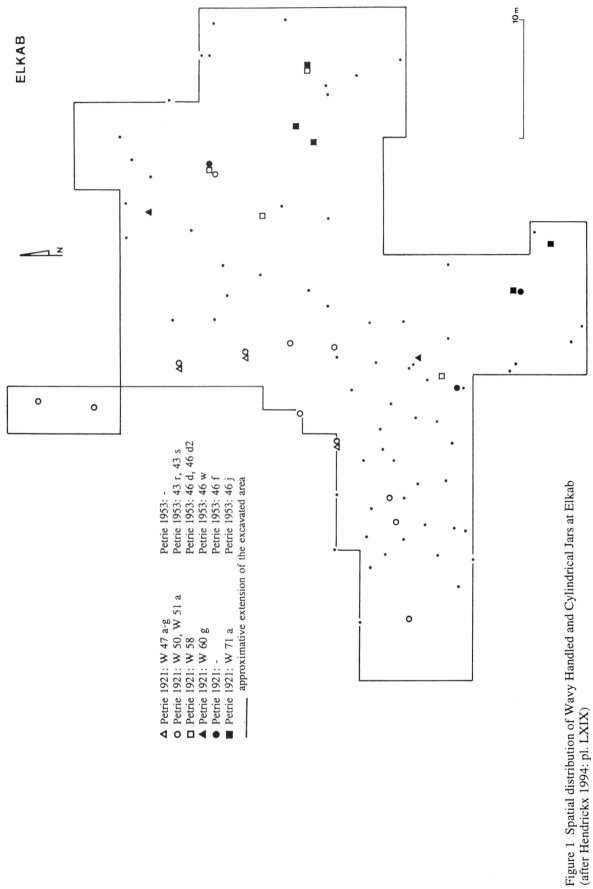

ELKAB

△ Petrie 1921: W 47 a-g   Petrie 1953: –
○ Petrie 1921: W 50, W 51 a   Petrie 1953: 43 r, 43 s
□ Petrie 1921: W 58   Petrie 1953: 46 d, 46 d2
▲ Petrie 1921: W 60 g   Petrie 1953: 46 w
● Petrie 1921: –   Petrie 1953: 46 f
■ Petrie 1921: W 71 a   Petrie 1953: 46 j
—— approximative extension of the excavated area

Figure 1 Spatial distribution of Wavy Handled and Cylindrical Jars at Elkab
(after Hendrickx 1994: pl. LXIX)

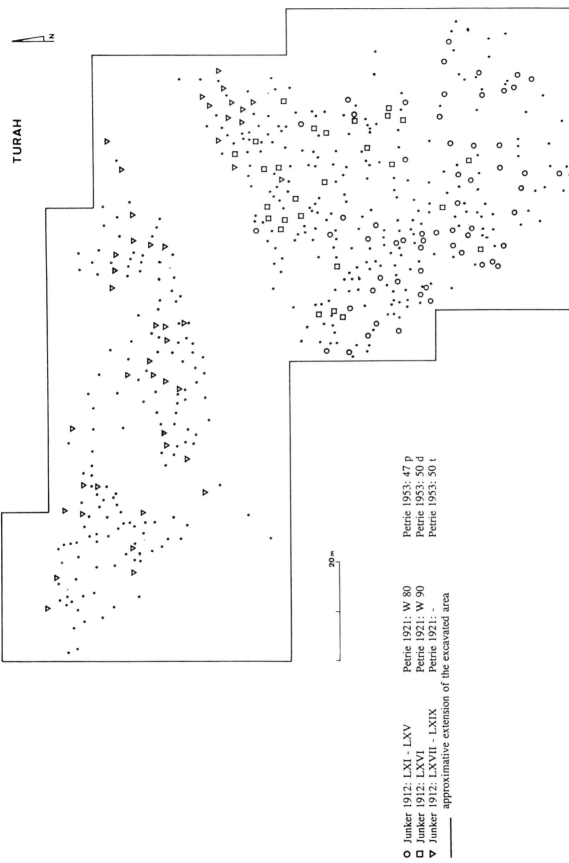

TURAH

20 m

○ Junker 1912: LXI - LXV   Petrie 1921: W 80   Petrie 1953: 47 p
□ Junker 1912: LXVI   Petrie 1921: W 90   Petrie 1953: 50 d
▷ Junker 1912: LXVII - LXIX   Petrie 1921: -   Petrie 1953: 50 t
———— approximative extension of the excavated area

Figure 2 Spatial distribution of Cylindrical Jars at Turah (after Junker 1912)

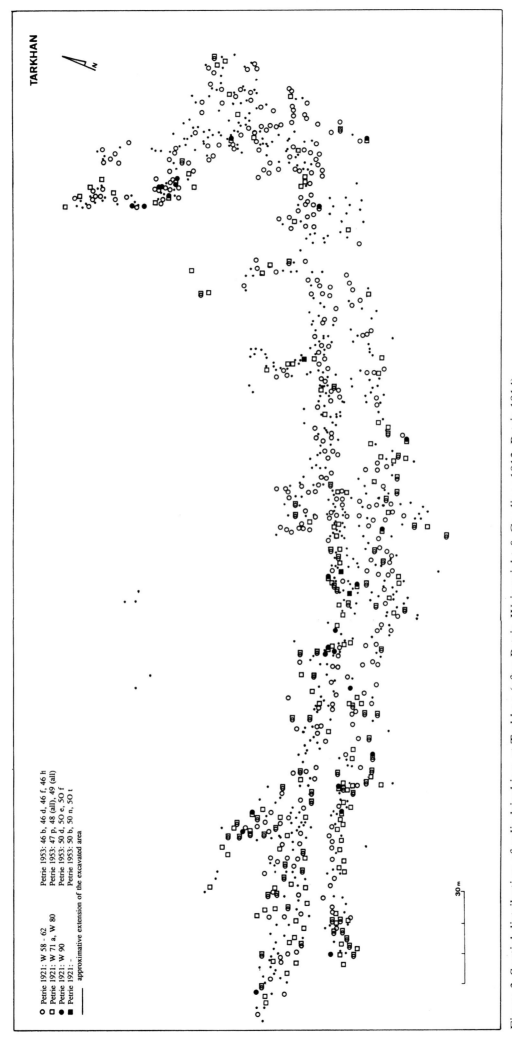

TARKHAN

N

○ Petrie 1921: W 58 - 62   Petrie 1953: 46 b, 46 d, 46 f, 46 h
□ Petrie 1921: W 71 a, W 80   Petrie 1953: 47 p, 48 (all), 49 (all)
● Petrie 1921: W 90   Petrie 1953: 50 d, 50 e, 50 f
■ Petrie 1921: -   Petrie 1953: 50 b, 50 n, 50 t
━━ approximative extension of the excavated area

30 m

Figure 3 Spatial distribution of cylindrical jars at Tarkhan (after Petrie, Wainwright & Gardiner 1913, Petrie 1914)

When studying the spatial distribution at the Naqada III cemetery of Elkab (Hendrickx 1994: 205-16) four groups of graves could be distinguished, both by their contents and by their spatial distribution (fig. 1). The homogeneity of the distribution of the Wavy Handled types within these graves was quite remarkable, and within material characteristic for Kaiser's *Stufe* IIIa2, two groups could be distinguished.[29] Because of this observation and the above-mentioned problems with the *Stufen* IId2-IIIa1, the most recent group distinguished within Kaiser's *Stufe* IIIa2 was readjusted to Naqada IIIA1 while most of the original *Stufe* IIIa1 types, together with a large number of the *Stufe* IId2 types, are considered characteristic for Naqada IID2.

In order to link the relative chronology of the Naqada period to historical times, the early dynastic cemeteries of Lower Egypt have to be taken into account, since well published large cemeteries from this period are not available for Upper Egypt. The switch from Upper to Lower Egypt should not be a fundamental problem, since it is generally accepted that, certainly by Naqada IIIA2, the whole country was already a cultural entity and probably also politically united (cf. Kaiser 1990). The cemeteries involved (note 16) have been published according to the 'protodynastic' and 'archaic' typologies, which offer a number of statistical advantages for seriation if compared with the 'predynastic' typology (cf. pp.44-7). Therefore, it was quite straightforward to identify groups of related graves, starting from a limited number of characteristic pottery types, mainly storage jars and the cylindrical jars which represent the final stages of the evolution of the Wavy Handled class. The evolution of the cemetery at Turah is particularly clear. This was noted by the excavator himself (Junker 1912: 1), and later also by Kaiser (1964: 108-9). The spatial distribution of this cemetery displays three clear zones (fig. 2), which are characterised by the difference in late types of Wavy Handled jars.[30] The southern part of the cemetery (zone 1) is dominated by Junker's types LXI-LXV (= W 80 = 47 p), the central part (zone 2) by Junker's type LXVI (= 50 d) and the northern part (zone 3) by Junker's types LXVII-LXIX (= 50 t). The spatial distribution at Tarkhan Valley Cemetery [31] is less obvious, but still allows two large groups of tombs and two or three smaller ones to be distinguished (fig. 3). The cemetery seems to have developed along a 'path' running SW-NE. The first group, dominated by 46 b-h (= W 58-62), is situated immediately to the north and south of the 'path', with the most marked concentrations in the central and north-eastern sections (zone 1). The second group, dominated by 47 p, 48-49 (= W 71 a, W 80, W 85), is situated further away from the path, with the most marked concentrations in the south-western and southern sections (zone 2). Two small zones, one in the central section to the north of the 'path' and one in the north-eastern section (zones 3-4), are characterised by the presence of 50 d-f (= W 90).

Groups of related graves could be distinguished at all of the large cemeteries, and a number of groups from Tarkhan Valley Cemetery, Turah and Abu Roash Cemetery 400 show very close parallels. It was, therefore, a rather simple matter to draw up one typo-chronological framework which gives a global image of the chronological evolution in Lower Egypt. Five periods are distinguished, three of them represented at the cemetery of Turah which is under discussion. Of these five periods, two show archaeological characteristics which are very similar to two most recent periods distinguished for the Naqada cemeteries of Upper Egypt, i.e. Naqada IIIA2 (Tarkhan, zone 1) and IIIB (Turah, zone 1; Tarkhan, zone 2). The three remaining periods for Lower Egypt were labelled Naqada IIIC1 (e.g. Turah, zone 2; Tarkhan zones 3-4); Naqada IIIC2 (e.g. Turah, zone 3) and Naqada IIID (e.g. Abu Roash, cemeteries 0 and 800). Naqada IIIC1 and IIIC2 are related to one another by the cylindrical jars, which become gradually less carefully made and which disappear during Naqada IIID. The relation between these periods and Kaiser's extension of his original *Stufen* chronology is summarised in table 7.

7. Correlation between Naqada IIIA2 - IIID and the First Dynasty

A number of tombs from Lower Egyptian sites, as well as from the royal tombs at Abydos,[32] can be connected by inscriptions or seal impressions with the early dynastic kings.[33] Only those tombs for which both inscriptions with royal names and the (partial) archaeological material are known, are taken into consideration.[34] The chronological position of these tombs was in most cases defined when studying the spatial distribution within the Naqada III cemeteries of Lower Egypt. However, a number of tombs from other sites are dated by typical objects they contained.

Saqqara	S 3120	Qa-a	IIID [35]
Saqqara	S 3121	Qa-a	IIID [36]
Saqqara	S 3500	Qa-a	IIID [37]
Saqqara	S 3505	Qa-a	IIID [38]
Abydos	Q	Qa-a	IIID [39]
Abydos	U	Semerkhet	IIIC2/D [40]
Saqqara	S 3038	Adjib	IIIC2 [41]
Saqqara	S 3111	Adjib	IIIC2 [42]
Saqqara	S 3338	Adjib	IIIC2 [43]
Abydos	X	Adjib	IIIC2 [44]
Saqqara	190	Den	IIIC2 [45]
Saqqara	230	Den	IIIC2 [46]
Abu Roash	M 25	Den	IIIC2 [47]
Saqqara	S 3035	Den	IIIC2 [48]
Saqqara	S 3506	Den	IIIC2 [49]
Saqqara	S 3507	Den	IIIC2 [50]
Saqqara	S X	Den	IIIC2 [51]
Saqqara	S 3036	Den	IIIC1/2 [52]
Abydos	T	Den	IIIC2 [53]
Tarkhan	1060	Djed	IIIC2 [54]
Saqqara	S 3504	Djed	IIIC2 [55]
Abydos	Z	Djed	IIIC2 [56]
Turah	235	Djer	IIIC1 [57]
Saqqara	S 3471	Djer	IIIC1 [58]
Saqqara	S 3503	Djer	IIIC1 [59]
Abydos	O	Djer	IIIC1 [60]
Tarkhan	300	Hor-Aha	IIIC1/2 [61]
Zawiyet el-Aryan	Z 2	Hor-Aha	IIIC1 [62]
Naqada	'Royal Tomb'	Hor-Aha	IIIC1 [63]
Abu Roash	402	Hor-Aha	IIIC1 [64]
Saqqara	S 3357	Hor-Aha	IIIC1 [65]
Abydos	B 10/15/19	Hor-Aha	IIIB/C1 [66]
Tarkhan	1982	Narmer	IIIC2 [67]
Minshat Abu Omar	44	Narmer	IIIC1/2 [68]
Tarkhan	414	Narmer	IIIC1 [69]
Tarkhan	415	Narmer	IIIC1 [70]
Tarkhan	1100	Narmer	IIIC1 [71]
Abydos	B 17-18	Narmer	-
Tarkhan	412	*Horizont* B	IIIC1 [72]
Turah	313	*Horizont* B	IIIC1 [73]
Tarkhan	261	Ka	IIIC1 [74]
Helwan	1627	Ka	IIIB/C1 [75]
Helwan	1651	Ka	IIIB/C1
Abydos	B 7/9	Ka	IIIB [76]
Tarkhan	1549	Horus Crocodile (?)	IIIB/C1 [77]
Tarkhan	[315 ?]	Horus Crocodile (?)	IIIA2/B [78]
Minshat Abu Omar	160	Horus Crocodile (?)	IIIB/C1 [79]
Abydos	B 1/2	Irj-Hor	IIIB [80]
Turah	64	*Horizont* A	IIIB [81]
Turah	89	*Horizont* A	IIIB [82]

Turah	54	*Horizont* A	IIIB [83]
Tarkhan	1702	*Horizont* A	IIIB [84]
Abydos	U-t	-	IIIB [85]
Abydos	U-s	-	IIIA2 [86]
Abydos	U-j	Scorpion I	IIIA1 [87]

Whenever the distribution of the pottery from the mastabas at Saqqara is arranged according to the sequence of kings from whose reign the mastabas date, a clear chronological distribution arises for a fair number of pottery types. As an example, the important groups of large storage jars and the cylindrical jars are presented in table 8. Let us keep in mind, however, that this image might be idealised by the degree of variation which Emery allows within the types (cf. above, p.47).

A similar investigation, which will not be discussed here, has also been made for the stone vessels from Saqqara, from which it has become clear that the presence or absence of a decorative band on cylindrical jars cannot be used as a chronological indicator, since both types occur from the time of Hor-Aha until Qa-a.

8. Absolute chronology.

The most recent interpretation of the available C^{14} dates for the entire Naqada culture, as well as for the kings of the First Dynasty in particular, has been made by F. Hassan (Hassan 1980, 1985, 1988, Hassan & Robinson 1987). These results have been combined in table 9 with the relative chronology established by the present study. However, this is to be considered only as an initial attempt. The number of available C^{14} dates remains limited. In some cases, the relative chronological period of the sampled archaeological material cannot be determined beyond doubt. Finally, the position of certain kings within the relative chronology should be more securely defined to make optimum use of the possibilities offered by the C^{14} dates. It is, therefore, beyond doubt that the need for C^{14} dates for all periods of the Naqada culture still remains very urgent.

9. Regional differentiation.

An important question is whether or not local or regional differences can be distinguished, as was the case for the lithics of the Naqada culture studied by D. Holmes (1989). Basically, two different kinds of regional differentiation might be found to occur. On one hand, different types of objects might occur at different sites, whilst on the other the same types of objects might occur at all sites, but in other combinations, or with differences in their absolute chronology. Unfortunately, there are several reasons which make it very difficult to get a clear picture of eventual regional tendencies among the gravegoods.

Regarding the possibility of different types occurring at different sites, an impression of uniformity among the cemeteries might be the consequence of the registration system used by Petrie and the other excavators during the first half of this century. They were making up their grave registers by referring to an already existing typology, and therefore it may well be supposed that they forced a kind of uniformity on the entire Naqada culture. Since Petrie's typological corpus and the Sequence Dating were developed on the combined information from the excavations in the region of both Diospolis Parva and Naqada, it has to be accepted that possible regional peculiarities were obscured from the beginning.[88]

Leaving aside possible typological errors, it is possible to compare the combination of types of objects in graves of different cemeteries, although this is hampered by the large number of types. Of course this kind of comparison is only meaningful for frequently occurring types. In an attempt to see whether certain pottery types are characteristic for a certain region, all cemeteries studied were grouped into four regions,[89] namely the Badari district,[90] the region around Abydos,[91] the Naqada cemeteries [92] and finally the cemeteries of Armant.[93] For pottery types represented five or more times in total, a

Kaiser 1957, 1990	Stufe	Hendrickx 1989	Naqada
-	-	no cylindrical jars	IIID
50 t	IIIc3	50 b-c, h-t	IIIC2
50 d	IIIc2	50 d-g	IIIC1
48 s,t/49 d,l/50 d	IIIc1	-	-
48 s,t/49 d,l	IIIb2	-	-
47	IIIb1	47 r-t/48 s/49 d,g	IIIB
W 50/51 a/55/56 g/61-62	IIIa2	W 55/58/60-62	IIIA2
-	-	W 49/50-51/56 a,g	IIIA1
W 41/43 b/47 g	IIIa1	-	-
W 41/43 b/47 g	IId2	W 41/42/43 b/47 a,g,m	IID2
W 24/25	IId1	W 24/25/27	IID1
W 3/19	IIc	W 3/19	IIC

Tab. 7. Relative chronological periods as distinguished by Kaiser 1957, 1990 and Hendrickx 1989, illustrated by the types of Wavy Handled / Cylindrical Jars.

type	#	Hor-Aha	Djer	Djed	Den	Adjib	Semer-khet	Qa-a
A01	637	-	138	64	434	-	-	1
A02	804	-	2	-	475	66	-	261
A03	819	-	23	419	347	30	-	-
A04	108	-	1	61	40	2	-	4
A06	167	-	-	167	-	-	-	-
A07	25	-	-	24	1	-	-	-
A08	166	-	-	162	-	-	-	4
A09	2	-	-	2	-	-	-	-
A10	7	-	-	-	-	-	-	7
A11	12	-	-	-	-	-	-	12
A12	2	-	-	-	-	-	-	2
B01	114	-	-	8	26	72	-	8
B02	85	-	-	-	56	-	-	29
B03	16	-	-	-	5	1	-	10
B04	94	-	-	35	35	-	-	24
B05	17	-	-	-	-	-	-	17
B06	126	-	-	120	-	-	-	6
B07	1	-	-	-	-	-	-	1
B08	12	-	-	-	4	-	-	8
B09	21	-	-	-	16	-	-	5
F01	174	-	-	-	103	71	-	-
F02	2	-	-	-	-	-	-	2
F03	67	-	1	65	1	-	-	-
F04	46	-	-	-	43	-	-	3
F05	38	-	-	-	-	-	-	38
F11	ca. 700	ca. 700	-	-	-	-	-	-

Tab. 8. Occurrence of cylindrical jars and large storage vessels in the 1st dyn. tombs at Saqqara (after Emery 1938-58).

check was made of their presence or absence in the four regions. Out of 339 types,[94] 103 occur in all four regions, 129 in three, 77 in two and 30 in one only. A far greater homogeneity than these figures suggest is to be inferred, since both the earliest and the most recent phase of the Naqada culture is not represented at Armant (out of 129 cases where only three regions are represented, Armant was the missing region in 81 instances), and since only a very limited number of Rough types is known for the cemeteries at Naqada (cf. p.43). From 96 Rough types, only 53 are represented at Naqada. Finally, the majority of the 30 types which occur only at one site are types which have been added to Petrie's original typology. Since Brunton allowed far less variation within one type than Petrie, it may well be supposed that parallels for many (?) of these new types did exist at Naqada or Abydos but were attributed by Petrie to related types. All in all, it cannot be denied that the uniformity of the gravegoods in the Naqada cemeteries of Upper Egypt, over a distance of nearly 400 km, is remarkable.

As mentioned above, related groups of types are present in different cemeteries. In this respect there are no obvious shifts in the appearance or disappearance of certain pottery types, except for the possibility that Black-Topped pottery seems to have disappeared earlier at Armant than, for instance, in the Abydos region. This seems to be confirmed by the results of Friedman's study of the Naqa ed Der cemetery (Friedman 1981: 35-6).

As for possible absolute chronological differences, it has already been said that the information in this field is very scanty and therefore does not allow any conclusions regarding the problem of possible regional differentiation.

Nevertheless, it would be surprising if all cemeteries developed along exactly the same lines and there is indeed a fairly good chance that regional differences have been obscured until now. But the question will have to rest until more data are available on old or new excavations.

The Naqada III cemeteries of Lower Egypt (cf. note 19), are located within a relatively small area. The distance between the most southern cemetery, Tarkhan, and the most northern, Abu Roash, is some 60 km. Also it may be assumed that the cultural unity had grown through political unification. This seems to be supported by the observation that the gravegoods of the burials at Tarkhan, for instance, show a striking homogeneity. Therefore, the possibility for regional variation seems of little importance. As for comparison with the late Naqada III cemeteries from Upper Egypt, nothing definite can be said for the time being because of the lack of data from Upper Egypt.

10. Conclusions

With regard to the terminological confusion mentioned at the beginning of the present article, it seems best for a discussion of the material culture to distinguish periods within the Naqada culture down to the time of the Second Dynasty.[95] There are two principal reasons for this. First, when no written information is available, which is nearly always the case, the archaeological material does not allow a precise assignment to the reign of a particular early king of Egypt. Secondly, there is no break in the material culture of Upper Egypt at the beginning of the historic period. As a matter of fact, obvious differences in material culture, meaning the development of typical Old Kingdom types of objects, can be observed to start during the final stages of the Naqada culture, but the results of this only become important after Naqada IIID.

It is more than obvious that working with information from old excavations, which are in nearly all cases incompletely published, causes great problems, especially for seriation. For this reason, the methodology presented by Kaiser over 35 years ago still seems to be valid. However, the possibilities offered by seriation (cf. Seidlmayer 1990) cannot be ignored, but they should be integrated with the study of the spatial distribution, without using one of the two systems merely as a control for the other.

The investigation of the relative chronology (Hendrickx 1989), of which some results have been presented, follows similar divisions to Kaiser's, but does not coincide completely with the *Stufen* chronology. The most important differences are situated in Kaiser's *Stufen* IId2-IIIa2 as well as in the *Stufen* which Kaiser added recently to his system (cf. table 7). These differences are caused mainly by the fact that Kaiser tries to define transitional periods (e.g. *Stufe* IIIc1), while my own study focuses on archaeologically clearly distinguished periods. As a result, Kaiser distinguishes more periods within

Naqada III. Nevertheless, it should be remembered that the definition of a relative chronology cannot be a goal in itself, but is only an indispensable tool for studying several aspects of the history of a given period. Therefore, it seems appropriate to distinguish only archaeologically well-defined and characteristic periods.

For the Naqada III period, which was the main topic of interest in this article, the following summary can be given (table 9). The earliest royal tombs at Abydos date to Naqada IIIA2. Naqada IIIB can be linked with the earliest tombs for which *serekh's* are known and thus also with Kaiser's *Horizont* A. Two of the kings of Dynasty 0, Irj-Hor and Ka, are also to be placed in Naqada IIIB. Since the inscriptions which were previously attributed to Scorpion are now no longer considered to belong to his reign, no inscriptions of this king remain, except of course on the Hierakonpolis mace head, nor is his tomb known at Abydos. Therefore his very existence becomes questionable. Naqada IIIC1 is certainly identical with the reigns of Narmer, Hor-Aha, and Djer. Naqada IIIC2 covers the reigns of Djed, Den and Adjib. The very limited evidence available for Semerkhet, from tomb U at Umm el-Qaab, does not allow a choice between Naqada IIIC2 and IIID. Naqada IIID might be found to commence with Semerkhet, but it can certainly be recognised already in the tombs attributed to the time of Qa-a. Because of the lack of historically dated material from the early Second Dynasty, a limit to Naqada IIID cannot be defined.

Period	Cal BC	Kings
Naqada IIID	from ca. 2900 onwards	[Semerkhet]/Qa-a - 2nd dyn
Naqada IIIC2	ca. 3000-2900	Den - Adjib
Naqada IIIC1	ca. 3100-3000	Narmer - Djed
Naqada IIIA1-IIIB	ca. 3300-3100	Horizont A - Irj-Hor/Ka
Naqada IIC-IID2	ca. 3650-3300	-
Naqada IA-IIB	ca. 3900-3650	-

Tab. 9. Absolute chronology of the Naqada culture.

The inconsistencies regarding the archaeological description of the differences between the principal periods of the Naqada culture are important enough to enforce a change in terminology. However, it seems to be too early to do so. It is to be expected that more data will become available within the next few years, than has through the last fifty years. These will come both from old excavations which still remain to be (re)published (el Ahaiwa, Mesaid, Mesheikh, Naqa ed Deir, Naga el Hay, Shurafa, Deir el Ballas, Hierakonpolis, cf. note 9), and from recent ones (Minshat Abu Omar, Abusir, Umm el Qaab, el Adaïma, Elkab, Hierakonpolis). Therefore, it is better to wait until the chronological consequences of these data have been evaluated before accepting a far-reaching change, such as proposing a new chronological terminology.

Acknowledgements

I wish to thank W.V. Davies and the staff of the British Museum for the perfect organisation of the symposium on Early Egypt. Many thanks are due especially to Dr. A.J. Spencer, who was so kind as to improve my English text. I am also greatly indebted to Prof. Dr. W. Kaiser, E.C.M. van den Brink and Dr. T. Wilkinson for their comments on an earlier draft of the present article.

Notes:

1. The term Naqada culture will also be used for the early dynastic period, i.e. the First and Second Dynasty (cf. pp. 63-4). An historical overview of the research for the relative chronology of the Naqada culture will also be found in Payne 1990 and Patch 1991: 153-170.

2. The following tombs are involved. D 10 m: Armant 1530, Badari 3753, Mustagedda 229. D 49 b: Abydos Cemetery E 340. D 63 a: el Amra Cemetery A 118, Cemetery B 021, 230, Armant 1458, 1547, Naqa ed Deir 7117, Hierakonpolis Fort Cemetery 70, Mustagedda 1626, 1633, Naqada Main Cemetery 524.

3. For the cemeteries studied by Hendrickx 1989 (cf. note 15) the occurrences for these types are: P 40 g1: 1; P 40 e1: 1; P 40 q: 5; P 46 b: 5; P 24 q: 1.

4. The *Horizonten* were conceived by Kaiser as a preliminary system only, based on limited evidence (pers. comm.). For discussion of a number of problems related to the *Horizonten*, see van den Brink (1996, this volume).

5. Recently, Kaiser seems to have omitted *Horizont* C (Kaiser 1990: Abb. 1) and probably also revised the archaeological characteristics of *Horizont* B.

6. Kaiser 1990 gives no archaeological description for these new *Stufen*, neither does he discuss the way in which they have been distinguished. Therefore, table 7 is based on personal information supplied by Kaiser (Poznan symposium 1992, letter 30 Oct. 1993). The following correlation with the early kings of Egypt can be made: *Stufe* IIIb2 = Irj-Hor and earlier; *Stufe* IIIc1 = Ka - Narmer; *Stufe* IIIc2 = Hor Aha - Djer; *Stufe* IIIc3 = Djed/Den until the end of the 1st dynasty.

7. B 19 a, B 25 f, B 25 g, B 53 a, B 53 c, B 57 b1, B 58 a, B 68 b, D 68 a, L 12 d, L 16 b, L 30 g, L 7 b, P 23 a, P 23 b, P 24 m, P 24 n, P 80 s, R 21 b, R 24 a, R 3 a, R 3 c, R 65 b, R 66 a, R 66 p, R 67, R 69 b, R 81, R 84, R 84 d, R 84 e, R 93 c, W 19, W 24, W 43 b.

8. On the other hand an important number of excavations carried out before 1957 still remain to be published. For instance the Italian excavations at Gebelein between 1910 and 1937 (Marro 1920, 1929; d'Amicone 1988); the excavations of Reisner and his assistants on behalf of the Hearst Expedition and the Harvard Boston Expedition at el Ahaiwa (Reisner 1900-1; 1936: 377-8), Mesaid (Reisner 1936: 371-7; Brovarski 1982: 300; Needler 1984: 138-45), Mesheikh (Fisher 1913), Naga el-Hay (Freed 1974), Shurafa (Mortensen 1991: 36) and Deir el-Ballas (Reisner 1936: 55-6, 379; Podzorski 1988: 260); C.S. Fisher's work at Dendara between 1915 and 1918 (Fischer 1969: 1-2); the Metropolitan Museum excavation carried out at Hierakonpolis by Lansing in 1935 (Lansing 1935). For additional bibliography concerning individual sites, see also Hendrickx (1995).

9. For a number of excavations, so little has been published that only some very general conclusions can be made. The most important excavation in this respect is of course the huge cemetery at Helwan, where 10,258 tombs were excavated by Z. Saad between 1942 and 1954 (Saad 1947, 1951, 1969). Furthermore, there are for example a number of smaller excavations of the Egyptian Antiquities Organisation at Abu Umuri (1936, cf. Kaplony 1965; Kromer 1973), Naga el-Gaziriya (1938, 1944, cf. Kaiser 1961: 20-1), el-Qatta (1948-52, cf. Brunner 1952-53; Leclant 1950, 1952, 1953, 1954; N.N. 1952), Tura (1957-79 ?, cf. Leclant 1961; el-Khouly 1968; Leclant 1973, 1978, 1979, 1980; Yacoub 1981, 1983), Hawashim (1965-8, cf. el-Sayed 1979: 254), Nag' el-Hagg Zeidan (1975, 1980-1, cf. Maher 1977), Edfu (1983-4, cf. Leclant & Clerc 1994: 427), el Adwa (1988, cf. Leclant & Clerc 1994: 427), Helwan (1966, cf. Leclant 1968; el-Banna 1990), Khozam (1989, cf. Shehata 1989). Among other excavations for which hardly anything is known, an early dynastic cemetery at Mendes (Hansen 1967: 16) and another one in the neighbourhood of Qasr el Sagha (Puglisi 1967) can be mentioned as well as the work of Debono in the Wadi Hammamat (Debono 1951) at Esna (Debono 1971) and at Adaïma (Debono 1971; Sauneron 1974). Finally, nothing at all is known for excavations at Naqada by the University of Alexandria (1971-2, 1981 ?, cf. Leclant 1973, 1974, 1982).

10. Since only the Naqada culture is under discussion, the publication by the DAI of the excavations at Merimde, Maadi, Wadi Digla, el Omari and Heliopolis are left aside.

11. Cemeteries at Sayala and Qustol (Williams 1986), Wadi Allaki (Piotrovski 1967), Faras-Gamai (Nordström 1972).

12. An extensive analysis of a similar problem concerning Late Old Kingdom - First Intermediate Period objects was made by Seidlmayer (1990: 8-12).

13. The additional types can be found in the following publications: Randall-McIver & Mace 1902: pl. XIII-XV; Ayrton & Loat 1911: pl. XXVIII-XXXVIII; Petrie, Wainwright & Mackay 1912: pl. IX-XII; Naville, Peet, Hall & Haddon 1914: pl. V; Peet 1914: pl. XXVII; Engelbach & Gunn 1923: pl. XXVI-XIX; Brunton & Caton-Thompson 1928: pl. XXXV-XIVL; Mond & Myers 1937: pl. XXIII-XXVIII; Brunton 1937: pl. XI-XIII; 1948: pl. XXXIII-XXXV.

14. The same observation was made by Seidlmayer (1990: 10) for the difference between the typological identification of late Old Kingdom - First Intermediate Period objects by Petrie and Brunton.

15. This is based on the data from: Abydos Cemeteries I and X (Randall-McIver & Mace 1902: 53-5; Petrie & Mace 1901: 11-2), Abydos Cemetery U (Peet 1914: 14-6), Abydos Cemetery E (Naville, Peet, Hall & Haddon 1914: 12-7; Peet 1914: 17-9), Abydos Excavations Frankfort (Frankfort 1930: 213-5), el-Ahaiwa (Reisner 1936: 377-8), el-Amrah (Randall-McIver & Mace 1902), Armant (Mond & Myers 1937), el-Badari (Brunton, Gardiner & Petrie 1927; Brunton & Caton-Thompson 1928), Elkab (Hendrickx 1993), Hammamiya (Brunton, Gardiner & Petrie 1927, Brunton & Caton-Thompson 1928), el-Mahasna (Ayrton & Loat 1911), Matmar (Brunton 1948), Mesaid (Reisner 1936: 371-7), el-Mustagidda (Brunton 1937), Naqada (Petrie & Quibell 1896, Petrie 1920: pl. LI, Baumgartel 1970b, Hendrickx 1986, Payne 1987), Qaw el-Kebir (Brunton & Caton-Thompson 1928), Salmany (el-Sayed 1979). The 'Fort' cemetery at Hierakonpolis is not included since the typological identifications of the objects are not solid enough (Adams 1987: 2). Cemetery N 7000 at Naga ed Der is not included since the unpublished tomb register (Friedman 1981) was not yet available to the author at the time when this was studied.

16. When comparing the archaeological material from Umm el Qaab with that from Tarkhan by means of the 'protodynastic' typology, there seem to be hardly any likenesses between the two, since the types present at Umm el Qaab rarely occur at Tarkhan. However, this is a false picture. The pottery from Umm el Qaab was not really 'integrated' in the 'protodynastic' corpus, since nearly all of the vessels received a separate type number. It is beyond doubt that Petrie would have identified many of these pots with already existing types if they had been found at Tarkhan.

17. The additional types can be found in the following publications: Engelbach & Gunn 1923: pl. 30; Petrie 1923: pl. LII-LIII; Brunton 1927: pl. XIII-XVI; Mond & Myers 1937: pl. XXIX-XXX; Brunton 1937: pl. XXI; 1948: pl. XLIV.

18. This is based on the data from: el-Badari (Brunton, Gardiner & Petrie 1927), Hammamiya (Brunton, Gardiner & Petrie 1927), Matmar (Brunton 1948), el-Mustagidda (Brunton 1937), Qaw el-Kebir (Brunton, Gardiner & Petrie 1927), Tarkhan (Petrie, Wainwright & Gardiner 1913, Petrie 1914), Tura (Junker 1912, Petrie, Wainwright & Gardiner 1913).

19. Wilkinson is only interested in comparing his results with Kaiser's. Therefore, the data are not taken from the original publication (Mond & Myers 1937), but from Kaiser (1957: 77, note 67), which implies that a small number of types is omitted.

20. The spatially isolated group of graves in the southern part of the cemetery, is seriated in the following manner:

grave	1.	2.	3.	4.	grave	1.	2.	3.	4.
1559	138	47	12	144	1590	145	8	148	134
1558	140	12	15	149	1518	146	42	98	123
1594	141	30	41	148	1595	147	75	84	147
1592	142	41	8	115	1593	148	13	147	84
1583	143	10	110	111	1591	149	25	63	131
1557	114	15	36	65					

1. position in Kaiser 'seriation'

2. position according to 'best polished result' (.POLISH) with initial orders being shortest hamiltonian circuits (.HAMIL).

3. position according to 'best hamiltonian circuit' (.HAMIL)

4. position according to 'best polished result' (.POLISH) using Kaiser's original order as starting order.

21. This study is not yet published and therefore the following summary has kindly been provided by T.A.H. Wilkinson (October 1993). Since the study itself has not been seen by the author no further comments can be made for the time being.

22. Tarkhan Hill and Valley Cemeteries, Turah, Matmar Cemeteries 200/3000-3100/5100, Mustagedda Cemetery 1600-1800, Mahasna, el-Amrah Cemetery b, Armant Cemetery 1400-1500, Hierakonpolis Fort Cemetery.

23. E.g. Abydos graves E75, E169, E4034, E4344 (Naville, Peet, Hall & Haddon 1914: 15-16; Peet 1914: 17-19), el Mahasna graves 48, 83, 107, 115, 120 (Ayrton & Loat 1911), Hierakonpolis tomb 100 (Payne 1973), Elkab grave 85 (Hendrickx 1994: 194-6). The presence of enormous numbers of identical (?) vessels is also typical for the First Dynasty mastabas at Saqqara (cf. table 8).

24. This does not imply that the same pottery is present in the cemeteries as well as in the settlements. On the contrary, settlement pottery shows very distinct characteristics.

25. With reservation, a correlation with the relative chronology suggested by the author (cf. infra), can be made: Group 1a = Naqada IIC-IID1, Group 1b = Naqada IID1, Group 2 = Naqada IIIA1, Group 3a = Naqada IIIA2, Group 3b = Naqada IIIB, Group 3c = Naqada IIIC1-IIIC2, Group 4 = Naqada IIID.

26. From information supplied by van den Brink, a tentative correlation with the relative chronology suggested

by the author (cf. infra), can be made. Group I-II = Naqada IIIB, Group III-IV = Naqada IIIC1.

27. The following cemeteries, from north to south, are involved: Matmar, cemetery 2600-2700 (Brunton 1948: pl. VIII-IX, XIX), el Badari, cemeteries 3700 and 3800 (Brunton & Caton-Thompson 1928: pl. III, XXXII-XXXIII), Hammamiya, cemetery 1500-1800 (Brunton 1927: pl. VI, X-XI; Brunton & Caton-Thompson 1928: pl. XXX-XXXI); Qaw el-Kebir, cemetery 100 (Brunton & Caton-Thompson 1928: pl. III, XXX), el-Salmany (el Sayed 1979), Naqada Main Cemetery (Petrie & Quibell 1896: pl. LXXXII-LXXXIII; Baumgartel 1970b; Hendrickx 1986; Payne 1987), Armant cemeteries 1300 and 1400-1500 (Mond & Myers 1937), Hierakonpolis, locality 27, 'Fort Cemetery' (Adams 1987), Elkab (Hendrickx 1994), Kubbaniya, South cemetery (Junker 1919). The data concerning cemetery N 7000 were not yet available to the author at the time when the study was carried out. The 'predynastic' cemeteries located north Asyut have not been taken in to consideration. They are to be studied separately since they come from a different region and in Lower Egypt the possibility of influences by the Maadi-Buto culture exists, also they represent only the second part of the Naqada culture. Nevertheless, the spatial distribution in the cemeteries of Gerzeh (Petrie, Wainwright & Mackay 1912), Abusir el Meleq (Scharff 1926), Harageh (Engelbach & Gunn 1923) should also be investigated and compared with Upper Egypt. Also, it would be most useful to make a comparison with the cemetery of Minshat Abu Omar, where chronological groups have already been distinguished (Kaiser 1987; Kroeper 1988).

28. The following cemeteries, from north to south, are involved: Abu Roash, cemeteries 0, 300, 400-500, 800-900 and M (Klasens 1958-61), Saqqara, cemetery west of Serapeum (Macramallah 1940), Turah (Junker 1912), Tarkhan, Valley cemetery, cemeteries A, F, G, H, J and Q (Petrie, Wainwright & Mackay 1913, Petrie 1914). Although maps are available for a part of the excavations at Helwan (Saad 1947) and also some information on the gravegoods, this is far too limited for an investigation of the spatial distribution. Also, the excavations at Abu Roash by Montet and Lacau in 1913-4 are published (Montet 1938, 1946) in a manner which does not allow their integration in the present study.

29. This was also observed by Kaiser (pers. com.) for other cemeteries.

30. Junker developed his own typological apparatus when publishing this cemetery (Junker 1912: 31-43). As a matter of fact his typology consists only of a number of broad types which allow much variation within each of the types. Petrie made tables of concordance with his own typology (Petrie, Wainwright & Gardiner 1913: pl. LXII-LXIII, LXV, LXVII-LXVIII).

31. On the map of the Valley Cemetery (Petrie 1914: pl. XLVI) 1064 numbered graves are indicated. The tomb register (Petrie, Wainwright & Gardiner 1913: pl. LX-LXVII; Petrie 1914: pl. XXXII-XLIII; contains information for only 712 of them.

32. The best information concerning the correlation between archaeological material and the earliest Egyptian rulers might be expected to come from their own tombs at Abydos or the mastabas at Saqqara which most probably belonged to their highest officials. However, these tombs have anciently been heavily looted. Also, the first excavations at Abydos, by Amélineau (1899a, 1899b, 1902, 1904), resembled very much a large scale plundering (Maspero 1912; Petrie 1901: 2). Furthermore, the results of Petrie's excavations are only partially published as far as pottery and stone vessels are concerned (Petrie 1900, 1901, 1902). Finally, the modern excavations by the DAIK are not yet published in detail (Kaiser & Grossman 1979; Kaiser & Dreyer 1982; Dreyer 1990, 1993). As for Saqqara, the excavations and publications by Emery (1938-58) are well produced, but the typological system used by Emery for the publication of the objects causes problems. The objects found for each of the tombs were in most cases illustrated by the reproduction of standard drawings. More important is the fact that it can not be denied that Emery allowed rather wide differences within one type. Naturally, this does not allow detailed typological research. cf. p. 47.

33. In the present context, the inscriptions are only of interest because of their chronological information and therefore their content etc. will not be discussed.

34. A number of tombs are excluded since the archaeological material is insufficiently known. E.g. tombs from the time of Den, excavated at Abu Roash (Montet 1938, 1946); a tomb from the time of Djed at Nazlet Batran (Daressy 1905) and especially a number of tombs at Helwan (cf. Kaplony 1963: 81, 133, 136, 141, 149). As far as can be judged from the excavation reports, the archaeological material from these tombs fits well in Naqada IIIC2 and therefore seems to support the correlation between this period and the reigns of Djed and Den. On the other hand, a tomb at Abu Roash attributed to the time of Djer or Djed (Klasens 1959: 58; Kaplony 1963: 85) is not included since the attribution seems to hold no ground. Two tombs at Abusir el-Meleq (tombs 1021 and 1144) containing pottery with uninscribed serekh's are not included because the contents of the tombs are insufficiently known (Scharff 1926: 20, 35, 150-1, 162-3, tf. 11, n° 28). These tombs are attributed by Kaiser & Dreyer (1982: 266-7) to Horizont A, and date probably to Naqada IIIA2 and/or IIIB.

35. Emery 1949: 121-44.

36. Emery 1949: 116-20.

37. Emery 1958: 98-109.

38. Emery 1958: 5-36.

39. Petrie 1900: pl. XXXIX-XLIII.

40. Petrie 1900: pl. XXXIX-XLIII. The very limited evidence available does not allow a choice between Naqada IIIC2 and IIID.

41. Emery 1949: 82-94.

42. Emery 1949: 95-106.

43. Emery 1949: 125-9.

44. Petrie 1900: pl. XXXIX-XLIII

45. Macramallah 1940: 58.

46. Macramallah 1940: 66.

47. Klasens 1961.

48. Emery 1938.

49. Emery 1958: 37-72.

50. Emery 1958: 73-97.

51. Emery 1949: 107-15.

52. Emery 1949: 71-81. This tomb contained only a limited variation of pottery types which does not allow a clear choice to be made between Naqada IIIC1 and IIIC2.

53. Petrie 1900: pl. XXXIX-XLIII

54. Petrie, Wainwright & Gardiner 1913: pl. LXIV.

55. Emery 1954: 5-127.

56. Petrie 1900: pl. XXXIX-XLIII

57. This tomb contained only a few objects which are not exclusively typical for Naqada IIIC1. However, considering the localisation within the cemetery, the tomb may in all probability be placed within this period. For the attribution to the time of Djer, cf. Kaiser 1964: 102-3.

58. Emery 1949: 13-70.

59. Emery 1954: 128-70.

60. Petrie 1900: pl. XXXIX-XLIII.

61. While studying the spatial distribution at Tarkhan, this tomb was attributed to Naqada IIIC2. However, the objects are not typical for this period alone, but might also occur during Naqada IIIC1. The problem cannot be solved beyond doubt, since tomb 300 does not occur on the maps of the cemeteries at Tarkhan. Because of its number, the tomb has to be sought in cemetery A (Naqada IIIB-IIIC2) or L (IIIA2-IIIB). However, since the vessel with Hor-Aha's name on it does not occur in the tomb register (Kaiser & Dreyer 1982: 267e), an error by Petrie might not be excluded.

62. Dunham 1978: 1. Among the gravegoods are four cylindrical jars, belonging to the type 'protodynastic' 50 g (Naqada IIIC1).

63. de Morgan 1897: fig. 562-73; Quibell 1905: CG 11.665-8, 11.760-8, 11.873-7.

64. Dunham 1978: 1.

65. Over 700 cylindrical vessels are mentioned for this tomb, which should belong to type F 2 (Emery 1949: 152). However, the type was still ill-defined at the moment of the excavation, and a comparison with the published objects (Emery 1937: pl. 16; Zaki & Iskander 1942: fig. 52-3) shows that they belong in reality to type F 11 (Klasens 1958b: fig. 13) (= 'protodynastic' 50 d, 50 f), which is typical for Naqada IIIC1.

66. Petrie 1900: pl. XXXIX-XLIII; Kaiser & Dreyer 1982: 227-8, Dreyer 1990: 64-7. The very limited evidence and the extensive disturbance of the tomb, does not allow us to choose between Naqada IIIB and IIIC1.

67. Petrie, 1914: pl. XLIII. This is the only tomb where the king's name is not written in ink on a jar or impressed on a seal, but it occurs, very carefully written, on a calcite cylindrical jar. This precious object might well have been used for a considerable time before becoming part of the equipment of a tomb. The Naqada IIIC2 date might therefore not apply to the vessel with Narmer's name.

68. Only the vessel with the inscription is published (Wildung 1981: Abb. 33). It belongs to the 'archaic' type E 22 (Naqada IIIC1) and is placed by Kroeper (1988: fig. 141) in 'group 3c', which matches with Naqada IIIC1/ C2.

69. Petrie, Wainwright & Gardiner 1913: pl. LXI.

70. Petrie, Wainwright & Gardiner 1913: pl. LXIV.

71. Petrie 1914: pl. XXXVIII.

72. Petrie, Wainwright & Gardiner 1913: pl. LXI.

73. Junker 1912: 74.

74. Petrie, Wainwright & Gardiner 1913: pl. LXI.

75. For both the tombs Helwan 1627 and 1651, only the vessel with the inscription is known (Saad 1947: pl. 60). They belong to the 'archaic' type E 22/22a (Naqada IIIB-IIIC1).

76. Kaiser & Dreyer 1982: 229-30, tf. 58.

77. Petrie 1913: pl. XL. The inscriptions from this and the following grave were originally read as Scorpion (Kaplony 1963: 1090; Kaiser & Dreyer 1982: 266-7), but are now attributed to Horus Crocodile, a king from Lower Egypt who may have been a rival to the Abydos kings (Dreyer 1992b). This interpretation is somehow corroborated by the presence of a seal impression of 'Horus Crocodile' in tomb 414 at Tarkhan which also contained several inscriptions of Narmer. For Tarkhan 1549, six objects are in the tomb register (Petrie 1914: pl. XL), among them two cylindrical jars ('protodynastic' type 50 d, 50 e) characteristic for Naqada IIIC1 besides the cylindrical jar on which the ink inscription occurs, which belongs to type 49 l, characteristic for Naqada IIIB. Since jars with inscriptions are exceptional objects, it is not impossible that the object only became a funerary gift at a later stage. The inscription may therefore date to either Naqada IIIB or IIIC1. The earlier date of this jar was already suggested by Kaiser (1964: 104, note 2) and is also confirmed by Dreyer (1992b: 260).

78. For Tarkhan 315, three cylindrical jars are mentioned in the tomb register (Petrie, Wainwright & Gardiner 1913: pl. LX), belonging to the 'protodynastic' types 46 b, 46 f and 46 k, which date the grave to Naqada IIIA2. The ink inscription is published (id. pl. XXXI,66) without drawing of the vase or reference to a type. However, according to Dreyer 1992b: 260), the type is 49 l. This type, which is characteristic for Naqada IIIB, differs considerably from 46 b etc. and can therefore hardly be one of the vases mentioned by Petrie. Unfortunately, it is possible that a mistake was made in the excavation report and that the ink inscription cannot be connected with Tarkhan 315.

79. Only the jar, 'archaic' type E 22 (Naqada IIIC1), with the inscription, is published. (Wildung 1981: Abb. 33). Dreyer 1987: 42 mentions for this tomb cylindrical jars which are typical for Naqada IIIC1. Kroeper 1988: fig. 95 places the object in 'group 3b' which matches with Naqada IIIB. The possibility that the inscription also belongs to the newly identified Horus Crocodile is suggested by van den Brink (this volume).

80. Petrie 1900: pl. XXXIX-XLIII; Kaiser & Dreyer 1982: 230-1, tf. 58. See also Wilkinson 1993b.

81. Junker 1912: 64; Petrie, Wainwright & Gardiner 1913: pl. LXII.

82. Junker 1912: 65; Petrie, Wainwright & Gardiner 1913: pl. LXII.

83. Junker 1912: 63; Petrie, Wainwright & Gardiner 1913: pl. LXII.

84. Petrie 1914: pl. XL.

85. Dreyer 1993: 31, 48.

86. Dreyer 1990: 57-8.

87. Dreyer 1992a, 1993: 34-5, 40-9.

88. As already stated by Mortensen 1991: 15, Petrie did not seem to realise this problem.

89. Another region might be distinguished for Hierakonpolis - Elkab. However, this was of no use in the present context since the Elkab cemetery represents only Naqada III and at Hierakonpolis are hardly any tombs published for Naqada I, although they were certainly present in this region (e.g. at el-Mamariya, cf. de Morgan 1912: 30-8; Needler 1984: 90-103).

90. This group includes all cemeteries of Matmar, el Mustagidda, el Badari, Hammamiya and Qaw el Kebir.

91. This group includes all cemeteries of el Mahasna, Salmany, Abydos, el Amrah, el Ahaiwa and Mesaid. At the time when this was worked out, the information on cemetery 7000 at Naqa ed Der was not at our disposal. Had this been so, another group could have been distinguished, consisting of the Naqa ed Der cemetery in combination with the few graves known for el-Ahaiwa and Mesaid, which are included in the Abydos group, but which are numerically of minor importance.

92. This group includes all cemeteries of Naqada and Deir el Ballas.

93. This group consists only of the cemeteries at Armant.

94. In reality 361 types occur five or more times, but a number of uncharacteristic shapes (e.g. R 1, R 3) was left aside.

95. Terms such as 'Amratian' or 'Gerzean' are to be omitted because they incorrectly suggest different cultures.

Minshat Abu Omar - Burials with palettes

Karla Kroeper

Minshat Abu Omar is situated on a 'gezira' hill (sand island) located in the North - Eastern Delta region, about 150 km from Cairo, in an area where previously the now defunct Pelusiac Nile branch was flowing (fig.1). Nowadays the height of the site reaches only about 2.5 metres above the surrounding cultivated land. The hill extends at the south from the edge of the modern village of Minshat Abu Omar, about 550m north to north-east and is surrounded by cultivated fields.

The site was identified in 1966 (Müller 1966) during a survey attempting to localise the place of origin of predynastic finds being sold in Europe and America.; Minshat Abu Omar was noted as a potential excavation site due to surface finds dating to the Early Dynastic Period. After receiving a licence from the Egyptian Antiquities Service for the site, excavations were commenced in 1978 and continued until 1991, by which time the intact part of the cemetery site was fully excavated.

Although other ancient sites have been found in the Delta in recent years (e.g. van den Brink 1992c: 43ff.), Minshat Abu Omar remains the only Pre-Early Dynastic cemetery so far excavated totally and therefore provides the only available data base of material for comparison with Upper Egypt in the late Predynastic/Early Dynastic Period. At present the final publication of the material and analysis of the cemetery is being prepared (Kroeper and Wildung 1994).

During excavations it became clear that the northern part of the hill was mostly covered by a settlement dating to the Greco-Roman Period (Kroeper-Wildung 1985: 8ff.). The southern part of the hill on the other hand was used as a cemetery and 420 graves of the Predynastic-Early Dynastic period, as well as 2630 graves dating from the Late- to the Roman period were excavated so far; evidence for the use of the cemetery in the intervening time was not found. Possibly geomorphologic factors may have made the area uninteresting as a burial site in the time between the 2nd and 26th Dynasty.

The older graves in Minshat Abu Omar date from the late Naqada II period (ca. 3300 BC) up to the middle of the first Dynasty. The greater majority of the burials were undisturbed with the grave offerings (ranging from 0 to 120 in number) still *in situ* around the body, providing an opportunity to compare the local burial practices in the Delta with those from other, mostly upper Egyptian sites.

As general information concerning the cemetery as a whole has been published elsewhere (Kroeper 1988, 1989a,b, 1992; Krzyzaniak 1992, Kroeper-Krzyzaniak 1992), here only a small specific group of graves, namely those containing palettes among the grave goods, shall be considered.

Palettes are part of a very old African tradition and occur already in the Early Khartoum and Neolithic Period of Nubia and the Sudan (e.g. in Kadero [Krzyzaniak 1991] ca. 4500 BC). Examples are also known from the Neolithic period in Egypt (Caton-Thompson and Garner 1934: pl.XII nrs. 21-25; 27-30) where they display more similarities with the Nubian than with the later Egyptian tradition. The oldest samples in Egypt and the Sudan are mostly of rectangular or slightly rhomboidal form, rather plump, reminiscent of small grindstones and are made from a variety of raw materials, including granodiorite, limestone and quartz. Palettes were found rarely in the graves of Wadi Digla and Maadi, but much more frequently in the settlement. There, 17 rhombic and 20 unworked slates were found; the former are being interpreted as Upper Egyptian imports, the latter as local products. The large number of irregularly shaped unworked limestone slabs found in the settlement may also have been used as palettes (Rizkana-Seeher 1988: 47ff.). By the end of Naqada I, use of the raw material called 'schist' for palettes became more or less standardised in Egypt, however in Nubia the use of other materials as well as a variety of shapes, especially a variant of the rhombic palette, continued in use into the early Dynastic period (see, e.g. Spencer 1980: 80).

The shapes of the palettes in Egypt are chronological markers, the rhomboid shape, in some cases with engraved decorations, being the oldest (after the more or less rectangular or irregular shape of the Neolithic). Similarly shaped palettes, decorated at the top with the profiles of birds or other motifs,

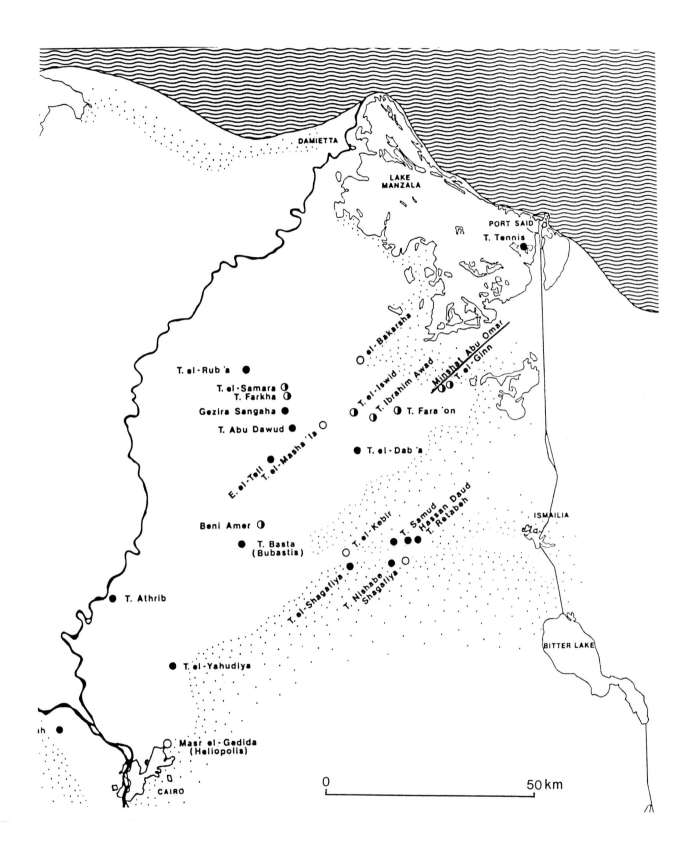

Figure 1 Map showing the location of Minshat Abu Omar and nearby sites

seem to have developed from the previous form. These occur in part together with, and are later completely replaced by, animal-shaped theriomorphous pieces.

The intended symbolism inherent in the animal shaped palette was probably to increase the healing power of the minerals/medicines that were ground on them. Whether this symbolism can be extended to include an interaction between the human eye and god's eye, and if the animals represented by the palettes are to be considered 'sun animals' (acting in defence of the sun god's eye: Westendorf 1982: 654f.) remains to be further investigated. Also the implication that the disappearance of the palettes at the beginning of the Dynastic Period may be connected with a change in the relationship sun to sun animal, must remain open (Westendorf 1982, 654f.).

The decorated/votive palettes occur only over a very short period of time, approximately at the time when animal-shaped palettes became rarer and before the onset of the decorated rectangular palettes (Kaiser 1964: 110; Abb. 6). Geometric palettes, first decorated then plain, bring to a close the sequence of palettes at beginning of the Early Dynastic period.

The function of most palettes, as evidenced by the wear traces on many of them, was to grind small amounts of mineral matter. Frequently these pigments were applied to the eyes as stated in (the much later) Papyrus Ebers (von Deines et. al. 1958), where these pigments are specially mentioned as parts of the ingredients of recipes for the treatment of eye sicknesses. The recommendation for a growth on the eye, for example, suggests to apply 'lower Egyptian mineral *sj3*, red ochre *mnšt*, green eyepaint *w3dw* and honey' (von Deines et al. 1958: Eb.336 (55,20-56,6) p.46). A recipe for the removal of blood from both eyes suggests:'*trw* (red) mineral, green mineral, black mineral, *ḥt-ʿw3*, *d3r.t* and water finely ground and applied to the eyes.' - applied to the outside of the eyes (von Deines et al. 1958: Eb.348 (57,6-8) p.47).

That pigments were also used for purely decorative purposes may be presupposed but contextual evidence is lacking. The application of paint to the lips may seem equally likely on the evidence of the many statues with red painted lips; however only one representation of a woman applying paint to the lips (by means of a brush) is known (Omlin 1973: pl.18a).

In Minshat Abu Omar thirty-seven palettes (or fragments of palettes) were discovered in 32 graves of the Pre-and Early Dynastic Period. All palettes found are made of siltstone, a material often called schist in literature. Recently however it was shown that the material should be, more correctly, classified under siltstones (Klemm and Klemm 1993: 369ff.). All palettes discussed here have a greenish gray colour, ca. Munsell 5Y 5 - 4/1 gray-dark gray, often with some whitish-grayish marbling. Generally they are very slightly plano-convex with pointed edges. If decoration is present it usually occurs on one side only, thereby clearly marking this side as the upper side. Also characteristic is that almost all the palettes are in some way damaged, the corners are especially frequently broken or chipped, indicating a frequent handling and/or use before deposit in the graves.

The palettes were found in various grave types belonging to different chronological groups, as briefly described below.

Grave group MAO I, dated to the late Naqada II Period

Grave 63 (fig.2 and pl.6a)
The grave was located in square 6/23 and lay 1,17m below the present surface. Around the grave pit a light gray discolouration was noted indicating the remains of a roof of organic material (probably made of mats). The burial was placed on the right side in a lightly contracted position. The orientation of the body was N-S, the head in the north, facing west. The human remains were identified as female between the ages of 14-20 years.

Eleven offerings had been placed in the tomb distributed as follows: four ceramic vessels in front of the body and behind the head including one wavy-handled jar; one small stone bowl grasped by the deceased with the left hand. Other offerings found in front of the body consisted of one aspatharia shell, a small stone jar, a grinding pebble and one bracelet of various stone beads, as well as a palette. The palette has roughly the form of a slightly asymmetrical oval with one remaining bird's head carved out of the top edge of the oval, on one side; the opposite edge shows that another bird's head was probably intended but was not finished or broken while being worked on. In the middle of the upper part of the palette a suspension hole has been bored. A small oval depression made through use can be seen in the middle of one side of the palette.

Palette-size: height 16,6 cm, width 9 cm , thickness 0,5 cm

Grave 305 (fig.2 and pl.6b)

The grave was located in square 4/22 and lay ca. 1,80m below the present surface. No pit was noticeable before the appearance of the burial. The body is oriented slightly NE-SW, placed on the right side, facing west, tightly contracted with the hands in front of the face. The age of the buried individual was 13-14 years, and of indeterminate sex.

Six offerings were deposited with the burial, consisting of four ceramic vessels, including one small red-painted pot, a piece of galena and one palette. The palette is fish-shaped (identified by A. von den Driesch as *Tilapia*), the body approximately elliptical with the tail fins worked out of the stone. No other internal decoration (i.e. eyes or mouth) are present. At the top, in the middle of the fish's back, a string hole was bored through the palette (pl.11a). No traces of use remain.

Palette-size: height 12,7 cm, width 8,7 cm thickness 0,7 cm

Grave 816 (fig.2 and pl.6c)

The grave was located in square 6/21 and lay ca. 1m below the present surface. The pit was lightly discoloured a reddish brown, possibly indicating a wood coffin or thick cloth around the body. The upper part of the body was destroyed by a later (greco-roman) grave.

The orientation of the grave was approximately N-S (possibly NE-SW) with the body having been placed on the right side facing west or north-west. The burial, probably a female, between 20 to 60 years of age was accompanied by a total of 20 offerings. Eleven ceramic vessels were found near the legs and partly in the pit of the later grave which had destroyed the upper part of this burial. In front of the middle part of the skeleton 6 stone vessels partly covered with or containing large lumps of galena were found, as well as a rubbing stone and some stone beads.

A crescent-shaped palette (pl.11b) with a string hole in the middle of the upper edge was also found in front of the body. The palette was undecorated and lacked any traces of use.

Palette-size: height 8,7 cm; width 14,5 cm; thickness 1 cm

Grave 1282 (fig.2)

The grave was found in square 9/20 and lay 1,45m below the present surface. The pit size was not noticeable in the soil. The burial was oriented N-S with the body placed on the right side, the head to the north, facing west. The badly preserved human remains were of an individual between 18 and 25 years old, of indeterminate sex.

Besides the palette also one ceramic vessel, two amulets, as well as some stone beads were found in the grave. The palette, in the shape of a fish, is badly preserved and summarily executed. The body is roughly elliptical with the tail end finished vertically and decorated with two diagonally placed cut notches on either side indicating the tail fins. A borehole (only slightly sunk) on each side of the palette nearer the pointed end of the ellipse is intended to represent the eyes of the fish, possibly they may have been inlaid at one time. At the top of the back of the fish-shape one string hole has been bored through the palette. On one side of the palette a deep oval depression resulting from intensive use can be seen, and it still contains some remains of black pigment.

Palette-size: height 9,6 cm; width 7,2 cm; thickness 0,8 cm

Grave 1340 (fig.2 and pl.6d)

The grave was located in square 11/20 and lay ca. 1,40m below present surface. The burial was oriented N-S, resting on the right side of the body, facing west. The human remains were identified a (probably) female ca. 16-18 years old. Seven offerings were placed near the head including two ceramic vessels, one stone vessel, beads and pendants and a flint scraper as well as a palette.

The original form of the palette is difficult to reconstruct since it is now broken on practically all sides. At the top the remains of a string hole can be noted. A least two deep depressions made by rubbing can be seen. One is localised in the centre of the remaining palette, whereas the other depres-

73

sion is at the edge of a large break. Possibly the palette was broken through intense use at this place and may originally have been of oblong shape. Some remains of black pigment (galena?) can be seen on the surface.

Palette-size: height 11,6 cm; width 8,2 cm; thickness 1 cm

Grave group MAO III, dating to Dynasty '0'

Grave 44 (fig.3)
The grave was located in square 8/23 - 8/24 and lay 2,38m below present surface. The walls of the approximately oval pit (ca. 1,75x 0,75m) were reinforced with compact mud. The burial was oriented NE-SW and the body had been placed on the left side in a tightly contracted position, facing south. Due to the fragile condition of the human remains, the sex could not be determined but the age of the individual was estimated to be between 20-40 years.

In total nineteen offerings, including two palettes, were found distributed near the head and the feet of the burial. Twelve ceramic vessels, including one jar with a *serekh* containing the royal name 'Narmer', and the larger palette were placed above the head. A group of more valuable objects consisting of a small calcite jar with lugs and copper lid, a small calcite bowl as well as the smaller palette and a pebble probably used as a grinder, were found near the feet. Carnelian beads were found in the head and chest area. The smaller palette (fig.3 [g.44], left) is rectangular or slightly trapezoid and decorated with two parallel engraved lines along the four edges of one surface. No traces of use could be seen

Palette-size: height 10,6 cm, width 8,7 cm, thickness 0,5 cm.

The larger palette (fig.3 [g.44], right) has an elongated rectangular shape and is decorated with four parallel lines engraved around the four edges of one side. Again, no traces of use could be seen.

Palette-size: height 25,7 cm, width 15,9 cm thickness max. 0,9 cm.

Grave 50 (fig.3)
The grave was located in square 8/24 and lay 1,23m under the present surface. The outline of the burial pit was noted due to a light grayish discolouration which represented the fragile remains of organic material, probably matting used as roof covering. The burial is oriented NE-SW, the body having been placed on the left side facing southeast, in a middle-tight contracted position. The human remains were identified as being probably those of a female, 20-40 years old.

Six offerings had been placed in the grave distributed as follows: three ceramic vessels in front of the body, one ceramic pot and the palette behind the head, carnelian beads near the head and the chest.

The palette is of elongated rectangular shape with two to three irregularly applied parallel engraved lines around the four edges of one surface (pl.11f). No traces of use were found on the surface

Palette-size: height 18,8 cm, width, 9 cm, thickness 0,5 cm.

Grave 73
The grave was located in square 7/23-7/24 and lay 1,28m below present surface. Thick remains of matting were found covering the body and the pots. The burial was placed on the left side, tightly contracted the head to the east, facing south. The human remains were identified as those of a female 20-40 years old. Twelve offerings had been placed in the grave distributed around the body. These consisted of seven ceramic vessels, one stone pot, one copper bracelet, one palette and a rubbing stone as well as a necklace of stone beads.

The palette is rectangular in shape and its edges are decorated with three parallel engraved lines. Some traces of use (rubbing marks) can be seen in the middle of one side.

Palette-size: height 17,3, width 12,8 cm, thickness 1,2 cm

Grave 127
The grave was located in square 8/23 and lay ca. 2,30m under the present surface. The size and orientation of the pit was not visible due to considerable disturbance caused by later grave pits which had cut grave 127. Tiny fragments of bones were collected throughout the pit but not enough remained in

order to determine the sex or age of the burial.

Fragments of thirteen offerings were encountered, including remains of twelve ceramic vessels and one small corner-fragment of a palette. The palette corner hails from a rectangular palette on which the remains of three parallel engraved lines along the edges of the upper side can be seen.

Grave 160 (fig.3 and pl.7a)
The grave was located in square 5/23 and lay 1,68m below present surface. The pit was recognisable at the top by a slight yellowish discolouration. Slightly above the skeleton a white-greyish rectangular/oval discolouration typical of the remains of matting (ca. 1,90m x 1,20m) appeared. The burial was oriented E-W, placed on the left side, middle-tightly contracted and facing south. The body was that of a person of 20-30 years of age of undetermined sex.

Altogether seventeen offerings had been placed around the body. Six stone vessels were found near the head, whereas the seven ceramic pots were found in various positions: one ceramic vessel with the Horus name of a king (probably 'Scorpion') was found at the foot end of the grave. Other grave goods included a necklace and bracelet of various stone beads, a fragment of a flint blade and a palette.

The palette has an irregular oval form. Following the edges of the palette are two continuous parallel engraved lines filled by a lightly engraved zigzag design.

Palette-size: height 19,6 cm, width 16,8 cm, thickness 1,6 cm.

Grave 400 (fig.4 and pl.7b)
The grave was located in square 6/22 and lay 1,60m below present surface. The burial was oriented E-W, the body having been laid on the left side, tightly contracted, facing south. The human remains were identified as female, 20-40 years old. Around the body thirteen offerings had been placed, made up of seven ceramic vessels, one bone needle, some carnelian beads, as well as two stone vessels. Also included among the goods were two palettes of different shapes.

The larger rectangular palette (fig.4 [g.400], right) is decorated with four lightly engraved parallel lines around the edges. Some grinding traces as well as remains of red pigment (ochre?) are noticeable in the middle of the palette.

Palette-size: height 17,8 cm, width 12,4 cm, thickness 1,5 cm

The second palette is of an irregular oval shape with two parallel engraved lines following the curve of the edges; between these lines some small triangles have been applied (fig.4 [g.400], left and pl.11c). Some traces of use are also noticeable on the decorated side.

Palette-size: 15,7 cm width 9,9 cm thickness 1,3 cm

Grave 434 (fig.4)
The grave was located in square 7/22-8/22 and found 2,10m under present surface. A slightly yellow discolouration in the sand indicated a rectangular pit ca. 160x95 cm in size. At the depth of the burial, a darker oval discolouration appeared around the skeleton indicating the remains of a container for the body. The orientation of the burial was NEE-SWW, with the body having been placed on the left side, tightly contracted, head to the east facing south. The burial was that of a female between the ages of 20-30 years.

Fourteen offerings had been placed in the grave, consisting of five ceramic vessels, two stone pots, a copper dish, a copper bracelet, a diadem and necklace made up of different stones, a rubbing stone and some galena. Additionally two palettes of similar shapes had been placed one behind the head and one behind the body.

One palette is of a rectangular/trapezoid shape, decorated with three parallel irregular engraved lines along the four edges (pl.11d).

Palette-size: height 18,1 cm; width. 14,6 cm; thickness 1,1 cm

The second palette is of a rectangular shape with slightly convex sides (fig.4 [g.434], left). It is decorated with two very irregular, badly applied parallel engraved lines around the edges of one side.

Palette-size: height 21,2 cm; width 16,9 cm; thickness 1,3 cm

Grave 550

The grave was located in square 10/24 and lay 2,67m below the present surface. The pit was rectangular, ca. 3,10 x 2,10m in size, and the walls were reinforced with a layer of compact mud. On top of the mud and on top of the remaining offerings, a thick white layer of matting, probably remains of the roofing material, was preserved.

The orientation of the grave pit was NE-SW, but no bones remained *in situ* due to robbers' activities. Only a few fragments of human remains (of undetermined sex and age) were collected from the filling of the grave. Despite the fact that the grave had been robbed, fifty-one offerings were still present, consisting of thirty-five ceramic vessels, fragments of nine stone vessels, two shells, one copper bowl and two flints. Some of the objects were found standing on the floor of the pit, in their original positions, others were collected in the loose sand of the robbers' pit.

Also found in the pit-fill was a small corner fragment of a palette decorated with three parallel engraved lines around the edges..

Grave 741 (pl.7c)

The grave was found in square 9/23 and lay 1,90m under present surface. The pit was of rectangular shape (1,4 m x 0,80 m) with the typical light grey discolouration indicating organic material. Over and under the skeleton a roughly rectangular brown discolouration (110 x 50 cm) appeared in the sand, indicating a decomposed container of organic material, probably a wooden coffin.

The orientation of the burial was NE-SW, with the head to the northeast, facing southeast. The body was placed on the left side, medium-tightly contracted. The burial was that of a male, 20-40 years old. Above the head area, eleven offerings had been deposited, consisting of six ceramic vessels, three stone pots, one needle fragment and one palette.

The palette is rectangular with the corners slightly chipped and with three, sometimes four irregular engraved lines parallel to the edge of one side. A slight concave depression in the middle of the decorated side indicates use.

Palette-size: height 17,2; width 14,7 cm; thickness 1 cm.

Grave 758 (fig.4 and pl.7d)

The grave was located in square 5/21-5/22 and lay 1,14m under present surface. The rectangular pit walls (160 x 125 cm) were reinforced with a mud packing and also thick remains of white organic material (mats) were visible. Over the skeleton an oval darker discolouration (150 x 85 cm) was visible which may indicate the presence of a container or cloth for the body.

The orientation of the grave is NEE-SWW with the body having been placed on the left side, head to the east facing south. The burial is that of a female, 20-30 years old and it contained eleven offerings, consisting of seven ceramic vessels placed above and behind the head, one stone vessel by the legs and some carnelian beads near the upper body.

The palette found behind the head was of a simple rectangular form (edges slightly convex) without decoration and without any traces of use.

Palette-size: height 16,8 cm; width 12,5 cm; thickness. 1,4 cm;

Grave 862 (pl.8a)

The grave was located in square 7/21 and lay 2,22m below present surface. The pit was surrounded by a very faint white rectangular discolouration (170 x 130 cm), probably remains of a mat used for the roofing.

The orientation of the burial is NE-SW, with the body having been placed on the left side facing east (SE?). The human remains were of an individual 13 to 14 years of age, of unknown sex. Although disturbed, the grave still contained ten offerings, consisting of one rubbing stone and one composite vessel near the feet, one ceramic vessel as well as five stone vessels, carnelian beads and a palette near the head.

The palette is rectangular with slightly convex sides and is decorated with three parallel engraved lines along the edges; no wear from use is noticeable but the surface is damaged.

Palette-size: height 19,2 cm; width 15,5 cm; thickness 1,2 cm

Grave 866 (fig.5)

The grave was located in square 6/21-7/21 and lay 2,40m below the present surface. The rectangular pit (175 x 160 cm) was reinforced with mud, and at the bottom, the remains of a coffin (brown discolouration 125 x 55 cm) was found.

The orientation of the burial is NE-SW, with the body having been placed on the left side, medium-tightly contracted, with the face to the south. The human remains are of a female, 20-35 years of age. The burial was surrounded by twenty-seven offerings distributed as follows: around the edges of the grave fifteen ceramic vessels had been lined up, whereas near the feet of the body two palettes, six stone vessels, and two copper dishes had been placed. On the body carnelian beads were found and a metal bracelet (silver?) was found near the arm.

The larger of the two palettes (fig.5 [g.866], left) is rectangular and decorated with three engraved lines parallel to edges; a minimal rubbing depression indicates wear from use.

Palette-size: height 27,5 cm; width 19,5 cm; thickness 1,3 cm

The second (smaller) palette (fig.5 [g.866], right), is of the same form and carries the same decoration as the first palette.

Palette-size: height 14,5 cm; width 10,2 cm; thickness 1,1 cm

Grave 1045

The grave was found in square 8/22 and lay 2,30m below present surface. The original pit size seems to have been approximately 200 x 140 cm, roughly rectangular, but toward the bottom more trapezoid. The pit walls were also reinforced with mud. At the bottom, remains of (probably) a wooden coffin (100 x 50 cm) were found. The orientation of the pit is NE-SW, with the burial having been placed on the left side, fairly strongly contracted, head to the NE facing east. The body is that of a 20-40 year old female.

Ten offerings including seven ceramic vessels were placed over the head outside the coffin. One stone pot, a shell and the palette were found inside the coffin area. The palette is of rectangular form and decorated on one side with three engraved lines parallel to the edge.

Palette-size: height 14,2 cm; width 10,9 cm; thickness 1,2 cm

Grave 1050 (fig.5 and pl.8b)

The grave was located in square 9/22 - 9/23 and lay 1,56m below the present surface. At first appearance the pit was of a large size (max. 3,60 x 2,50m) and an irregular, rectangular form. At the bottom of the pit the typical brown discolouration indicating a wooden coffin (110 x 60 cm) appeared. The orientation of the burial was NE-SW, with the body having been placed on the left side facing east in a tightly contracted position. The burial is of a male, between the ages of 20-40 years.

Twenty-six offerings had been deposited in the grave, the smaller of the seventeen ceramic vessels inside of the coffin, the larger at the outer edges of the pit. Three stone vessels as well as the palette were placed at the head and at the foot of the coffin. Four copper tools were found in front of the face as well as a necklace of carnelian beads.

The palette is of an elongated rectangular form with slightly convex sides. Around the edges there are engraved irregularly 3-4 parallel lines; in the middle some grinding traces could be noted.

Palette-size: height 32 cm; width 15,1 cm; thickness 1,4 cm

Grave 1127

The grave was located in square 8/21 and lay 2,90m under the present surface. The grave was badly disturbed in the central area by robbers' pits. The orientation of the pit was NE-SW and it was approximately rectangular in form at the top (220 x 150 cm). Mud reinforcement of the walls was noted at a deeper level. Only small pieces of human bone, too fragmentary to determine the sex or age of the individual, could be collected in the robbers' pit.

Remains of nineteen offerings were discovered, consisting of fourteen ceramic vessels, two fragments of stone vessels, a knob-like object made of siltstone, as well as some stone beads. A corner-fragment of a rectangular palette which is decorated with 2-3 parallel engraved lines was also among the finds.

Grave 1194

The grave was found in square 10/21 and lay 1,75m under the present surface. Remains of dark grey-black mud fragments were found lining the oval (ca. 100 x 80 cm) pit. The pit was much disturbed by pits of later graves. The outline of the pit was oriented approximately E-W but no bones remained *in situ*. Four offerings were retrieved from the pit, two ceramic vessels, one stone vessel and one palette. The rectangular palette with slightly convex sides is decorated with three engraved parallel lines along the edges on one side. In the middle of the decorated side, in a slight concave depression, a reddish discolouration can be seen, possibly traces of red ochre.

   Palette-size: height 16,5; width 13,5; thickness 1,2 cm

Grave 1287 (pl.8c)

The grave was found in square 10/20-21 and lay ca. 1,93m under the present surface. Dark compact mud reinforcement around the pit walls (ca. 105 x 175 cm in size) was noted, as well as the remains of white organic material, probably a reed mat (95 x 165 cm). Around and over the skeleton a dark discolouration seems to indicate remains of some sort of cloth. The grave was orientated NE-SW, the body placed on the left side, middle-tightly contracted and facing southeast. The human remains were of a woman 20-25 years of age.

   Eighteen offerings including sixteen ceramic vessels, a rubbing stone and one palette were distributed near the head and the feet of the body. The palette is of an elongated rectangular shape, slightly trapezoid. At the shorter edges six irregularly parallel lines have been engraved whereas the longer sides have been engraved with four parallel lines. One corner is broken; no use traces are present.

   Palette-size: height 18,6 cm; width 10,3 cm; thickness 1,3 cm

Grave 1295 (pl.8d)

The grave was located in square 9-10/20 and lay 2,34m below surface. The pit is of rectangular shape with pointed corners marked by a strong white discolouration indicating organic material (mats). The orientation was NE-SW, the body having been placed on the left side, facing south. The sex of the badly preserved skeleton could not be determined, but the age was between 20-30 years.

   Twenty-three offerings consisting of nineteen ceramic vessels, two stone vessels, one set of beads and a palette, were included with the burial. The palette was of an elongated rectangular shape with slightly curved edges which were engraved with three parallel lines. No use traces were present (pl.11e)

   Palette-size: height 19,2 cm; width 11,1 cm; thickness 1,2 cm

Grave 1455

The grave was located in square 10/22-11/23 and lay 2,72m below the present surface. The size of the pit at first appearance was rather large, ca. 370 x 240 cm, but it had been disturbed by grave robbers. Later, (at a deeper point) a strong white discolouration with pointed corners appeared. Around the pit walls near the body, traces of white and red plaster were preserved. The orientation of the pit was NE-SW. The body had been placed on the left side, in a contracted position. The upper part of the body had been completely destroyed by grave robbers. The human remains were identified as female, 30-40 years old.

   Remaining in the robbed tomb were thirty-six offerings consisting of twenty-four ceramic vessels, two copper objects and remains of six stone vessels, as well as pendants and carnelian beads. Also found were small fragments of a palette (two corner pieces) with remains of incised decoration consisting of four parallel lines around the edges

Grave 1666 (pl.9a)

The grave was located in square 11/24 and lay 2,40 under the present surface. The pit, at the top, had a size of ca. 280 x 170 cm and at the bottom, a white discolouration indicating a mat ca. 210 x 75 cm in size was found. Remains of rosé coloured plaster indicated the presence of a (probably wood) coffin covered with plaster. The grave was oriented E-W, the body having been placed on the left side, tightly contracted, facing south. The burial was that of a female 20-40 years old.

   The twenty offerings placed in the grave consisted of eleven ceramic vessels, three stone vessels, four copper objects and a large quantity of beads. The palette found in the grave is of rectangular shape with three parallel engraved lines along the edges. No traces of use were noticeable.

Palette-size: height 26 cm; width 18,1 cm; thickness 1,2 cm

Grave 2200 (pl.9b)
The grave was located in square 12/24 and lay 2,56m under the present surface. The very large conical pit ca. 4m x 3m at the top, with some triangular extensions, was badly disturbed by many later graves. The pit walls were reinforced with mud, and at the bottom a rosé discolouration, possibly indicating plaster around the wall, and the remains of a coffin, divided the grave in two parts. The orientation of the grave was NE-SW, the body having been placed on the left side in a middle-tightly contracted position, facing south. The body was of a female 20-40 years old.

The grave contained twenty-five offerings including fourteen ceramic vessels, four stone vessels, two ivory needles and a spoon, one copper object and beads. The two palettes included in the burial are both rectangular. One palette is incised/engraved with three irregular, parallel lines around the edges.

Palette-size: height 29,3 cm; width 12,5 cm; thickness 1,2 cm

The second palette is plain on both sides, with a string-hole at one of the smaller sides of palette, not centred. No traces of wear (depressions) were found on either, although some reddish discolouration on the second palette can be seen. However it was not possible to determine with certainty if these are remains of pigment or a discolouration in the stone itself (pl.11h).

Palette-size: height 18,8 cm; width 13,7 cm; thickness 1,4 cm

Grave group MAO IV dated from the First Dynasty to the middle of the Second Dynasty

Grave 322 (fig.6 and pl.9c)
The grave was located in square 6/22 and lay 1,26m under present surface. Around the almost rectangular pit (165 x 100 cm) remains of mud reinforcement of the pit walls was found. The burial was oriented NE-SW placed on the left side facing east, in a middle-tight contracted position. The human remains were identified as female, 20-40 years of age.

In front of the body, thirty-five offerings were distributed in various layers. Among the grave goods were found sixteen ceramic vessels, thirteen stone pots, one palette with rubbing-stone, an ivory needle and a necklace of carnelian and faience beads. A particular interesting and unique find among the offerings was a stone vessel in the form of a papyrus bark, with delicately-worked details of papyrus reeds and ropes. The palette is of a simple elongated rectangular shape with slightly rounded corners. It is undecorated but bears some traces of use, in the form of a slight depression on one side caused by grinding.

Palette-size: height 16,6 cm, width 8,9 cm, thickness 1,4 cm

Grave 1030 (fig.6 and pl.10c)
The grave was located in square 9/22 and lay 3,06 cm under the present surface. A light discolouration indicated that the size of the excavated pit was 190x130 cm. Toward the bottom of the pit remains of a (probably) wooden coffin with reddish coloured plaster was found. The orientation of the pit was NE-SW. The body was placed on the left side, medium-tightly contracted, facing east. The human remains indicate a female burial of between 20-40 years of age.

The twenty-five offerings found in the grave were distributed in two concentrations: inside and outside of the coffin area. Of the sixteen ceramic vessels, all but two were placed at the foot end of the pit. Six stone vessels and some stone beads, as well as the palette, had been placed near the head inside of the coffin. One of the larger schist bowls was found to contain the remains of the head of a pig. Another of the stone vessels seems to have been placed in the left hand of the deceased.

The one small rectangular palette in the grave is of an unusual shape. Flat and plain on the back, it is decorated on the front with raised mouldings around the four sides, making a kind of very flat container. It would seem from the size of the object that it was probably not used like the other palettes i.e. for grinding minerals, but more probably as a container for mixing the already-ground minerals similar to the depressions found on writers palettes, used to mix water with pigments.

Palette-size: height 8,6 cm; width 5,4 cm; thickness 0,7 cm

Grave 1147 (fig.6 and pl.9d)

The grave was located in square 10/22 and lay 2,56m below the present surface. The pit was noted by its grey discolouration 180 x 120 cm in size, indicating organic material. At the bottom, remains of a rectangular coffin (125 x 95 cm) covered with pink plaster were found. The orientation of the pit was NE-SW, the body having been placed at the bottom on the left side, tightly contracted, with the head to the northeast, facing east. The human remains were of a female, 20-40 years of age. Twenty-seven offerings had been placed around the burial. Most of the nine stone vessels (including a composite vessel), the palette and the beads were found in front of or behind the head, whereas the fourteen ceramic vessels were placed in front of the body and in the area of the feet of the burial. Also included among the grave offerings was a small, flat trapezoid stone possibly used for grinding (fig.6 [g.1147], right) and a rubbing-stone.

The palette is of an elongated rectangular shape with slightly rounded corners and is undecorated (fig.6 [g.1147], left). In the middle of one side a slight concave depression indicates use wear.

Palette-size: height 16,3 cm; width 9,5 cm; thickness 1,7 cm

Grave 1150 (fig.7 and pl.10d)

The grave was located in square 8/22 and lay 2,16m below present surface. The pit, noticeable through a slightly darker colour than the surrounding sand, was ca. 160 x 100 cm in size. Over the skeleton remains of a slight brown-violet discolouration (remains of cloth ?) were noted. The orientation of the grave was NE-SW. The body had been placed on the left side, head to the northeast, facing south in a tightly contracted position. The human remains were of a 20-40 year old female.

Twenty-five offerings had been placed near the head and the feet of the body. The offerings consisted of ten ceramic vessels, three stone vessels, a necklace, an amulet, a copper pin and a palette. Also included was an ivory box and lid (?) in which six miniature stone vessels had been placed. The palette is of an unusual form: one side of the rectangular piece of siltstone is flat and undecorated whereas the other side is divided into four rectangular compartments, created by two rows of stepped mouldings. Probably this palette, like the one above in grave 1030, was used as a flat container for the mixing of various coloured pigments at the same time, similar perhaps to a modern watercolour box. No traces of use were found in the four compartments (pl.11i).

Palette-size: height 16 cm; width 9,9 cm; thickness 1,6 cm

Grave 1363 (fig.7 and pl.10a)

The grave was located in square 11/21 and lay 2,53 cm, under present surface. The rectangular pit (200 x 150 cm) was reinforced with mud and at the bottom the remains of a wooden coffin, (brown discolouration, 170 x 70 cm) covered with pink-reddish plaster were found. The orientation of the burial was NE-SW, the body having been placed on the left side, lightly contracted, facing southeast. The body was of a female between 20-40 years of age.

Thirty-nine offerings had been placed in two concentrations in the grave: nineteen stone vessels as well as an ivory/bone spoon, two ivory/bone needles, a flint, a rubbing-stone and beads were placed in the coffin over the head, whereas thirteen ceramic vessels were put at the foot end of the grave. The palette found behind the head was of a rectangular form with slightly rounded corners, and was undecorated (pl.11h).

Palette-size: height 18,4 cm; width 10,7 cm; thickness 1,2 cm.

Grave 1430 (fig.7 and pl.10b)

The grave was located in square 12/20 and lay 2,20m below present surface. The pit (size 190 x 135 cm) was rectangular and the pit walls were reinforced with a mud packing. At the bottom, remains of a rectangular coffin (brown discolouration, 115 x 60 cm in size) covered with pinkish plaster was noted. The orientation of the pit was NE-SW, the burial having been placed on the left side, medium contracted, facing southeast. The human remains were identified as female, 20-25 years of age.

Twenty-seven offerings made up of twenty ceramic vessels, five stone pots and beads of various stones as well as a palette had been included in the burial. These were distributed mainly in front and near the feet of the burial. The palette is of an elongated, somewhat irregular, rectangular type without decoration. On one side remains of red pigment (ochre?) were found.

Palette-size: height 14 cm; width 8 cm; thickness 1,5 cm.

Summary and conclusions

Typologically the palettes can be divided roughly into three groups (fig.8):

figurative:
1 ovoid with birds' heads on top
2 fish-shaped

rectangular/square (30 pieces):
22 decorated with 2-4 engraved parallel lines
6 without decoration:
4 with rounded corners
2 unique types

unusual shapes:
1 crescent-shaped
1 drop-shaped (?) without decoration
2 oval forms with decoration

The chronological sequence of the palette forms found in Minshat Abu Omar corresponds to those at other sites and to the internal chronology of the MAO grave groups as determined through analysis of ceramic and other finds. However the volume of palettes occurring in the older *versus* younger graves in Minshat differs noticeably from other sites. In less than one percent of the graves of group MAO I, (the oldest grave group made up of 255 graves) did the few animal-, crescent- and drop-shaped palettes occur.

On the other hand, in the graves of group MAO III, with a total of 86 graves dated to the very beginning of the dynastic period, 21 graves contained palettes. This represents a high percentage (24 %) especially at a time when, at other sites, palettes are rapidly disappearing (e.g. Turah 3% [Junker, 1912:57]).

Within group MAO III the rectangular decorated palette is the most frequently occurring type. The variation in size (largest 32 cm x 15,1 cm in grave 1050, smallest 10,6 cm x 8,7 cm in grave 44) and the proportions,(length to width) as well as the variation in engraved decoration seem to be without chronological significance. It is interesting to note that in two cases oval-shaped palettes with decoration occur in this grave group, in one case together with a rectangular palette. These two graves, according to the ceramics also found in the grave, belong to the older graves within the group whereas two graves of group MAO III in which undecorated rectangular palettes were found can be assigned, also according to other criteria, to the younger graves of the group.

The chronologically youngest group of graves to which 73 graves have been assigned (MAO IV) dates to the time-period of Dynasty I down to the middle of Dynasty II. Only six palettes were found in this grave group. The four undecorated rectangular palettes have in common the slightly rounded corners and plumper forms than the decorated rectangular palettes. The two unusual palettes of graves 1030 and 1150 are more similar to flat containers than palettes (e.g. Helwan [Saad 1951: 33, pl.XXXVII] two compartments and lid).

The low number of palettes found in group MAO IV corresponds with the situation concerning finds at other places where the flat slab-shaped palettes disappear after the Early Dynastic period.

The chronological distribution of the occurrence of palettes at the site of Minshat Abu Omar is therefore somewhat different from other sites:

-in Minshat Abu Omar only a small number of palettes occur in the oldest grave group, a large increase of palettes can be seen in Dynasty '0' graves and a rapid decline follows in the later phase of the cemetery. Why palettes reached the height of popularity in Dynasty '0' in Minshat Abu Omar is unclear. At other sites a steady decline in the numbers of palettes from the older period to the younger period is more common.

Distribution and Social differentiation

The distribution of palettes in the graves according to the sex of the burial shows a clear preponderance of palettes in graves of females.

MAO I	MAO III	MAO IV	Total
2 female	11 females	6 females	19 females
2 children	5 children		7 children
	2 males		2 males
1 unknown	3 unknown		4 unknown

The horizontal distribution of graves in the field with palettes, (fig.9) indicates no clustering, the only noticeable feature being the lack of palettes in the extreme north and in the extreme south. Graves with palettes are evenly spread over the whole of the middle part of the field, about one grave with a palette occurs every 10 sq.m.

Deposition of palettes in the graves shows some variability but the favoured position in the grave was near the head.

That the palettes were usually kept in the hand (Asselberghs 1961: 256) could not be confirmed in Minshat Abu Omar

Location of palettes in the grave:

16	x	near the head
8	x	near the feet
6	x	in front of the body
1	x	behind the body
1	x	in the hand
5	x	fragments in the pit, not *in situ*

The presence of palettes is not limited to any particular type of grave: palettes were found in burials of the poorer group (although never the very poor) as well as in the very rich group (but not the richest). The greater majority of palettes was found in the middle-rich grave groups with the total amount of offerings varying from 11 to 40 pieces.

Distribution of palettes in rich vs. poor graves:

no. of offerings: in graves	no. of graves with palettes in this group
0-1	0
2-5	2
6-10	6
11-20	12
21-40	11
41-80	1
81-126	0

Also noticeable is the rather low percentage of graves containing palettes at all namely only 7,6%. The object group itself (38 pieces) represents a minuscule part (less than one percent) of all offerings found in graves. This stands in marked contrast to Petrie's statement concerning graves in Naqada (1920: 36f.) 'slate palettes are the most frequent object in prehistoric graves after pottery, usually accompanied by a pebble of jasper for grinding.' The difference is particularly noticeable in the oldest (late predynastic) grave group MAO I where only five palettes occurred among a total of ca. 800 offerings.

Table 1: contents of all graves of group MAO I

offering type	% of all offerings
ceramics	ca., 74%
jewellery	ca., 10%
tools	ca., 6,5%
varia	ca., 6,5%
stone vessels	ca., 2,54%
palettes	ca., 0,65%

Some variance in the distribution of grave goods in graves with and without palettes can be noted from the following tables.

Table 2: offerings found in the 32 graves containing palettes (MAO I, III, IV)

offering type	% of all offerings
ceramic	ca., 58%
stone vessels	ca., 22%
flint	ca., 1%
copper	ca., 1%
ivory	ca., 1,5%
beads	ca., 4%
rubbing-stones	ca., 1%
minerals	ca., 0,5%
varia	ca., 11,5%

Table 3: offerings found in all graves (420)

ceramics	ca., 70%
stone vessels	ca., 15%
flint	ca., 2%
copper	ca., 2%
ivory spoons/needles of ivory	ca., 1%
beads	ca., 3%
rubbing-stones	ca., 0,5%
mineral	ca., 1%
varia	ca., 5,5%

Whereas in the oldest grave group MAO I (table 1) jewellery is the second most frequent object found after ceramics, stone vessels appear as the second most frequent group of objects in MAO III and IV. This clearly reflects the general increase in wealth (or the trend to display wealth) after MAO I. The fact that graves with palettes contain an even higher proportion of stone vessels (table 2) than all graves (table 3), ca. 22% as opposed to ca. 15%, probably reflects the fact that stone vessels occur in higher numbers in graves of females, as do the palettes. Also visible in the table is that while rubbing-stones do occur more frequently in graves with palettes the same cannot be said of minerals. Lumps of minerals, such as galena, ochre or malachite, occur in Minshat Abu Omar in twenty-nine graves, but only twice in graves with palettes. A necessary association of the two (palette and minerals) cannot therefore be presupposed.

As regards shells (especially *aspatharia*), which are often supposed to have been used as a container for mixing ground pigments with adhesive, the same pattern emerges: shells were found in twenty-eight graves in Minshat Abu Omar but only in two cases did these graves also contain palettes; characteristic for shell finds is that the large majority (19) occur in child-burials of the oldest grave group, MAO I.

MAO I

Grave 63

Grave 305

Grave 816

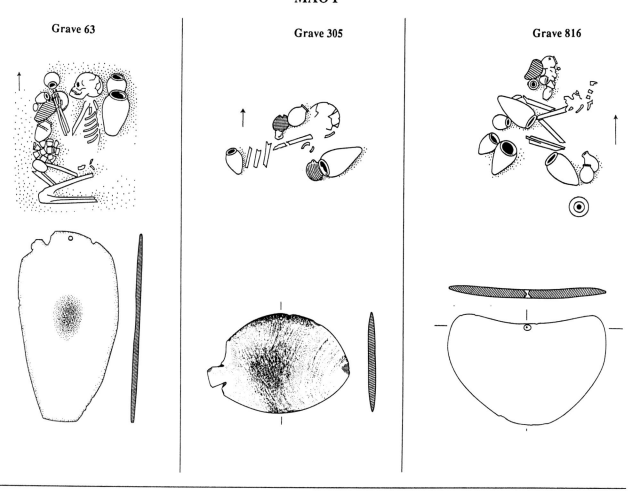

Grave 1282

Grave 1340

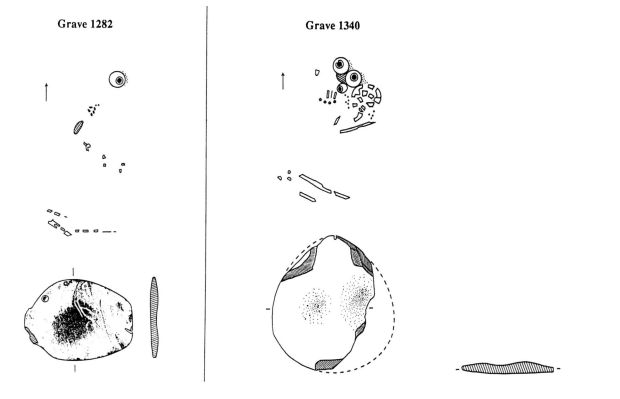

Figure 2

MAO III

Grave 44

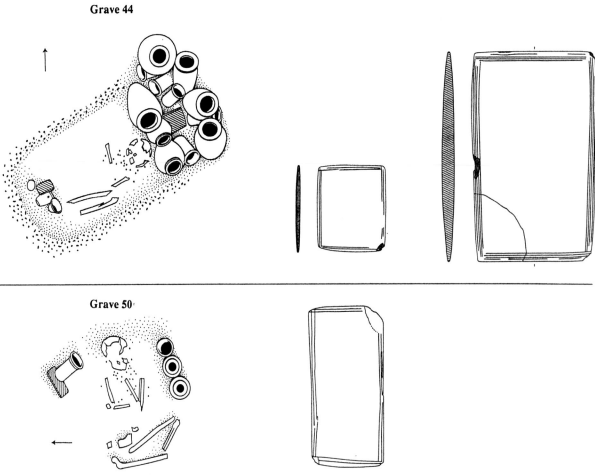

Grave 50

Grave 160

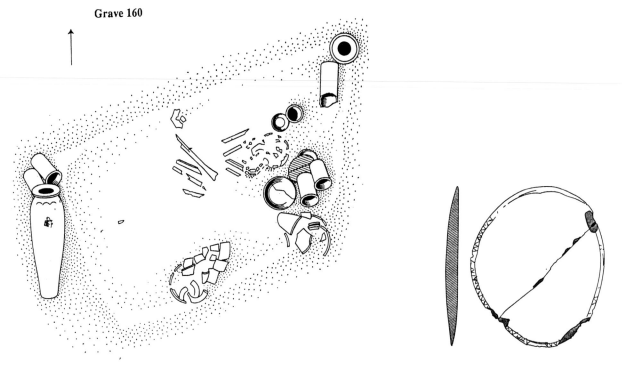

Figure 3

Grave 400

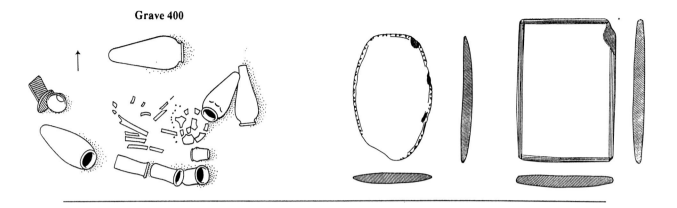

Grave 434

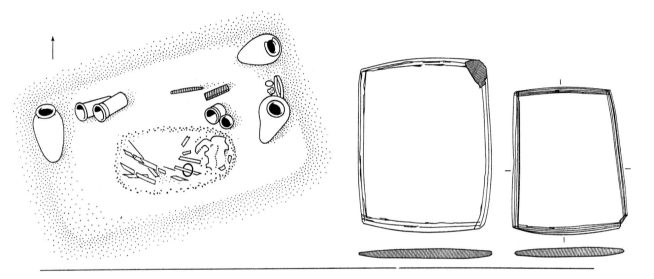

Grave 758

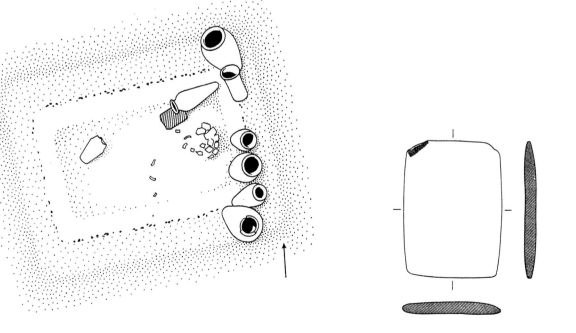

Figure 4

Grave 866

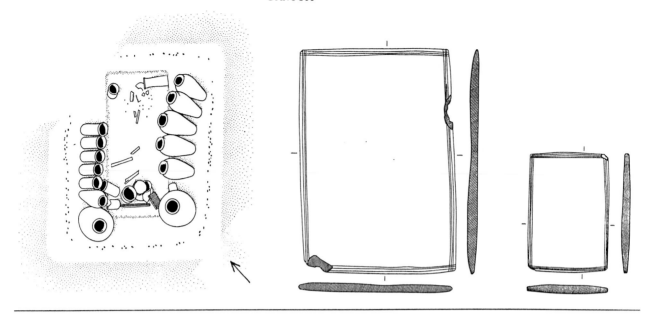

Grave 1050

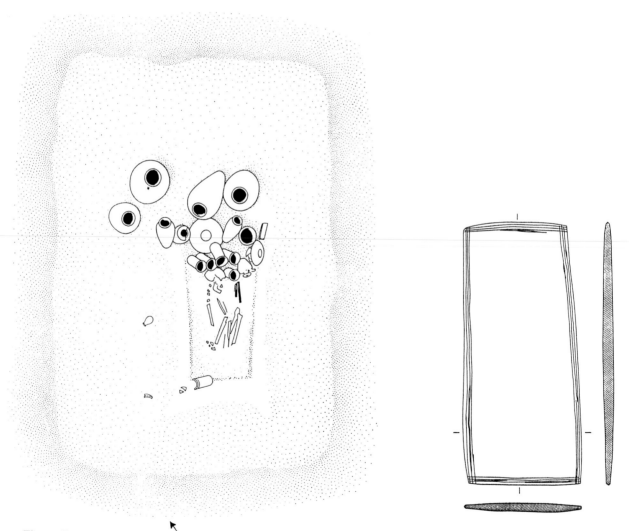

Figure 5

MAO IV

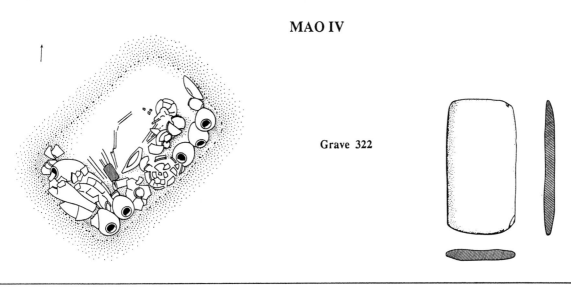

Grave 322

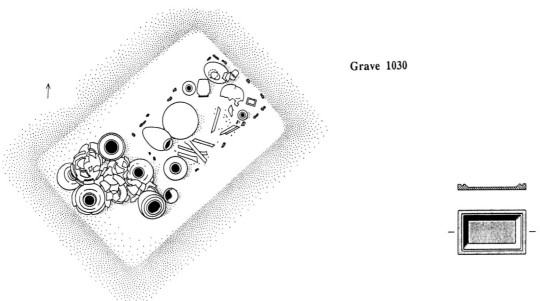

Grave 1030

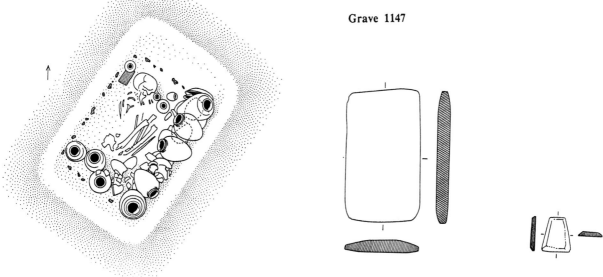

Grave 1147

Figure 6

Grave 1150

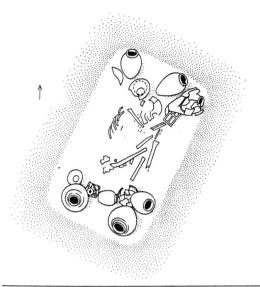
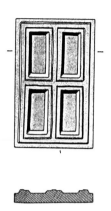

Grave 1363

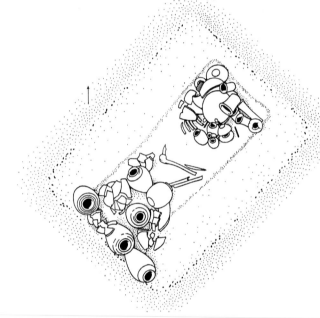
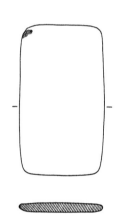

Grave 1430

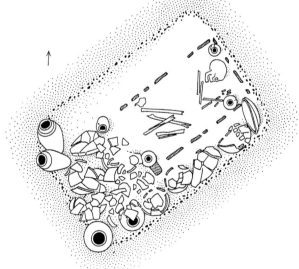
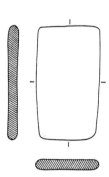

Figure 7

MAO I

63   305   1282   816   1340

MAO III

160   400

44   44   50   73   400   434   434

741   862   866   866   1045   1050

1194   1287   1295   1666   2200   2200   758

MAO IV

322   1147   1363   1430   1030   1150

Figure 8

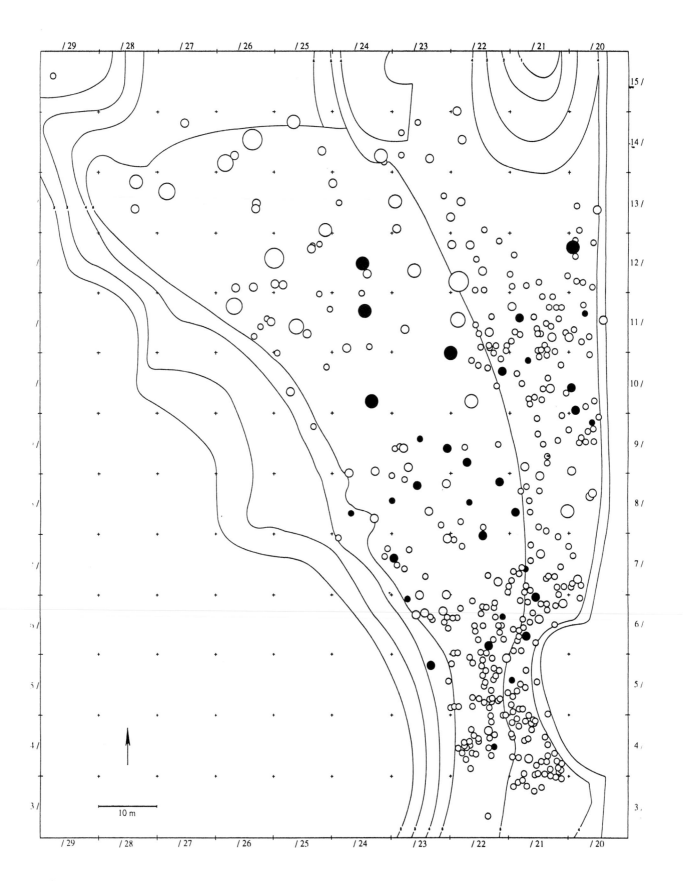

Figure 9 Minshat Abu Omar: distribution of graves with palettes

The Predynastic Site of Adaima: Settlement and Cemetery

B. Midant-Reynes,[*] N. Buchez,[**] Eric Crubezy,[***] T. Janin[****]

The predynastic site of Adaima is located on the West bank of the Nile, about 8 km south of Esna and approximately 25 km north of Hierakonpolis (see map, fig.1). It consists of a very plundered tomb set and a settlement, appearing as a large area with artefacts scattered all over the surface, extending for about 1 km along the cultivated land (pl.12a). The site, which covers about 40 ha (settlement : 35; cemetery : 5), was discovered at the beginning of the century by Garstang (1907). Henri de Morgan (1912) excavated a part of the settlement and some of the plundered tombs. Most of the associated finds are now in the Brooklyn Museum (Needler 1984).

The next excavation took place in 1973. F. Debono (1971), who worked for the French Institute of Archaeology in Cairo, excavated thirty badly plundered tombs in an area of the cemetery which is now destroyed.

In 1986 and 1987, we could see that the site was in the same state as in 1973, with the trenches of Debono's excavation still visible. But in 1988, a large part of the cemetery had been completely destroyed by the modern extension of the cultivated land and it was threatened with complete extinction.

The tombs excavated by Debono were cut in the mudterrace. We noted at the beginning of our work in Adaima that the presence of these types of graves is marked by a characteristic shallow pit, the result of their later disturbance. Therefore, the only chance to find undisturbed burials was in the sandterrace where no traces of interference were visible. All the new tombs discovered until last year were simple pits dug in the sand. Last year, we discovered not far from the settlement a set of tombs of a new type, different from those we had excavated so far. This new set of tombs, which will be discussed later, are similar to those excavated by Debono.

The present excavation was planned within the activities of the French Institute of Archaeology in Cairo, and the work began in 1989. At first a systematic sampling of the surface material allowed us to gain a great deal of information which would normally only have become available through excavation. It concerns the spatial distribution of several classes of archaeological material. The application of this method to the site of Adaima enabled us to follow a complex development of the settlement, which obviously made a shift from the desert to the valley during the Naqada period and down to the First Dynasty (Midant-Reynes, Buchez, Lechevalier, Hesse 1990; 1993a).

The artefacts found scattered all over the site exhibit all the characteristic features of a predynastic settlement, from the typical Amratian sherd (pl.3a) to the clay seal of the final phase of the period (pl.3b). We have to mention for instance Gerzean sherds (pl.3c), incised pottery (pl.3d), planes (pl.3e), partially polished axes on pebble, heat-treated blade-cores (pl.3f), sandstone grindstones, limestone spindle-whorls and bone-needles.

The settlement includes two geomorphologically distinct parts on each side of a small artificial depression which crosses the site westward. On the northern side, gravel and silt terraces outcrop with innumerable traces left by the *sebakh*-diggers. At the southern side, a thick level of sand slopes down gently to the south.

Excavations in the northern part revealed, beside the numerous *sebakh*-diggings, occupation features dug into the gravel terrace: trenches and holes smeared with Nile mud. The trenches, perpendicular or parallel to each other, constituted three areas which were associated with 73 mudholes (pl.12b). The diameter of these mudholes varied from 13 to 145cm, and averaged about 45cm; they varied from 2 to 19cm deep, averaging about 8cm. As noted by M. Hoffman (1982a: 11) for Hierakonpolis: 'The trenches are perhaps remains of reed fences plastered with mud and occasionally reinforced with wooden posts', as found also in Maadi (Rizkhana and Seeher, 1989). More enigmatic are the mudholes, which could be interpreted in some cases as post-holes, but most of them are too large and not really deep enough.

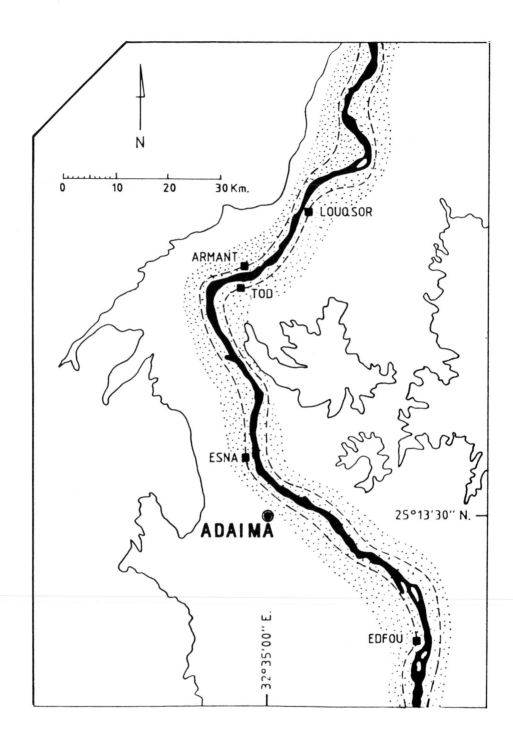

Figure 1 Map

In the case of plate 13a, the hole offered the appropriate dimensions for a post-hole and an elongated rod-shaped granite hammerstone played the role of a wedging-stone. But the one illustrated on plate 13b is certainly not a post-hole and not really a hole at all. It looks like a small basin smeared with mud. Another one had been filled with ashes.

Botanical material was recovered by flotation from the filling of these mudholes (see C. de Vartavan, in Midant-Reynes et al. 1991). Among the seeds, *Triticum monococcum* and *Hordeum sativum* have been identified. It may be hypothesised that some of these holes have been used as mortars cut in the hard gravel terrace; the absence of big grindstones among the surface material and the presence of the elongated rod-shaped granite hammerstone in one of these holes argue for this possibility. Hermann Junker (1930) described similar features at Merimde Beni Salâme.

Based on the sherds found in the filling of the trenches and the holes, these structures can be dated from the end of Naqada I to the middle of Naqada II. This shows a clear difference with the very mixed surface material which, however, was never found to go beyond the First Dynasty in date.

The excavation in the southern part of the site revealed the existence of an undisturbed domestic area of special interest with hearths, storage jars (among which was a large Black-Topped vessel with a vegetal temper) and a large granite milling stone.

Remains of a living floor (pl.14a), consisting of consolidated sand dug with several irregular small depressions have been identified. The process of formation of these blocks of compact sand is probably double: natural and man-made. The presence of organic material in the sand has favoured the formation of moisture in the soil. The depressions, which in some cases could have been remains of post-holes, are therefore mainly remains of irregular small pits caused by rotten organic material (decayed wood, dung, meal waste...). Under this living floor an earlier level of occupation is constituted by small wooden posts (pl.14b), which allows us to infer the presence of a superstructure of light timbers and reed. These two archaeologically attested occupational phases have been confirmed by the ceramic analysis. Therefore, the interpretation and the cross-connection of all the remains is still a difficult problem, which will require more work. The whole surface excavated in this area covers 925 square metres.

Beside the 'architectural' elements, the ritual and symbolic aspects of the site have been revealed by a newborn child skeleton, a young adult skull and two animal skeletons. The newborn child was associated with a small vessel inverted over a Nile shell (*Etheria elliptica*), which was probably used as a spoon. The young adult skull had been deposited with animal bones. Lastly, burials for a dog and a pig had been dug in the virgin soil, apart from the other settlement remains. Like some of the human bodies of the cemetery, these animals had been buried in leather bags.

From the faunal remains (W.Van Neer in Midant-Reynes et al. 1993b) it appears clearly that the activities of the inhabitants of Adaima were centred on fishing and husbandry. The domestic stock (cattle, goats, sheep and pigs) was the principal source of animal protein at the site.

Turning next to the cemetery, 220 graves have been excavated up to the present day out of an estimated 1500, and 25 of them were found intact. Some others are completely destroyed but the majority of them had been disturbed during predynastic times, allowing observations to be made about the skeletons and the funerary offerings.

Two 'field anthropologists' (E. Crubezy and T. Janin) carry out the excavation in Adaima. As explained by Duday et al. (1990), the understanding of mortuary practices requires a methodology which recognises the importance of both the position of the skeletal remains and the taphonomy of the cadaver. The chronology of articulations dislocated during the decomposition of the body served as a basis for demonstrating the nature and evolution of burials. It is the aim of field anthropology to reconstruct the original position of the body, the arrangement of any pieces of clothing, ornament or other furnishings. Furthermore, it is the field anthropologist who must define the architecture of the tomb and the precise nature and circumstances of decomposition. This requires the reconstruction of the burial itself in terms of the conditions surrounding the body, e.g. if it was directly covered by soil or surrounded by free space, in order to identify effects these contribute to the position of skeletal remains.

From the point of view of the mortuary practices, two kinds of burials can be distinguished: simple and multiple burials. In all the cases of intact burials, the bodies were buried in a mat.

The first group (simple burials) made up two-thirds of the funerary set. They included those with offerings (up to 30 vessels for one tomb) and those without gifts (two were undisturbed). We obtained last year the proof that these simple burials without gifts were really predynastic thanks to the fact that one of them had been cut by a Naqada III grave.

The multiple burials included double burials (two were intact, pl.14c). We found an interesting case with five bodies associated with a big hearth, which was already in place before the burial, and in which the five bodies had been placed (pl.15a). Some months to some years later, the tomb had been badly but only partially plundered, giving the picture of ashes mixed with broken human bones. Could not such finds be responsible for theories on 'cannibalism' during predynastic times? With regards to the chronology, this tomb is as yet the oldest in the necropolis. It has been dated to Naqada Ic (see S. Hendrickx in Midant-Reynes et al. 1992)

We have already mentioned the human skull buried in the settlement. We found in Adaima two simple burials *without gravegoods and without the head* (pl.4a). In these cases, plundering is not responsible for the absence of the skull, as it is in some other cases. Here, we did not find any remains of skullbones, which could point to a selective plundering. The sand all around these burials has been carefully screened. *It appears that the skull had been taken away after the corpse was totally decomposed.* The discovery under the settlement floor of the remains of a mat containing a human face (pl.4b) suggests human intervention and the collecting of human bones from corpses totally decomposed in predynastic times in Upper Egypt.

A few cases of infectious diseases have been identified, which bring an interesting light on this pre-urban period. A case resembling tuberculosis is among the oldest known in the world (Crubezy and Janin, in press): a woman suffering from this illness was completely hunchbacked. An offering was associated with her: a pot which had been deformed before baking. One cannot help wondering whether both facts might be connected.

Lastly we would like to mention certain burials we found for the first time last year, which consist of tombs in the mudterrace (pl.15b). We have just excavated four of them and intend to carry out excavation in this area during the next campaign.

It was noticed immediately how different they were from the former ones, not only because of their geomorphological location, but also because they include other types of burial: a pot-burial, in which the body of a very young child was enclosed by a pot inverted over the body, and burial in a clay coffin, as in certain graves found in Debono's excavation.

All the main Naqadian pottery categories are present on the site, but no indications have been found which could confirm production activity. Perhaps this fact shows that some workshop may have produced ceramics for several settlements? The comparison between the pots of the cemetery and those of the settlement offered interesting information about chronology and allows a better understanding of the funerary practices. We can establish that the pottery was deposited in the graves after having been used as cooking pots. But one can suppose that as a funerary offering the *function* of the vessel played a role. However we found in the settlement an important proportion (15%) of a kind of pottery exclusively used for cooking and which is not represented in the graves.

From the point of view of the chronology, the cemetery had been used *in continuum* from Naqada IC (the tomb with five bodies) until Naqada IIIB and the First Dynasty (for the chronology, see S. Hendrickx, this volume).

Turning to the settlement, we have a similar evolution from the end of Naqada I to the First Dynasty. Six C^{14} dates have been obtained from charcoal. They spread from 4765 ± 50 BP[1] to 4420 ± 55 BP,[2] which means between 3671 to 3387 Cal. BC for the earliest date and between 3307 and 2923 Cal. BC for the latter.

The multi-component character of Adaima, with its functionally specific activity areas and its domestic units, make it an important site for gathering data on Egyptian prehistory, the palaeo-environment and subsistence strategy. The site includes cemetery and settlement which cover the same periods of the predynastic age and, therefore, allow comparisons between the two areas. Even partially disturbed, they offer information of special relevance to those interested in pre-urban patterning, daily life and mortuary practices. The lithic industry and the ceramics will permit comparison with other sites in the Nile valley.

Notes:

* URA 995 du CNRS, Paris.
** Céramologue
*** Laboratoire d'Anthropologie de Bordeaux, URA 376 et GDR 742 du CNRS.
**** UPR 290 et GDR 742 du CNRS.
1. Centre de Datation par le Radiocarbone. Département des Sciences et de la Terre. Université Claude Bernard Lyon 1. Echantillon Ly 5832.
2. Echantillon Ly 5207.

Imported Pottery with Potmarks from Abydos

Barbara Adams and Naomi Porat

It has long been recognized that certain pottery vessels discovered in the Early Dynastic tombs and the cemetery at Abydos in Upper Egypt by Amélineau (1899a, 1902, 1904) and Petrie (1900, 1901, 1902) at the beginning of this century were foreign imports. This catalogue of examples was expanded over the years from excavations in the north at Saqqara (Emery 1938, 1949, 1954, 1958; Macramallah 1940), Turah (Junker 1912), Tarkhan (Petrie 1914), Lahun (Petrie 1923), Abu Roash (Klasens 1961), Abusir el Meleq (Scharff 1926), and more recently from Minshat Abu Omar (Kroeper in prep.) and Tell Ibrahim Awad (van den Brink 1988b). The types of these Abydos ware pottery jugs and flasks were outlined by Hennessey (1967) who showed that they were first imported during the reign of Djer and restricted to Dynasty I.

Neither stump based vessels or painted vessels appear before the reign of Den. Hennessey conducted a series of chemical analyses of sherds from Egypt and Israel provided by the Ashmolean Museum Oxford which confirmed their origin in Palestine and divided them into two main groups: a) a high calcium group which equated with the painted wares and b) a burnished ware group.

As part of the current renewed interest in the process of unification in Egypt at the end of the Predynastic period, in the light of new discoveries in the Delta, and the part played by international contact in the formation of the state, there is also a renewed interest in the enigmatic potmarks found on pottery in Egypt (see especially van den Brink 1992b: 265-296), the meaning of which can not be explained by reference to hieroglyphic signs. There has been much speculation about the purpose of potmarks, which is best summarised in van den Brink (1992b: footnote 4, quoting van den Berg 1989).

These interpretations range from property marks, content descriptions, capacity indications and source notations to an argument that they are a younger Lower Egyptian ('Butischen') script (Helck 1990), which was superceded by an Upper Egyptian script. As potmarks are known from many sites in Upper Egypt, both prior to and during the spread of the southern Predynastic culture into the Delta from Naqada IIcd, the latter interpretation seems unlikely.

The quantity of Early Dynastic potmarks available for study is fairly daunting. Petrie assiduously collected and published over 1500 marks from the Umm el Qa'ab cemetery at Abydos (Petrie 1900, 1901). These and published examples from later excavations have been assembled in a corpus of 907 types in 97 groups by van den Brink (1992b), who has tried, wherever possible from the information supplied by the excavators, to relate the potmarks to the type of pots into which they were incised, realising the importance of this information if their true meaning is ever to be interpreted.

Potmarks were usually made with a sharp or blunt instrument into the wet clay of the pot before firing, but there are examples which were scratched into the fired pot. Caution is required, however, in the acceptance of some of the scratched examples because at least some of those with the *serekh* of Semerkhet have proved to be faked, or much later additions, albeit marked onto genuine, if inappropriate vessels (Adams 1993b). The group studied here presents such an example: the hieroglyphic group which is probably meant to signify *sntr* (incense), incised into a red-coated and burnished imported sherd (fig.1Q, UC.36609, Petrie 1901: pl.LVB, 206), which is highly unlikely to have been contemporary with the pot.

Imported jugs and flagons are one class of pottery found in Dynasty I tombs that are sometimes found with potmarks (Petrie 1901: pl.LIV; Petrie 1902: pl.VIII; Klasens 1961: fig. 3; Bonnet 1928: tafel 25), and the character of these potmarks seems to be wholly Egyptian; in other words they were applied to the surface of the vessels after they reached Egypt. There are certain particular examples of these added potmarks: a fragment of a net-burnished vessel from a tomb dated to the time of Djet at Tarkhan has a falcon scratched into the surface (UC.17089, Petrie 1913: pl.XVI,4, XXX, 6-7; Amiran 1968), and a jug from the Tomb of Hemaka, an official of Den at Saqqara, has an incised design of two parallel lines above a crocodile (Zaki Saad in Emery 1938: 12, pl.41).

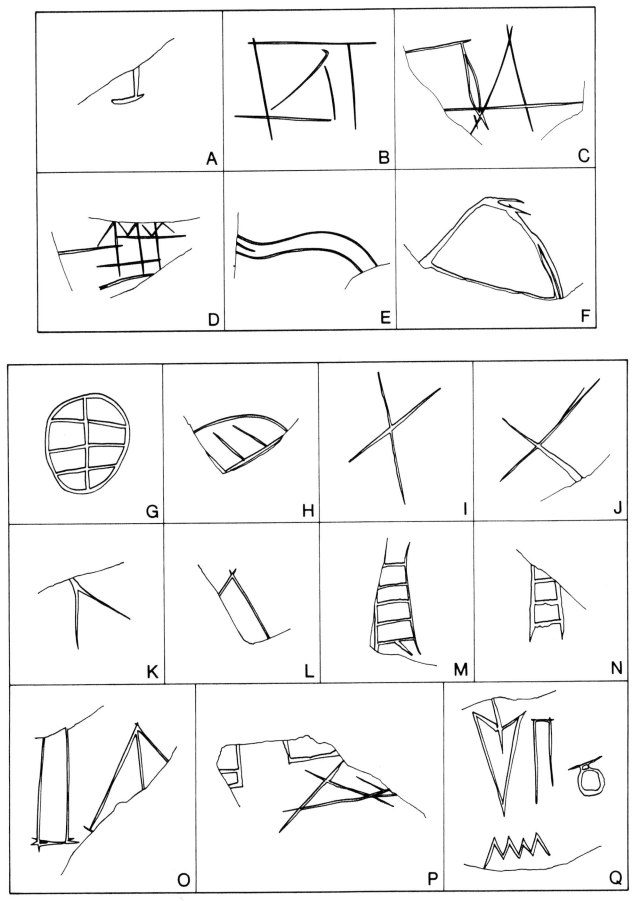

Figure 1 A) UC.36617 B) UC.17387 C) UC.36615 D) UC.36614 E) UC.17407 F) UC.17390 G) UC.36610 H) UC.35785 I) UC.17428 J) UC.17429 K) UC.17422 L) UC.17437 M) UC.17427 N) UC.36611 O) UC.36616 P) UC.36613 Q) UC.36609.

An important exception here, UC.17387 from the Tomb of Djer, has a potmark on the base which was incised before firing (fig.1B), indicating that it was applied at the point of manufacture and, surprisingly, examination of vessels in the Ashmolean Museum has revealed that this is not the only example, see below.

In addition to the published corpus, there are over 100 potmarks on sherds in the Petrie Museum of Egyptian Archaeology, University College London, from the Umm el Qa'ab cemetery for which Petrie did not publish drawings. During an initial sort of these unidentified potmarks a number of sherds were discovered that did not seem to be of Egyptian manufacture. There are a number of foreign sherds which have been known for some years in the Petrie Museum [Tomb of Djer UC.17385-17399, UC.17402-17437; Tomb of Den: UC.17408-17412, UC.17420; Tomb of Semerkhet: UC.17422-17434, UC.36758; Tomb Unknown: UC.17400-1, UC.17404-7], and these examples can now be added to that group, although the tombs from which they originated cannot be identified.

This small group of potmarked, imported pottery compiled from examples already registered and these new sherds (see Table 1) was sampled for petrographic analysis in the hope that it could: a) confirm that all the pieces were foreign, and b) identify the source of the clay from which the pots were manufactured; this information might then be a useful contribution towards the interpretation of the marks. Samples were taken for analysis by Naomi Porat, who has built up a large reference collection of thin section analyses from both Early Bronze Age sites in Israel and comparative material from Egypt (Porat 1989).

Petrography (Porat)

Fragments from 16 sherds with potmarks were thin-sectioned and analysed under the polarizing microscope. The sand-size minerals in the temper were identified and the silt-size minerals and the texture of the matrix were noted. The sherds can be divided into two distinct groups, differing in temper components, type of matrix and firing temperature. Details of the petrographic constituents and an estimate of the firing temperature for each sample are found in Table 2. The results are summarised below.

GROUP A: (Six samples belong to this group).

Temper:

The samples are sparsely tempered, the sandy components constituting up to 10% of the volume of the sherd. The temper minerals and rock fragments, in decreasing abundance, are:

Quartz: Quartz is found in most samples belonging to this group. It is sand-size, poorly sorted and subrounded (pl.19a). Occasionally, stable heavy minerals such as zircon and epidote are found.
Shale fragments: The fragments are oval or rectangular, with a laminar structure. Fine, silt size iron oxides are dispersed within the shales (pl.19a). Occasionally, the oxides are rhomb-shaped.
Siltstone: These comprise poorly sorted silty quartz cemented with clay minerals.
Oolites: Rounded, sand-size, opaque grains were identified as iron-rich oolites.
Volcanics: Highly weathered fragments with textures resembling volcanic rocks are found in most samples. Only rarely feldspar crystals can be identified. Usually the fragments contain two phases, an opaque one and a clear one (pl.19b). The opaque phase is rich in iron oxides. The clear phase is isotropic when viewed with a crossed polarizer.
Limestone: In most samples where limestone fragments could be identified, they had decomposed due to a high firing temperature, and their original texture is no longer visible.

Matrix:

The matrix surrounding the temper is clay-rich, with a calcareous component. In most samples it is milky and vitrified, due to a high firing temperature. The silty components of the matrix are:
Quartz: The silty quartz (pl.20a) often forms one continuous range of sizes with the sandy quartz temper. It was probably introduced into the clay together with the quartz or the siltstone temper.

100

UC.Number	Description	Incision	Tomb	Reference	Figure/Plate
17387	Brown-coated	Wet, triangle & rectangle?	Djer	cf.Ab I, pl.VIII, 8	1B/16b
17390	Red-coated	Dry, rounded triangle?	Djer	cf.Ab I, pl.VIII, 7, 8	1F/17a, 20b
17437	Red-coated & polished	Dry, triangle part?	Djer		1L/17c (rt.)
17407	Brown-coated & pattern-burnished	Dry, wavy lines			1E/16c (mid.), 19b
35785	Red-coated & polished, strap-handled	Dry, part hatched circle			1H/17b (left)
36609	Red-coated & burnished	Dry, *sntr* ? sign		RT II, pl.LVB, 206	1Q/18c
36610	Red-coated & polished	Dry, hatched circle			1G/17b (rt.)
36611	Red-coated & burnished	Dry, 'ladder'			1N/17c (left)
36613	Coated & burnished	Dry, ?rectangle & triangle			1P/16d (left)
36614	Brown	Dry, triangles & grid			1D/16d (rt.)
36615	Burnt	Dry, triangle & ?rectangle			1C/16c (rt.)
36616	Blackened	Dry, triangle & rectangle			1O/16c (left), 21
36617	Combed, cream-coated base	Dry, ?part rectangle			1A/16a
17422	Base	Dry, asterisk star	Semerkhet	cf.RT II, pl.LIV	1K/18a
17427	Painted	Dry, 'ladder'	Semerkhet	cf.RT II, pl.LIV	1M/17d
17428	Painted sherd	Dry, asterisk star	Semerkhet	cf.RT II, pl.LIV	1I/18b (rt.)
17429	Reconstructed ?painted	Dry, asterisk star	Semerkhet	cf.RT II, pl.LIV	1J/18b (left)

Table 1: Imported Jar Sherds with Potmarks in the Petrie Museum from Petrie's Work in the Umm el Qa'ab Cemetery, Abydos, 1900-1902.

Iron oxides: Finely dispersed oxides are found mainly in the samples which contain shale fragments.
Decomposed carbonate fragments: Like the limestone temper, the carbonate in the matrix was affected by the high firing temperature and can no longer be identified. Due to a reaction between the carbonates and the clay minerals the matrix has acquired a milky appearance.

Firing temperature:
As indicated by the isotropic, milky matrix and the decomposed limestone fragments, the firing temperature of the samples belonging to this group was higher than 850-900°C.

Source:
The raw materials used for producing these vessels were derived from continental, quartz-rich clastic rocks, associated with basalt flows. The only formation in this region which contains all the components found in the pottery is the Hatira Fm., of Lower Cretaceous age. This formation comprises iron-rich sandstone, siltstone and shales, with iron-bearing oolites, underlain by highly weathered basalt flows and overlain by limestone. The formation is exposed in the north-eastern part of Israel, around Mt. Hermon, and in Lebanon (Porat 1989).

The petrographic composition of Group A is remarkably similar to that of the Metallic Ware pottery, found in Early Bronze Age II and III sites in Northern Israel, such as Tell Dan, Tel Hazor and Megiddo. The group is also very similar to Abydos Ware jugs found in Early Dynastic tombs in Abydos and in other sites in Egypt (Group 2 in Porat 1989). The Metallic and Abydos Ware vessels were produced from the same type of raw materials, in a location somewhere in northern Israel or in Lebanon.

GROUP B: (Ten samples belong to this group).

Temper:
The samples are sparsely tempered, and the sand-size component constitutes between 5 and 10% of the volume of the sherd. The temper minerals and rock fragments are:
Calcite: The calcite fragments are often rhomb-shaped, broken along cleavage planes. They appear to be unweathered and they vary in size. Probably the calcite was freshly crushed and added to the clay.
Limestone: Limestone fragments are usually rounded, with micritic or sparry texture (pl.20b). Unlike the limestone in Group A, there is no evidence of destruction due to a high firing temperature.
Chalk: The chalk fragments are rounded, rich with foraminifera and are often stained with iron oxides.
Basalt: Basalt fragments are usually sub-rounded to sub-angular, containing unaltered minerals (Photo XV). Olivine phenocrysts are surrounded by iddingsite rims. Pale brown pyroxene and plagioclase laths comprise the groundmass.
Chert: Chert fragments are large and very angular (pl.20b).
Quartz: Rare grains of rounded quartz occur in most samples.

Matrix
The matrix in all samples is highly calcareous, rich in foraminifera (pl.21) and contains some well-sorted silty quartz.

Firing temperature
All samples belonging to this group were fired to a temperature below that of the decomposition of calcite, less than 750°C.

Source
The samples contain components derived mainly from carbonate rocks associated with fresh basalt flows. The composition and texture of the basalt fragments are very similar to Tertiary basalt flows which outcrop in the Lower Galilee and the Golan Heights. Chalk and limestone containing chert beds and nodules are very common in the Galilee and these crop out close to the basalt flows. The source of the quartz could be in the Miocene Hordos Fm, exposed mainly around Lake Kinneret.

SHERD #	FIG.	TEMPER											MATRIX				FT	GROUP
		QZ	CC	LS	CT	CK	SF	MB	BS	VL	OO	SS	QZ	CC	FR	OX		
17387	1B	+		+						+	++			+		++	H	A
17390	1F				++	+			++				++		+++		L	B
17407	1E	+++					++			+			+			+	M	A
17422	1K	(+)	++	+		++		+	+				+		+++		L	B
17428	1I	(+)	++	++		++		+	(+)						+++		L	B
17429	1J		++					++					+	++	+++		L	B?
17437	1L		++			+			+				+		+++		L	B
36609	1Q				+	+++			+				++		++		L	B
36610	1G	(+)				+++			+				+		+++		L	B
36611	1N							++	+				+		+++		L	B
36613	1P	(+)		+	(+)	+++			++				+		+++		L	B
36614	1D			++							+		++		++		H	A?
36615	1C	+++									++	+	+			++	M	A
36616	1O		(+)	+++	++	(+)			+				++		+++		L	B
36617	1A	+++								+	(+)		+	+		+	H	A
BM35549		+									(+)		+++				M	A

Table 2: Composition of individual samples. Temper components: QZ - quartz, CC - calcite, LS - limestone, CK - chalk, SF - shale fragments, MB - mud balls, BS - basalt, VL - volcanic, OO - oolites, SS - siltstone. Matrix components: QZ - quartz, CC - calcite and other carbonate fragments, FR - foraminifera, OX - iron oxides. FT - firing temperature: L - low (<750°C), M - medium (750-850°C), H - High (>950°C). Concentrations: +++ very common, ++ common, + occasional, (+) rare.

The roundness of some temper fragments indicate that the temper could have been collected from wadi beds or from the shores of Lake Kinneret. The clay was collected from marly formations, found in that same region.

Early Bronze Age pottery from several sites in the Lower Galilee, such as Beit Yerah, contains a very similar assemblage of sandy temper with components such as limestone, chalk, basalt, chert and quartz, in a calcareous clay. The proportion between the different components vary, but all are always present. Painted Abydos Ware from Abydos also contains similar temper components such as basalt and iron-stained chalk fragments, within a calcareous clay (Group 3 in Porat 1989). The vessels found in Abydos were probably manufactured in the Lower Galilee, perhaps in the vicinity of Lake Kinneret.

Interpretation

When the results of the petrographic analysis is related to the potmarked sherds, it can be seen that there is a difference in the potmarks which are scratched into the Group A and Group B sherds. The more highly fired pottery of Group A has potmarks which are geometric in shape, such as rectangles, squares, grids and triangles and this may be significant, although it may also be a function of the difficulty presented by a harder surface. The mark on one of them in Group A (fig.1B: UC.17387) was, as noted, wet incised. The sherds in Group B have potmarks which tend to be of three types: asterisk-stars, 'ladders' and crossed circles (three parallel lines and one cross line). A survey of the potmarks on vessels from other sites in the site reports seems to confirm these correlations, where they can be associated with a particular type of pot; potmarks are often recorded separately from the drawings of the pots on which they were incised, a frustrating feature also remarked upon by van den Brink. The crossed circles and the stars are particularly common on the painted pottery, found during the reigns of Den, Semerkhet and Qa'a in Upper and Lower Egypt. For example the vessel from tomb 38 at Saqqara (Macramallah 1940: pl.XLIV), which has a broken 'ladder' and an asterisk-star in a circle and the painted jug from tomb 9B-1 at Abusir (Bonnet 1928: taf.27) which has a asterisk-star.

This association of potmark type with fabric group was further tested by personal examination (Adams) of the imported pottery with potmarks from Early Dynastic contexts in the Ashmolean Museum. We are indebted to Helen Whitehouse, of the Department of Antiquities, for making these pots available for examination and for permission from the Visitors of the Ashmolean Museum to describe and figure the potmarks here. By using a hand lens and the ware criteria established by Porat it was possible to tentatively assign the pottery in Oxford as follows:

E.3160	Tomb of Djer, Abydos	*Abydos* I, pl.VIII, 4	Group A	Fig.2E
E.4034	Tomb of Djer, Abydos	*Abydos* I, pl.VIII, 8	Group A	Fig.2F
E.3245	Tomb Unknown, Abydos		Group A	Fig.2D *
E.1309	?Tomb of Semerkhet	*RT* II, pl.VII, 9	Group ?A	Fig.2C
E.3212	Tomb of Semerkhet	*RT* II, pl.LIV	Group ?B	
E.3216	Tomb of Semerkhet	*RT* II, LIV	Group B	Fig.2B *
E.3215	Tomb of Semerkhet	*RT* II, LIV	Group B	Fig.2A

The two pots, E.3245 and E.3216, marked with an asterisk, are part of a group which was sampled in Oxford for NAA analysis by Joan Huntoon some time ago, but not processed or published before she died. The unprocessed results have been passed onto Pat McGovern of MASCA and were made available to us by Helen Whitehouse for comparative purposes. Based on external macroscopic examination, E.3245 was placed in Group A and E.3216 in Group B. The chemical composition of these samples, chiefly the concentrations of the rare earth elements, may be compared to NAA results for samples with a known petrography from Abydos (Porat 1989, appendices 5b and 9). As mentioned above, Groups A and B of this work correspond to groups 2 and 3 of Porat (1989), respectively.

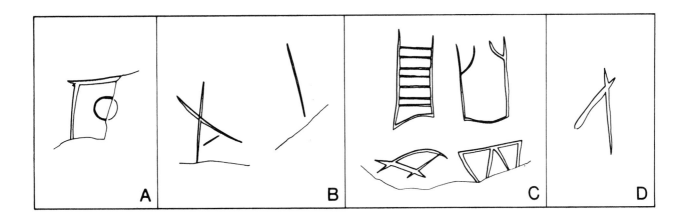

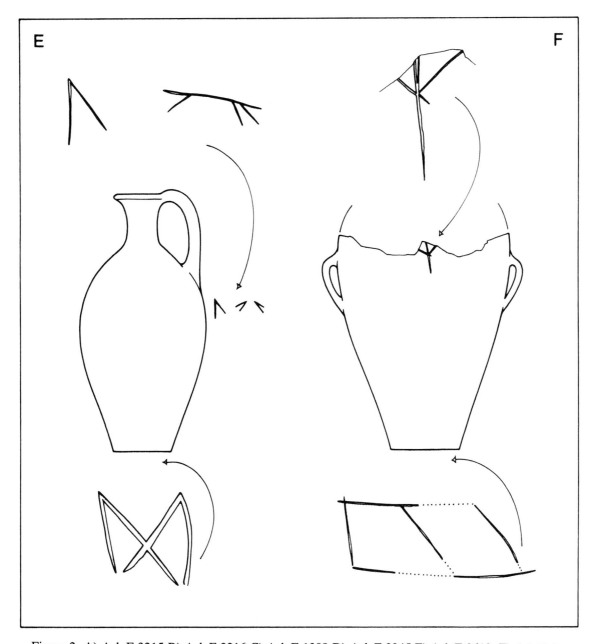

Figure 2 A) Ash.E.3215 B) Ash.E.3216 C) Ash.E.1309 D) Ash.E.3245 E) Ash.E.3610 F) Ash.E.4034.

The composition of E.3245 is very similar to that of sample 640, an Abydos jug painted with a net pattern which was found in the tomb of Semerkhet. The composition of E.3216 is remarkably similar to that of sample 633, a decorated Abydos jug found in the tomb of King Den. Sample 640 was placed by Porat (1989) in Group 2 (=A), whereas sample 633 belongs to Group 3 (=B). These NAA results confirm the macroscopic examination of the sherds with potmarks from the Oxford collection. Furthermore, these results show that the potmarked sherds are not different in any way from other types of Abydos Ware found in tombs at Abydos. This means that the correlation of particular types of potmarks with each type of fabric seems to be confirmed (but see the analysis of the British Museum vessel below). The potmarks associated with Group B ware sherds were as expected: part of a rectangle with a circle on Ash.E.3215 (fig.2A), an asterisk-star on which the lines do not properly overlap on Ash.E.3216 (fig.2B)) and a more complex sign group with a 'ladder', *ka* arms, a possible trap sign (cf. seals of Hor-Aha, Petrie 1901: pl.XIV, 101-104; Kaplony 1963: III, Abb.53-62) and two inverted triangles on the sherd Ash.E.1309 (fig.2C), which may be a later, more hieroglyphic addition like that on UC.36609 (fig.1Q).

The marks on the Group A pottery, equivalent to Abydos metallic ware (Porat 1989: 64 Group 2) proved to be most interesting. The sherd without a tomb context, Ash.E.3245, has the crater left by an applied handle beneath an applied horizontal ridge and a wet-incised, inverted V-shaped potmark applied to the left of the handle (fig.2D). Fortunately, in two cases, Ash.E.3160 and Ash.E.4034, virtually whole pots are available for examination and the dry incised potmarks on the shoulder of these vessels were checked against the published versions (Petrie 1902: pl.VIII, 4 and 8), and seen to be slightly different. On Ash.E.3160 the potmark consists of an inverted V-shape and a horizontal line with lines radiating from it at each end (fig.2E, top). On Ash.E.4034 the partial mark could be a square or rectangle with a bisecting line or a bisected triangle (fig.2F, top). There are also wet incised potmarks on the base of both these vessels, which seem to have been unobserved since they were excavated at the beginning of the century. The mark on Ash.E.3160 is like a bisected open square, or angular figure of eight, but with curved sides (fig.2E, bottom), and the mark on Ash.E.4034, although partially obscured by a carbonate concretion, is probably a rectangle with cross lines (fig. 2F, bottom). Both these pots have the remains of copious organic contents, now black and glistening, which Hennessey suggested was bitumen, but the effect observed is probably the result of burning.

An investigation of the contents of some of these Abydos ware jars has been undertaken by Margaret Serpico, with Raymond White and Gretchen Shearer, as part of her study of oils, resins and perfumes for her Ph.D. thesis at University College London (see Serpico and White, this volume). Her samples included three pots from the Tomb of Djer at Abydos with potmarks (the aforementioned Ashmolean E.4034 and E.3160 and BM.35549, Petrie 1902: pl.VIII,3,4,8), and one from the Tomb of Semerkhet in the Petrie Museum (UC.17422). The contents of UC.17422 were unfortunately indeterminate, probably due to contamination in the burial environment, but probably organic. Delwen Samuel examined the sample using a scanning electron microscope and observed fungus on the surface which confirms this.

The pot in the Department of Egyptian Antiquities at the British Museum (Spencer 1980: cat.no.328, pls. 42, 22) has the crossed circle type of potmark and is the only one with this potmark assigned to Group A ware by macro examination (pl.20a), which was subsequently confirmed from analysis of a thin section provided by the British Museum (see Table 2), although its fabric is a little different from the rest of the group. This might be explained by a re-use of the jar in Egypt, with the mark then referring to the contents, a possibility suggested by Serpico. The pots from the Tomb of Djer were burnt in antiquity which is an extra complication in analysis, but the contents of the pot in the British Museum and Ash.E.3160 have produced interesting and differing results (see Serpico and White, this volume, pp.128-139). The implications of these analyses for trading patterns and the kind of oils and resins in demand in the newly formed Egyptian state are obviously important.

A jug from the recent excavations of Tomb 1590 in the cemetery at Minshat Abu Omar in the Delta has a short stump base which, according to Hennessey's typology, places it after the reign of Den. Kroeper dates the tomb on Egyptian ceramic evidence to the middle of Dynasty I (Kroeper 1992). It has two potmarks incised into the surface on either side of the vessel. One of the potmarks is the 'ladder' sign and the crossed circle and the other a group of three signs which might be the hieroglyphs for *s* and *n* with three inverted triangles. According to analysis previously undertaken by Porat, the fabric of this pot does not equate with either Group A or B here. We are indebted to Karla Kroeper for providing a drawing of the pot from Minshat Abu Omar and for her permission to describe it here prior to her full publication of the material from the site. The stump base jug found by van den Brink at Tell Ibrahim Awad has a potmark consisting of *ka* arms and an inverted triangular sign (van den Brink 1988b: 80 fig.19;1992b: corpus III.12), a group which is also found on Egyptian 'wine jars' from Abydos and therefore seems in a different category. Analysis of this jug by Porat indicated that the fabric is equivalent to the northern Group A defined here.

As far as interpretation of these signs is concerned, there are still a number of possibilities. Van den Brink (1992b) suggests that: 'potmarks served an administrative function during the Protodynastic (Dynasty 0) and Early Dynastic periods in Egypt linked to centralized bodies responsible for the collecting and re-distribution of the commodities contained in these marked vessels for funerary use and that they were not connected *per se* with potters' workshops.' If this is the case, then there might be a chronological implication in the use of different potmarks for the Group A and B wares, in other words slightly different connotations may have been used during the reigns of earlier and later kings in the First Dynasty for the same category of import. It is possible of course that these potmarks were incised after re-use of the vessels in Egypt, after the imported commodity had been exhausted and that they relate to their subsequent disbursement, but both these suggestions seem unlikely. The potmarks of Group B ware do however appear as wet incised marks on Egyptian vessels in various combinations (see especially Petrie 1900, 1901 and van den Brink 1992b).

Another more likely possibility is that the potmarks link to the source of the pottery, or more likely to the commodity imported within the vessels. It certainly seems to be the case that the potmarks of Group A echo the marks applied at source in northern Israel or the Lebanon, even although these are merely indistinct geometric shapes featuring mainly squares and triangles. According to Yukutieli (1995): 'the custom of incising different kinds of designs, either before or after firing, on pottery jars is a common Egyptian Predynastic and Early Dynastic trait, while it is very rare on contemporaneous Canaanite vessels.' No wet incised potmarks have been observed on Group B sherds and these seem to have a wholly Egyptian repertoire of signs: the ladder, asterisk-star and crossed circle.The pots have of course been found in tombs in both Upper and Lower Egypt and not just at Abydos, which would seem to preclude designations of funerary distribution. If, for example, it was known to the Egyptians that the vessels which were manufactured in the north of Israel and the Lebanon contained a different commodity than those from the area of the Lower Galilee, then they might give them a different connotation. At this juncture, in relation to the potmarks and the sources of the pottery in the Levant now identified, it can be suggested that there is a correlation between source/content and potmark prior to or on import into Egypt, which was constant no matter what the ultimate funerary destination of the jar was to be.

Town and State in the Early Old Kingdom
A View from Elephantine

Stephan Johannes Seidlmayer

The fusion of predynastic chiefdoms to form a first national state in Egypt did not affect only the geographical size of the political unit(s); rather, it entailed profound changes in socio-economic structure, evident, among other indications, in the settlement pattern. Most conspicuous, archaeologically, are the remains documenting the establishment of the royal residence in the Memphite area, where the social élite and all expressions of high culture came to be concentrated; the rest of the country, including the former centres, sank to a level of provincialism. Social and economic relations of unprecedented asymmetry between centre and country provided the basis for the achievements of civilisation; on the condition, however, that a stable integration of the social system as a whole was still maintained.

One may wonder, indeed, whether Old Kingdom Egypt is more remarkable for her early success in meeting this requirement, or for her ultimate failure. Both the ability of the Egyptian state, during the Fourth Dynasty, to concentrate the forces of the whole country on constructing royal mortuary complexes of such astonishing dimensions, no less than the amazing fact of its dissolution during the First Intermediate Period, should alert the observer to the key question of Old Kingdom history: the organisation of social differentiation and integration in a nationwide perspective. Elucidating the political, economic, ideological and cultural relationships between the institutions of the centralised state and the country, which both depended on and influenced developments in the local communities, becomes therefore a task of crucial importance.

Urbanisation, as a way in which cultural complexity becomes manifest on a local level, is of immediate relevance to any consideration of this broader issue of structural history. Accordingly, the development of towns, the rôles they played within their regional context as well as the functions they fulfilled in the framework of state organisation and interests has attracted ever-growing scientific concern during recent decades (Bietak 1979, 1981, 1986, Hoffman 1982a: 122ff, Hoffman et al. 1986, Kemp 1977, Müller-Wollermann 1991, Uphill 1988, Wenke et al. 1988, Patch 1991). As a contribution to this discussion, I will attempt here a synthesis of the data pertaining to the early history of Elephantine. In fact, as a result of systematic excavation carried out on the site by the German Archaeological Institute on a regular basis since 1969 (see Kaiser et al. 1970-1995), a fairly coherent picture seems to emerge.

There is no such thing as *the* typical Egyptian town. Turning to an individual site, it should be borne in mind that, depending on its geographical setting and its historical background, probably each place has its own story to tell. This is particularly true for Elephantine. Forwarned against thoughtless generalisation of the findings, one should not overlook, however, that it is often atypical situations in archaeology which help to make typical matters visible.

Nature may often set the stage for history, and it seems important that Elephantine's geographical situation is fairly well understood, together with its ecological and political implications. Elephantine is situated at the southern border of Egypt proper, where an outcrop of the magmatic basement complex has created the first cataract of the Nile. The town was placed on the southern tip of a large island, lying where the river, after passing through the torrents and over the shoals of the cataract, takes up its tranquil course towards the north.

The prospects for an agrarian subsistence were meagre indeed. By far the largest expanse of cultivable land was available in the wide bay on the east bank, which is nowadays occupied by the modern town of Aswan; some fields could have been on the islands; at places, a narrow strip of fertile soil was available along the river-bank. Hunting in the adjacent desert areas and, most importantly, fishing in the river rounded off the diet available on the spot, as the remains of animal bones recovered in the excavation prove (Boessneck Von den Driesch 1982, Hollmann 1990, Katzmann 1990, Von den Driesch

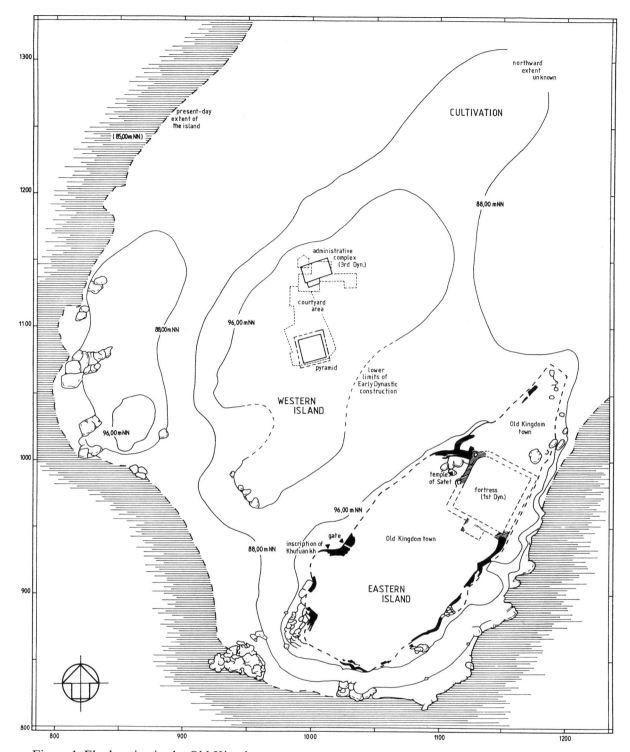

Figure 1 Elephantine in the Old Kingdom

1986). In comparison to other important provincial towns, which, even in southern Upper Egypt, govern vast expanses of cultivable land, Elephantine's situation may be termed rather extreme.

Aswan's riches did not lie in bread but in stone. Granite in the first place, indispensable for monumental architecture from Thinite times onwards (Arnold 1991: 36); but also various kinds of colourful crystalline rocks, highly valued for the production of stone vessels, which played so important a part in the élite culture of early Egypt.

Another aspect deserves to be mentioned. Elephantine is situated right in the zone of contact between Egypt and the Nubian people who settled the valley down to Kubanije, some eighteen kilometres north of Aswan. Thus, the place was predestined to serve as a basis for the trade in luxury items coming from subsaharan Africa, which was channelled to the mediterranean world through the Nubian 'corridor', as Adams (1977: 13ff) so aptly has termed it. And since military force was being used, whenever felt necessary, to back up the pursuit of the economic interests of pharaonic Egypt against interference from native groups (Redford 1981), this rôle implied some strategic importance as well.

Summing up, a rather unbalanced partnership seems to result: on one side a town, lacking a proper hinterland which could enable it to play a political rôle on its own; on the other hand the state and the ruling élite seeing important economic and political interests at stake in the area.

Quite naturally, therefore, one feels tempted to regard Elephantine as an Egyptian colony on foreign territory, founded to serve these interests, and integrated quite late, only during the Third Dynasty, into the framework of the Egyptian state (e.g. Helck 1974: 199). One of the results of the excavations at Elephantine has been to prove that this is not true. In fact, as Junker (1919: 5) had supposed, the settlement at Elephantine is very ancient. Some introductory remarks regarding the original topography of the site may be in order. Recent research by Ziermann (1993: 12ff, id. in Kaiser et al. 1995: 103ff., 121ff.) succeeded in confirming Haeny's earlier supposition (in Kaiser et al. 1974: 84) that originally, when the rock surface was not yet covered by settlement debris, the southern part of the island was bipartite, at least during the inundation of the Nile (fig.1). Probably until as late as the First Intermediate Period, a larger eastern and a smaller western island were separated by a temporary river-channel. Further, it may be assumed that the long tongue of alluvial land which accumulated downstream behind the rock-core of the island was still in the process of formation during the Old Kingdom; evidence which would allow this process to be traced in detail is still lacking, however.

The original settlement occupied the centre of the eastern island. The oldest layers hitherto uncovered in front of the temple of Satet (Lindemann in Kaiser et al. 1988: 141-4, Andraschko in Kaiser et al. 1995: 100-1) date back to Naqada IIc or IId. A few still older objects encountered in secondary position may indicate that the occupation had already begun by early Naqada II times.

Under the present conditions, only very limited areas of this early settlement are accessible to excavation. Assessing its original size remains therefore largely a matter of speculation. Certainly the village extended eastward to the river. Isolated finds could be taken to indicate that an early cemetery occupied the southern half of the island (Jaritz in Kaiser et al. 1970: 137ff, Rösing 1970), confining the settlement to its northern part. But this is still rather uncertain, and the early village may have been much larger (Ziermann 1993: 14-5). Its architectural layout was modest, of course. Arrangements of post-holes allow the reconstruction of reed huts (Lindemann in Kaiser et al. 1988: 141-4), but only from Dynasty 0 onwards does simple mudbrick architecture appear. Possibly of considerable consequence is the recent identification of a smelting furnace for copper along with some pieces of copper ore, proving the presence of industrial activity of some sophistication at the site. Comprehensive analysis of this material by the excavator is under way.

As a point of particular importance it should be noted that the cultural inventory so far recovered, – consisting mainly of pottery – while showing some admixtures of A-Group tradition, is in the main clearly of Egyptian type. One should think, therefore, for these early times not so much in terms of a clear-cut borderline between Egyptian and Nubian cultures, but rather in terms of a zone of contact of some width; an observation which, in view of the close connections between A-Group Nubia and late Naqada Egypt, is not too surprising.

The essential proof that this early settlement is really the ancestor of the later town of Elephantine, not a Nubian village supplanted later by an Egyptian foundation, is provided by the fact that the origin of the temple of Satet is securely tied to this context. Its earliest preserved architectural phase dates only from early Dynasty 1 (Dreyer 1986, corrected chronology id. in Kaiser et al. 1988: 140-1), but the way in which it is linked with the settlement shows clearly that the niche between huge granite boulders was considered a holy place right from the beginning.

It is well known, of course, that the architectural history of this sanctuary can be followed in an unbroken sequence down to Ptolemaic times (Kaiser in Kaiser et al. 1977: 65 Abb. 1), and that the peculiarities of its layout, even until the New Kingdom, derive directly from the ground-plan of the archaic temple: incontrovertible evidence that stages in the development of one and the same unit are involved.

The decisive turning-point in the history of this settlement came about during the First Dynasty, when, as Ziermann's (1993, id. in Kaiser et al. 1993: 136-41) excavations revealed, a fortress was constructed on the site; thorough analysis of the stratigraphic and, above all, ceramic evidence must be awaited before a more precise dating of its foundation can be offered (see Ziermann 1993: 139-41). Unfortunately, most of this building is now covered by the modern museum and its garden. Only parts of its north-western corner in front of the temple of Satet, and its south-eastern corner slightly north of the forecourt of the later temple of Khnum, were uncovered.

From these remains a building of approximately square layout, about 50 metres in length and width, can be reconstructed. It was situated prominently on an elevated part of the island, in the immediate vicinity of the best landing place, and would have controlled the business on the main river branch and on the area of low ground on the east bank, the site of later Aswan (Ziermann 1993: 32 Abb. 12).

The fortification consisted of double walls, originally at least three metres high, built in straight lines over the uneven, rocky ground and strengthened by short transverse connecting walls. Semicircular and (at least one) rectangular towers at the corners, and probably at regular intervals along the walls, completed the defence-work. Remains of what was probably a gate were uncovered in the middle of the south side, and another gate is to be assumed in the north. This construction was reinforced several times.

Only a small part of the interior of the fortress could be uncovered in its north-western part (see Ziermann in Kaiser et al. 1993: 136-41, 1995: 105ff.). The constructions encountered here bear no specifically military character; in fact, they do not differ from the huts found in the village outside. Unfortunately, it is impossible to be definite about the question of the origin of the garrison which manned this fortress. There are, however, arguments which suggest a provenance from outside Elephantine, even from Lower Egypt (Kaiser in Kaiser et al. 1988: 156).

It seems crucial to assess the relationship existing between the fortress and the earlier settlement. As Ziermann has remarked (1993: 133), the planning and construction bear witness to considerable know-how not previously attested on the site. Further, the project did not aim to fortify the existing settlement, which continued to be inhabited outside the fortress. Rather, the architects in charge chose the optimum location for their scheme, without caring too much about what had been there before.

The most flagrant example of this attitude is shown by the way they treated the temple, which was not included within the sheltering walls. Quite to the contrary, the fortification was allowed to run immediately in front of it, enforcing, at first, the removal of the entrance to the sanctuary to a rather inconvenient place at its northeastern corner, and later the cutting off of a substantial part of its forecourt in the course of reconstruction work done at the fortress.

In view of these facts, it seems fairly clear that the establishment of the fortress did not arise from an autonomous evolution within the local community, nor was it designed primarily to protect the residents from any dangers which might have arisen. Rather, the fortress at Elephantine was planned to play a part in the harsh policies the Thinite kings adopted in their attitude towards the south. As has been set out so clearly by Smith (1966: 118ff, 1991: 108), Nordström (1972: 29-32), and others, with the beginnings of the dynastic age the pharaonic state denounced Egypt's almost symbiotic relationship with A-Group Nubia, through which the southern people had prospered so much. From now on, supported by military action, Egypt pursued her economic interests on her own, without recourse to Nubian intermediaries (Redford 1981), a policy which brought about the collapse of the A-Group socio-economic system almost to the point of extinction (Adams 1977: 135ff, Bietak 1993, Nordström op.cit., Smith op.cit.; but see Seidlmayer 1992).

This nexus is demonstrated very clearly on a local level in the Aswan area. In fact, the predynastic settlement at Elephantine formed part of a well-established regional settlement pattern. The distribution of cemeteries shows that a series of villages was aligned along the river, spaced at regular intervals of about 6 km, taking advantage of patches of cultivable land which were available in the mouths of wadis or in desert-bays (fig.2). Khôr Bahan and Khôr Ambukol (Reisner 1910: 114-45), Shellâl cemetery 7 (ibid. 17-56), Elephantine, Kubanije South (Junker 1919) and Kubanije North (id. 1920: 163-8) are the sites in question. At about the time of the founding of the fortress at Elephantine, this pattern collapses all but completely (for evidence pointing to a slight Third Dynasty occupation at Kubanije South, see Seidlmayer forthcoming), to reassert itself, to a certain degree, only considerably later during the First Intermediate Period and the Middle Kingdom.

To appreciate the full significance of this course of events, apart from it being perceived as simply exhibiting the collapse of A-Group society in a regional perspective, it should be related to two other well established phenomena.

Bietak has recently (1993) drawn attention to the fact that the change in Egypt's attitude towards her southern neighbours was paralleled by a similar process in the north. Here, there existed in pre- and protodynastic times a broad border-zone occupied by intermixed Egyptian and native trading-posts and villages along the northern coast of Sinai, extending well into southern Canaan. This system disappears abruptly after the First Dynasty (Oren 1973, 1989, Ben Tor 1982, Mortensen 1991: 29). Undoubtedly, as in the case of A-Group Nubia, the fundamental reorganisation of Egypt's trading relations by the newly established state, as well as its emphasis on imposing territorial frontiers of a new political quality in the place of former, less clearly delimited ethnic border zones, is to be held responsible for this process.

Further, at several important sites in Egypt itself, most notably at Abydos (Kemp 1977) and at Hierakonpolis (Hoffman et al. 1986), a fundamental reorganisation of the settlement pattern in early dynastic times has been observed. At both places, a scatter of villages was replaced by a single large fortified town in which the regional population came to be concentrated, probably for defensive reasons (Trigger 1985: 348); at the same time, as Bietak (1986: 33) emphasised, facilitating control over the population through state authorities. Evidently, a whole range of historical factors must be taken into account in trying to understand the early history of settlement in the Aswân area; all of them coming together to demonstrate the fundamental nature of the change in traditional structures brought about by the establishment of the early dynastic state.

In the course of time, the original fortress underwent several phases of structural reinforcement. Early in the Second Dynasty (see Ziermann in Kaiser et al. 1993: 141), the fortification was extended in a less formal arrangement first northwards, and a little later also to the south, to include the settlement and the temple; and early in the Third Dynasty the walls of the old fortress, lying now amidst the town, were laid down to form a continuous settlement area.

It is this fortified town to which the title 'overseer of Elephantine' refers (Elephantine being written with the determinative for a fortress) which, in the Fourth Dynasty, the officer Khufuankh bears in his graffito near the south-eastern gate of the town (Habachi 1957a), and which is now attested on a seal-impression from the reign of Sekhemkhet (Pätznick in Kaiser et al. 1995: 181).

Functionally (or perhaps only nominally), it seems, Elephantine maintained its status as a fortress and accordingly it is found listed in the series of Nubian forts by the Ramesseum Onomasticon (Gardiner 1947: 11), in the Middle Kingdom and later (e.g. Urk. IV, 1122, 13), although nothing in its actual architectural appearance, especially when compared to the Nubian forts, would have suggested such a rôle.

Summing up this account, which began with a rather harsh interference by the state in village affairs - which party emerged as the winner? Both, it seems. Neither did the fortress remain an episodic project abandoned as soon as a stable situation was reached at the border, nor was the village simply brushed aside to make room for a strictly military installation in the style of the Nubian fortresses of the Middle Kingdom. Rather, the settlement, developing into a fortified town, took over a rôle in the context of state enterprise and organisation, thereby gaining for itself a new quality.

The early Egyptian state, therefore, appeared on stage at Elephantine right at the beginning of its history, displaying no mean resources and an overwhelming authority. Set against this background, observations relating to another key area in the town-state relationship gain critical significance: the

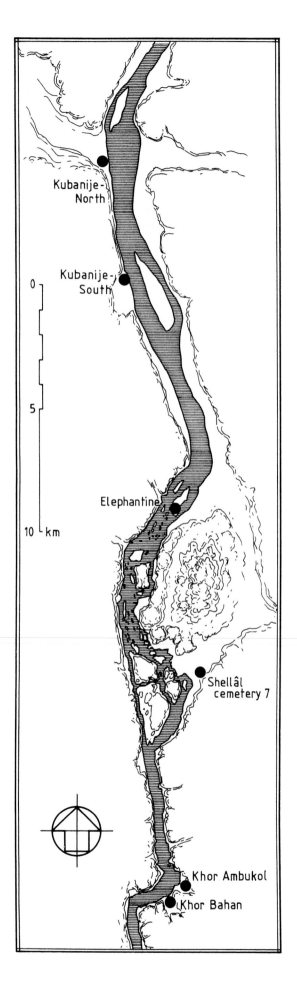

Figure 2 Distribution of predynastic settlement in the Aswan area

attitude of the state towards the temple of Satet during the Old Kingdom.

For the present Elephantine is the only site in Egypt where, thanks to a combination of lucky circumstances, the development of a provincial sanctuary can be followed from protodynastic times onwards (Kaiser in Kaiser et al. 1977: 65, Dreyer 1986: 12ff). Minor gaps in the series of building-phases recovered in excavation, produced by occasional levelling operations (Dreyer in Kaiser et al. 1988: 141), can be filled securely by reconstruction thanks to the morphological coherence of the developmental sequence.

In fact, throughout the Old Kingdom, the appearance of the temple remained basically unchanged: a small, hut-like sanctuary inserted into a natural niche formed by three enormous granite blocks, preceded by a square forecourt. This building, erected in plain mudbrick architecture throughout, exhibits nothing of the monumentality nor of the refinement characteristic of Old Kingdom élite culture.

As outlined above, the state's actions regarding this shrine are marked by utter neglect from the beginning. Constructing the defence-work of the fortress, a part of its forecourt was sacrificed; later, the temple seems to have been largely ignored.

Setting aside as disputable a faience-figurine deriving from a Sixth Dynasty deposit and interpreted by Dreyer (1981) as a representation of king Djer, a votive-plaque of Niuserre remains the first document of royal interest in the temple (Dreyer 1986: 148 No. 426). During the Sixth Dynasty, royal donations became more frequent, and included votive plaques of Pepi I and Pepi II and a monkey-shaped stone vessel inscribed with the name of Pepi I (Dreyer 1986: 148-52), the latter of a type well-known among the presents given also to important officials as a sign of the king's grace (Valloggia 1980, Fischer 1993).

The most important single item is surely the granite naos donated to the temple by Pepi I and reinscribed by Merenre (Ziegler 1990: 50-3), incidentally providing inscriptional proof from the Old Kingdom (overlooked by both Kemp 1989: 74 and O'Connor 1992: 93) that the shrine was indeed dedicated to the goddess Satet so early. Further, two rock inscriptions carved in the entrance passage, recording royal visits to the temple by Merenre and Pepi II, deserve to be mentioned (Dreyer in Kaiser et al. 1976: 79). These documents may serve as proof that the kings of the later Old Kingdom did at least take notice of the temple of Satet, and of course it was integrated within the network of state administration.

The first king, however, who attached so much importance to his relationship with the local cult that he took not only the trouble to erect a sanctuary, but also to document this fact visibly on the spot by including inscribed architectural elements, was $W3h$-$^c nh$ Intef II, and it may be said that he inaugurated a new epoch in the relationship between the kings and the sanctuary: all of his successors during the Eleventh Dynasty took an active rôle in providing for the temple, soon overshadowed, however, by Sesostris I, who erected a most magnificent shrine on an unprecedented scale for his divine mother (Kaiser in Kaiser et al. 1988: 152-7).

Kemp (1989: 65-83) has recognised the significance of these facts. Comparing the evidence from Elephantine and certain other Upper Egyptian temple-sites with the Old Kingdom monuments of the Memphite region, he drew attention to the tremendous difference in the style of cultural expression between the court culture of that time and that of the provinces. Accordingly, the establishment of the 'Great Tradition' of pharaonic culture throughout the country appears not as a simple, unilineal development, but rather as a drawn-out process of unequal pace: while the 'formal' style of cultural expression was developed at the court from Early Dynastic times onwards, most of the country remained on a 'pre-formal' level throughout the Old Kingdom, catching up with the 'early formal' style only during the Middle Kingdom. 'It means that for about a third of its history, Pharaonic Egypt was a country of two cultures.' (op.cit.: 83).

This interpretation addresses issues central to any attempt to understand Old Kingdom history, and therefore it is important to check its validity and to explore its implications. In a recent article, O'Connor (1992) made an important contribution to these matters. Basing his argument mainly on two sets of archaeological material, the monumental temples of the Early Dynastic period at certain sites in Upper Egypt, and the traces left by kings of the late Old Kingdom in the provincial temples, O'Connor emphasises the evidence for a royal presence in the temples throughout the country before the Middle

Kingdom. He proceeds to discuss whether these data can be made to support an alternative theory claiming, in principle, continuous court involvement in the local sanctuaries throughout the Old Kingdom.

Here, however, important gaps in the evidence become obvious. The situation at Elephantine, in particular, presents itself as an embarrassment. O'Connor (1992: 93-5) proposes the following hypothesis: the main Old Kingdom sanctuary is yet to be discovered; further, the principal temple should have been located then, as later, at the site now occupied by the temple of Khnum. A building lying to its south-east, referred to in the preliminary reports as *'AR-Heiligtum'* (Grossmann and Junge in Kaiser et al. 1976: 92-107), being oriented towards the alleged temple, would indicate the ritual importance of this location already during the Old Kingdom.

Indisputably, this building served the memorial cult of a private individual for a considerable time, but it remains totally unclear how it acquired this rôle. Comparing its massive architectural layout with the *k3*-chapels of private individuals discovered at Balât (Soukiassian Wuttmann Schaad 1990: 353ff), it seems highly unlikely that this can have been its original function. Aside from this, archaeological evidence has since become available which almost completely excludes O'Connor's hypothesis.

Recent excavation in the forecourt of the Late Period temple of Khnum revealed that the area was occupied by well-to-do living quarters during the late Old Kingdom (Kaiser et al. 1993: 153); its rear part, on the other hand, where earlier stratification seems to have been dug away for laying the deep foundations of the late temple, is situated in an area outside the limits of the Old Kingdom town. This place became available for construction only as a result of levelling operations carried out during the First Intermediate Period (Ziermann in Kaiser et al. 1995: 128-40), and accordingly, the sanctuary of Heqaib was not erected in this location beyond the Old Kingdom town walls until that time. The existence of an important Old Kingdom temple in this area can therefore safely be excluded.

In complete accordance with this state of affairs, the earliest secure evidence for an independent temple of Khnum at Elephantine dates from the Middle Kingdom, most probably from the reign of Sesostris I (Kaiser in Kaiser et al. 1993: 152-3). A fragment of a decorated block of fine limestone, found re-used in the foundations of the late temple of Khnum, may be taken to indicate that this king commissioned the first temple for Khnum as well as rebuilding the shrine of Satet. Until the earlier part of the Eleventh Dynasty, the cult of Khnum had been served in the precinct of Satet, as Kaiser (in Kaiser et al. 1993: 145-51) was able to prove through his reconstruction of the chapels formerly erected there by Intef II and Intef III.

It seems well-founded in archaeological evidence, therefore, that the temple of Satet may certainly be regarded as the main temple of the town throughout the Old Kingdom, quite in accordance with the pre-eminent position claimed for the goddess by her title as *nb.t-3bw* 'Mistress of Elephantine'.

It is, however, highly rewarding to have a closer look at the evidence discussed by O'Connor. There are, in the first place, the monumental temples of Dynasty 0 at Koptos and Hierakonpolis, recently reconstructed by Williams (1988). O'Connor (1992: 84-7) very convincingly pointed out the striking similarity in layout existing between the early temple at Hierakonpolis and early dynastic royal funerary monuments. Royal presence in the temple of Hierakonpolis is again documented in late Dynasty 2 by an important series of monuments of Khasekhem (see Quibell Green 1900-1902). Also, in the temple of Hathor at Gebelên, not too far from Hierakonpolis, a royal stela of late Second Dynasty date is attested (Galassi 1955: 64ff., Smith 1946: 137), and perhaps the chapel of king Djoser from Heliopolis (Weill 1912, Smith 1946: 133ff) should also be mentioned in this context.

Viewing these early monuments as a group, it seems important to make two points. In the first place, I would like to stress their specifity. The monuments are confined to places which are specifically linked to the emergence of pre- and protodynastic kingship and to periods of royal presence at or very near these places. The disappearance of monumental art at Koptos after Dynasty 0 and the reappearance of royal monuments in southern Upper Egypt during the late Second Dynasty seem particularly telling in this respect.

The two sites not entirely covered by this description, Gebelên and Heliopolis, on the other hand, held cults of Re and Hathor, the divine ancestors of the king. It seems, therefore, that this group of early temples provides evidence for royal court cults focusing very much on the ideological founda-

116

tions of divine kingship. The similarity in layout between the temple of Hierakonpolis and a royal ritual precinct highlighted by O'Connor seems of particular significance in this respect.

Accordingly, these archaic shrines should be regarded, along with the installations of the royal funerary cult, as the forerunners of Old Kingdom state and court religion. The developmental connections need further elucidation, of course. It seems safe to say, however, that this situation is something very different from the royal care attested in later periods for -in principle- every provincial cult.

Secondly, it should be underlined that this material is chronologically isolated. There is no archaeological evidence linking these early monumental temples to the well-attested royal activity in the provincial temples of the later Old Kingdom.

The available *in situ* evidence for Old Kingdom provincial temples has been discussed by Kemp (1989: 65-83) and reviewed by O'Connor (1992); the latter's assumption that in most cases the main temples simply remain to be discovered, remains strictly hypothetical. The material is sparse indeed, and to broaden the basis for the archaeological argument, we should pay attention to the distribution of inscribed architectural fragments and important royal votive objects discovered in secondary positions. Clearly, the temples in question would have been erected chiefly in mud-brick. Nevertheless, the use of inscribed stone elements (at least for pillars and door frames) may be considered a hallmark of the architecture in the 'formal' court style - and this is what our inquiry is all about. A comparison with the situation regarding Middle Kingdom temples serves to confirm the validity of this approach: most of our information about Middle Kingdom provincial temples derives precisely from the great wealth of architectural fragments found re-used in the buildings of later times. Systematic differences in the distribution of recovered items from the Old and Middle Kingdoms cannot therefore be ascribed simply to accidents of preservation, but rather must be taken to reflect historical reality.

A comprehensive review of the evidence is beyond the scope of this paper. In an attempt to assess at least the basic facts, the Delta must be set aside as presenting a rather specific situation. It is well known that from the New Kingdom onward, statues and architectural elements were transported in important numbers from monuments in the Memphite area in order to furnish the new Delta capitals, and even relocated there several times (Bietak 1975: 213-4, Sourouzian 1988). This seems particularly true for several Old Kingdom blocks dating back well into the Fourth Dynasty discovered at Tanis (Vandier 1955: 597ff, PM IV: 13ff) and Tell Basta (Vandier 1955: 602ff, PM IV: 27ff). None of the inscriptions suggest that these architectural elements were dedicated originally to a local temple. The only *in situ* remains of Old Kingdom temples in the Delta are, as far as I know, the *k3*-chapels of Teti (El Sawi 1979: 75-6) and Pepi I (Habachi 1957b: 11ff) at Tell Basta. Unfortunately, the original provenance of an offering-stand dedicated by Khephren to the sun-god, bought at Zagazig for the Metropolitan Museum of Art, remains unknown (Lythgoe 1907, Hayes 1953: 64).

Upper Egypt, on the other hand, presents a rather clear picture. The Third and Fourth Dynasties (setting apart a few minor objects) left no traces in the Upper Egyptian temples. The oldest inscribed architectural element to appear is a pillar of Userkaf from el-Tôd (Bisson de la Roque 1937: 61-2); further, the Fifth Dynasty is represented by a decree of Neferirkare from Abydos (Petrie 1903: Pl. 18), a statue of Niuserre from Karnak temple (Bothmer 1974), and a statue of Asosi, again from Abydos (Petrie 1902: Pl. 55,2). The dyad depicting Sahura and the personification of the Coptite Nome (MMA 18.2.4, Hayes 1953: 70-1) was bought at Luxor, so nothing is known about its provenance.

Only during the Sixth Dynasty, however, does royal presence become a regular feature at the Upper Egyptian temple sites. Royal statues, stelae, decrees and architectural elements are known at Hierakonpolis, Koptos, Dendera, Abydos, Heliopolis and Tell Basta, in addition to Elephantine.

As O'Connor noted in his discussion of the evidence, it appears from the texts of the royal decrees at Abydos, as well as from the inscriptions of the temples at Tell Basta, that royal *k3*-chapels played an important part in this context. In fact, further royal *k3*-chapels are attested in priestly titles, and Pepi I is known to have commissioned a whole series of *k3*-houses throughout the country.

The significance of this observation will be discussed later; here it may suffice to say that it seems tempting to connect the statues of Pepi I from Hierakonpolis (Quibell Green 1902: Pl. 50ff) and Dendera (Daumas 1953, 1973) with this project. In fact, most of the Fifth and Sixth Dynasty material could derive from royal *k3*-chapels. As far as I can see, only the naos of Pepi I from Elephantine and the relief-slabs of Pepi II from Koptos (Petrie 1896: Pl. 5.7-8, Stewart 1979: Pl. 2) undoubtedly formed

117

part of the local temple itself.

In view of this situation there can be hardly any doubt, I feel, that the negative evidence for state sponsored temple construction in the provincial towns during most of the Old Kingdom is very real, and virtually the same conclusion was reached already by Goedicke (1979), mainly on the basis of the written evidence. It would be erroneous, however, to conclude that the Old Kingdom provincial temples were unimportant to everyone. Scores of votive presents recovered from the temple of Satet (Dreyer 1986) afford tangible proof of the popular veneration this cult enjoyed throughout the Old Kingdom, very much reminiscent of the deep reverence known to have been felt for the 'local god' (nṯr nw.tj) in later times. Therefore, the rôle of the local cults as foci of personal loyalty and as an expression of the collective identity of the local communities must be regarded as a genuine element of Egyptian provincial culture.

Further, at several important Upper Egyptian sites, there is evidence forthcoming from the early Old Kingdom for priests of the local cults holding an elevated social position within the local context, as becomes apparent whenever their tombs are known. For Elephantine, we have at Sehêl island a graffito of a priest of Satet named Ḥwfw-wr from the second half of the Fourth Dynasty (H. de Morgan 1894: 88, no. 53, Weigall 1911: 171, Valbelle 1981: 1).

At Elkâb, an important mastaba can be assigned on the basis of a fragment of a statue-base to an overseer of priests K3-mn, whose funeral furniture includes a costly stone bowl inscribed with the name of king Snofru. Another large mastaba in the immediate vicinity, which belongs to an inspector of priests Nfr-šmm, is likely to be of similar date (Quibell 1898: 3-5; Fischer 1968: 18-9). Further, at Elkâb, a group of seal-impressions dating to the Second or Third Dynasty was excavated in the temple precinct; the inscriptions mention an 'inspector of the granary of Elkâb', attesting, it seems, the economic importance of the temple at that early date (Van de Walle 1940).

At Dendera, the most important early tomb belongs to a priest of Hathor named Nj-jb.w-njswt, dating probably to the later Fourth Dynasty (Fischer 1968: 14ff). The sculptured panel of his false-door stela (op.cit. Pl. 2), while certainly a piece of art much-admired in Fourth Dynasty Jwn.t, betrays unmistakably the craftmanship of a local workshop by its gauche style. At Qau, a priest called Nmtj-ḥtp occupied a stairway-mastaba in cemetery 400 in the vicinity of the ancient townsite, which contained a splendid group of stone and metal vessels dating to the second half of the Third Dynasty (Brunton 1927: Pl. 18).

As the title rḫ-njswt, born by Nj-jb.w-njswt, Nfr-šmm and K3-mn, as well as the royal gift in the latter's burial equipment indicate, these people at least were connected somehow to the central administration. At about the same time, an offering endowment, however modest, was presented by king Mycerinus to the cult of Hathor nb.t-r3-jn.t, as is recorded in the inscriptions of Nj-ᶜnḫ-k3=j at Tehna (Urk. I, 25). Nevertheless, it seems crucial that the evidence for early priests dates from a time *before* the widespread use of the provincial temples as administrative nodes in the network of the state economy during the late Old Kingdom. Therefore, this may be interpreted to indicate that the later, highly prominent, rôle of the temples as organisational nuclei on a local level is also to be regarded as an original part of their function.

Viewing these facts mainly, as Kemp did, with an intent to follow the formation of the 'Great Tradition' of pharaonic culture and its adoption throughout the country, the forms of cultural expression encountered in the provincial temples and in the monuments of the residence area respectively, will appear as stages in a developmental sequence, with provincial culture lagging behind. Accordingly, the terms 'pre-formal, early-formal, mature-formal' coined by Kemp tend to focus attention on this diachronic aspect.

While this point of view is perfectly valid, of course, we should not miss the synchronic aspects of the phenomena involved. From this perspective, the relationship between provincial temples and court culture appears as a structural pattern indicative of the state-province relations. With some simplification it seems possible to identify, in the course of time, three structural stages:

A first stage, during the Early Dynastic era, when the kings were involved in several temples connected specifically to the ideological foundations of divine kingship.

A second stage, covering the Third, Fourth and much of the Fifth Dynasty, when royal activity was almost completely withdrawn from the provincial sanctuaries.

A third stage, appearing during the Fifth Dynasty and covering the Sixth Dynasty, when the kings regularly displayed some care for the local cults, and were eager to have $k3$-houses for their own cults attached to them.

It seems evident that it would be inadequate to interpret these structural patterns simply in terms of differing rates of development. Concentrating on the second stage for the moment, it seems clear that the central state and the provincial communities did not lead a life of independent development side by side. On the contrary, the enormous achievements in monumental building, for example, prove that the Pharaonic state operated very efficiently on a national level precisely during this period, undoubtedly affecting the lives of everybody through its actions.

The difference in culture between court and country is therefore to be interpreted as an expression of the socio-political organisation of this state, characterised by a profound structural dichotomy. Evidently, state interests were pursued independently, without acknowledging the temples in their rôle as indigenous organisational and ideological nuclei of the local communities, and these shrines were not the places the kings chose to display their relationship to the local gods as a tenet basic to their ruling ideology. Consequently, it was felt unnecessary to adorn the provincial sanctuaries with carved and inscribed architectural elements which would have offered the possibility to express such a doctrine in visible and lasting form.

There remains to be considered another monument at Elephantine which, in my view, may shed some light on these matters; and in fact, its significance, which hitherto has remained rather enigmatic, can be appreciated to a certain extent within the present context. I am referring to the small step-pyramid situated in the north-western part of the site, and the contemporary building complex in its vicinity, discovered during our excavations (see for more detail Seidlmayer in Kaiser et al. 1982: 299-306, id. 1995, and forthcoming).

In 1908, the expedition of the Berlin Museum, turning over the site in search of papyri, encountered a massive building of granite blocks. Joseph Étienne Gautier, working for Clermont-Ganneau, cleared it in 1909 in the vain hope of finding on top of it the much-sought Jahu temple of Persian times. Nevertheless, as emerges from his unpublished letters, he recognised the monument as a pyramid of the early Old Kingdom, an identification which was confirmed in the course of Dreyer's re-examination (in Kaiser et al. 1980: 276-80, Pls. 86-70). The monument is situated on the highest ridge making up the rock-core of what was then the western island of Elephantine, originally in a very conspicuous position.

The uneven plot was levelled by constructing a platform of roughly broken granite blocks, 45 cubits square, and also, it seems, by flaking off protruding parts of the rock on its western side. On this platform, the pyramid was constructed entirely from unworked, naturally rounded blocks, but with truly remarkable accuracy. It still stands up some five metres high. The southern, western and eastern faces, which were covered until the early Middle Kingdom by settlement debris, are well preserved, while the northern face, which lay exposed well into the New Kingdom, is completely ruined. Here, Gautier dug a trench right to the centre to explore the internal structure of the monument and to locate the burial chamber.

Thanks to this act of vandalism, the construction of the pyramid is today quite clearly visible. It consists of a core and two accretion-layers, built in courses inclined to the centre, as were the great pyramids until the beginning of the Fourth Dynasty. The building can be reconstructed, accordingly, as an uncased, three-stepped pyramid, rising from a ground-plan 35 cubits square to a height of about 10 to 12 metres. Corridors or interior rooms are lacking; remains of a chapel, an enclosure-wall or other standard features are also completely absent.

There is, however, a conical granite-block, slightly larger than the ordinary building material of the pyramid, which is inscribed on its narrow face. The *editio princeps* is due to Goedicke (1956; see Dreyer Kaiser 1980: 57f. with further bibliography, and Seidlmayer 1995: note 37). The text was read and interpreted almost correctly by Lacau in 1909 as '*château du couronnement du roi Souten-he*' (quoted in a letter by Gautier). Henri Gauthier, who also knew of the block (*contra* Barta 1973: 2), proposed a little later '*faire tracer l'édifice du roi Souten-he.*' Kaiser and Dreyer gave the final version as the name of a building or institution *sšd njswt Ḥwj* 'Diadem of king Huni', followed by the determinative of a palace.

This block, which was found in the late Old Kingdom cemetery in front of the northern face of the pyramid, clearly must have been incorporated in some very massive building, for which the pyramid is the only candidate on the site. It might seem rather surprising to find the identifying name inscribed on the monument like on a door-plate, but a rather close parallel seems to be forthcoming from the Nubian diorite quarry near Tomas, whose name *ḥ3m.t-Ḥwfw* 'Fishing-net of king Kheops' was found inscribed on a stela set up in that place (Rowe 1938: Pl. 55). In later times, of course, this became common practice. It is impossible to reconstruct the original position of the block, but in view of its find-spot, a place on the northern face of the pyramid seems most likely. Such a position would agree well with the layout of other Third Dynasty pyramids, which have the cult-place on the north. It should be noted, however, that the main inscription in large sunk characters was re-cut over an earlier, smaller one executed in raised relief, of which only one line on the lower rim of the block is preserved. It gives again the name of the building exactly as the main inscription. Only regarding the last character does a slight uncertainty remain: it could have been an ^{c}ḥ palace sign as in the main inscription, but it could equally be read as an *wsḫ.t*-sign with battlements executed only on its top, as is attested in PT 636d (N). Maybe this re-working was caused by a change in the architectural setting (from a position in a closed chapel to an open air location for instance). In any case, the block provides an exact date for the monument in the reign of king Huni, last ruler of the Third Dynasty and predecessor of Snofru.

Matters are a little less straightforward regarding the building complex discovered some 40 metres north of the pyramid below strata of later occupation (Seidlmayer in Kaiser et al. 1982: 300ff, Abb. 12-3, Pl. 65a). In one excavation area, the situation was particularly well preserved, the walls standing to a height of about 1.5 m in some places (pl. 22). Here, in the north-eastern part, we see a building attached to a low granite ridge at the north. To the south, a long rectangular room can be discerned, which opens through a door, which was walled up later, to an open courtyard to the south and west. The rather undistinguished appearance of this room, with large granite boulders protruding into it from the south, and an added reinforcement wall running along its northern side, mark it as a room for technical or economic use.

The walls in the northern part were identified on closer examination as a system of retaining walls which formed a foundation terrace attached to the northern granite ridge; the chambers between them were filled in originally. To understand this situation, we must have a closer look at the topography (see fig.1 and Seidlmayer 1995: Abb. 2). In fact, we are dealing with a second granite ridge, parallel to the one on which the pyramid was erected, running along the northern bank of the western island of Elephantine. Between these two ridges, in a deep valley, a naturally sheltered courtyard area some 20 metres wide was available.

This northern ridge, where it formed a kind of plateau, was used as the emplacement for an important building, a part of whose foundation platform and subsidiary rooms we found. Unfortunately, this main building was completely destroyed in the course of later occupation, apart from the remains of one very massive wall, which provides the surviving evidence for its existence. Despite the destruction, the space available allows an estimate of the original size of about 15 by 25 metres.

The series of building phases, which bears witness to a continuous enlargement and reinforcement of this complex, need not concern us here in detail. But there is one important moment in its architectural history which calls for comment. At some point in time, the whole courtyard area between the northern and the southern granite ridges was artificially levelled by filling it with some thousand cubic metres of sandy material. Above this filling, the scanty remains of a new phase of the building were preserved on the same spot, following the outline of the former construction.

The extremely fragmentary state of this material makes interpretation difficult, but the size of the complex and its professional execution, which stand in marked contrast to what is encountered in the town, leave no doubt that some official building is involved. In order to get some idea of the activities which were carried out there, we must turn to the finds.

Most striking is a sealing from a papyrus-roll, bearing the seal-impression of a 'Lower Egyptian seal bearer' of the *pr-njswt*, the administration of the royal domain, from the time of the Horus *Z3-nht* (Seidlmayer in Kaiser et al. 1982: 304, Pl. 65b). This king is known from two graffiti in the Wadi Maghara and seal-impressions from Saqqara and Beit Khallaf, but his position within the Third Dynasty is disputed. Among other considerations (see Seidlmayer 1995: note 15, and forthcoming) in my view, a seal-impression from Beit Khallaf, now kept in Liverpool university (E5251; our pl. 23, cf. Garstang 1903: Pl. 19,7), is most decisive. It shows undoubtedly (*contra* Lauer 1954: 369, 1962b: 27 note 7) the end of a cartouche sign, the occurrence of which clearly indicates a date near the end of the Third Dynasty. The first kings to use the cartouche regularly are Huni and Snofru. Even if we do not assume that this 'Lower Egyptian seal bearer' officiated in the place, which does not seem very likely, the fact that a document bearing this seal was consulted there shows that the complex was directed by the royal domain.

Some twenty other sealings were recovered from the refuse layers (Seidlmayer 1995: Abb. 3). Their inscriptions contain names of private persons in the style of what is known from the Second and Third Dynasties, bearing such subordinate titles as *zš* 'scribe', *jrj-ht* and *mjtr*. Indications which could point to a Fourth Dynasty date, such as vertical dividing lines, are absent. These sealings derive from bags and jar-covers. It seems significant to me, that the only sealing of an official of the central administration stems from a papyrus document, not from the packing of products, as is the rule, for example, in the furnishings of élite-burials. This indicates that the complex at Elephantine did not receive goods from central magazines. Further, there are three short dockets inscribed on jars, for which Dreyer (1987) has given an initial interpretation. Their mode of dating to years of the 'following of Horus' and the 'appearance of the King of Upper and Lower Egypt' proves that they are to be dated before the Fourth Dynasty, as comparison with the Old Kingdom annals shows. The texts themselves, as far as they can be understood, name certain individuals and list for them quantities of goods, mainly cereals, in amounts clearly relating to the production or consumption of individual persons. So these dockets are evidently primary notes, later intended to be condensed to larger tables of food distribution (unless they are extracts derived from such tables) as are preserved among the Abusir papyri (Posener-Kriéger 1976: 323-39). In addition, it should be noted that one inscription lists the administrator (*hq3*) of a village called *jtj-t3.w* 'lord of the lands', a name very much reminiscent of the great domain of king Peribsen *jtj-wj3.w* 'lord of the ships' (Kaplony 1963: Abb. 282, 285-6).

The most important class of finds is, of course, the pottery (Seidlmayer 1995: Abb. 4). Looking at the material first from the functional aspect, we can say that it is made up entirely of good utilitarian ware and that especially fine pottery is absent. In comparison with other contexts, storage jars, as opposed to dishes and other forms related to the sphere of consumption, make up a substantial part of the assemblage. Truly astonishing is the number of bread-moulds and beer-jars, especially in the material from an ancient garbage-heap which was redeposited during the great levelling operation. Of both classes, several tens of thousands of items must have been present. This situation, which is significantly different from what is known from other Old Kingdom contexts at the site, indicates that rations for a substantial number of people were prepared and distributed here.

Regarding chronology, I can, in this context, only quote the available results (see Seidlmayer 1995 and forthcoming). According to the pottery, the occupation of the building complex falls into the second half of the Third Dynasty, not earlier than the reign of Djoser, and extends, after the levelling operation, possibly into the beginning of the Fourth Dynasty, but not later than the middle of the reign of Snofru. Afterwards, the occupation was discontinued and it is only in the late Fourth Dynasty that the next stratum, a series of workshops, is attested on the site. As a last word regarding the finds, the complete absence of anything which would indicate refined furnishing of the building, or the consumption of luxury items, may be emphasised.

In conclusion, it may be said that everything, both in the architecture and among the finds, points to economic activities, and the written documents prove the presence of the administration of the *pr-njswt*. It seems to me, therefore, not very far-fetched to conclude that we are dealing here with the administrative building of a royal domain or estate, as are attested already on seal-impressions of the Second Dynasty. In the context of this interpretation, the situation of the complex in a convenient place near the river and in the vicinity of the cultivable alluvial land accumulating to the north, deserves attention (fig.1).

From these facts it emerges that the northern building complex and the pyramid are not only situated in the immediate vicinity of one another, but also that both are in part contemporaneous. The administrative building seems to be a little older; in fact it represents the oldest occupation attested on the western island. There is no precise indication as to how the erection of the pyramid fits into the sequence of building phases of this complex; to me it seems most likely that it coincides with the great levelling operation, which provided easier access to the site of the pyramid. The pyramid would then be contemporary with the second main building phase of the northern complex. Like this building, the pyramid was abandoned during the Fourth Dynasty, the earliest tombs of the cemetery which came to occupy the area in the Fifth Dynasty being cut into its sides and its foundation platform.

The key-question now, of course, is what the addition of this small pyramid meant for the older estate and for the neighbouring town of Elephantine at large. Discussing this monument, we must mention in the first place that it is not unique; Sayce, already in 1909, recognised it as '*le frère de celui de El-Kolah*' (quoted in a letter by Gautier). Apart from Elephantine, such pyramids have been found near Edfu, Hierakonpolis, Naqada, Abydos, Zawjet el-Mejtin and Seila (fig.3). These buildings are, with the exception of that at Seila, so similar in size, design and construction, that they must have been erected, as Dreyer and Kaiser (1980: 54f; for Abydos/Sinki see Dreyer Swelim 1982) argued, as one single project in the reign of king Huni. Seila is slightly different, larger, and Swelim's excavations provided proof that it dates from the earlier part of the reign of Snofru (Lesko 1988, Swelim 1987, Leclant in *Orientalia* 57, 1988: 336, 58, 1989: 368).

The interpretation of these monuments is considered to be rather enigmatic. Since all of them lack burial apartments, they cannot have been tombs. Various ideas which have been proposed in the literature (see bibliography in Dreyer Kaiser 1980: 54, and Swelim 1983: 105ff), include the suggestions that the monuments were intended to mark places important in the myth of Horus and Seth (Maragioglio Rinaldi 1963: 70), or stages in the reconquest of Egypt by Khasekhemui (Lauer 1985: 65) - neither of them convincing nor in accordance with attested habits of pharaonic culture.

If we adhere to the parallel evidence for monuments of this type, namely the funerary pyramids and, in a wider sense, the solar temples of the Fifth Dynasty (for their connection to the royal mortuary cult see Kaiser 1956a, Winter 1957), there can be no doubt that these pyramids must have marked the locations of an official cult centered around the person of the king. The finds from Seila: stelae with the name of Snofru, fragments of a naos, a royal statue and an offering table (see *Orientalia 57,* 1988: Pl. 32), afford tangible proof for this proposition.

With the identification of this pyramid, there is now an attested monument of the royal cult at Elephantine, and the comparison with the contemporary temple of the local cult is most striking. The failure of the central authorities to care for this sanctuary was clearly not a matter of lacking funds (as envisaged by Kemp 1989: 83), but of a completely different ideological background.

In Egyptology, the royal cult is usually regarded primarily as a mortuary cult. This is true but not quite precise. Baer (1960: 45) has assembled evidence that the cult at the pyramids was celebrated already during the lifetime of the king. Further, a closer look at the decoration of the royal mortuary temples, especially the earlier ones, shows that they do not focus on *specifically* funerary topics (burial, funerary offerings). Instead, ritual duties and festivals of kingship play a prominent part, of which the sed-festival as a festival of the renewal of kingship takes pride of place (for details Seidlmayer 1995: note 61). Therefore, to find a cult for the king at several places and separated from the royal tomb does not seem absurd.

Apart from the similarities in design and situation between the small step pyramids and the funerary pyramids – they too are situated in areas which conform to the criteria which governed the choice of cemetery sites – possibly an ideological link can also be established between them.

The name of the complex at Elephantine *sšd-nỉswt-Ḥwj* '(palace named) Diadem of King Huni' recalls, as Arnold has remarked (Arnold 1974: 76 note 309; see also Goedicke 1956: 33, Kadish 1970: 100), the *ḥb-sšd*, the 'festival of the diadem', which is mentioned among the coronation rites on the Palermo stone in the first year of Shepseskaf (Schäfer 1902: 32). Again we find this festival in the depiction of such coronation rites in the temple of Hatshepsut at Deir el-Bahari (Naville 1898: Pl. 63), clearly derived from an ancient copy. Here we see the king, after having been crowned in two ^{c}ḥ-palaces with the crowns of Upper and Lower Egypt, proceeding, clad in a garment of the type he wears

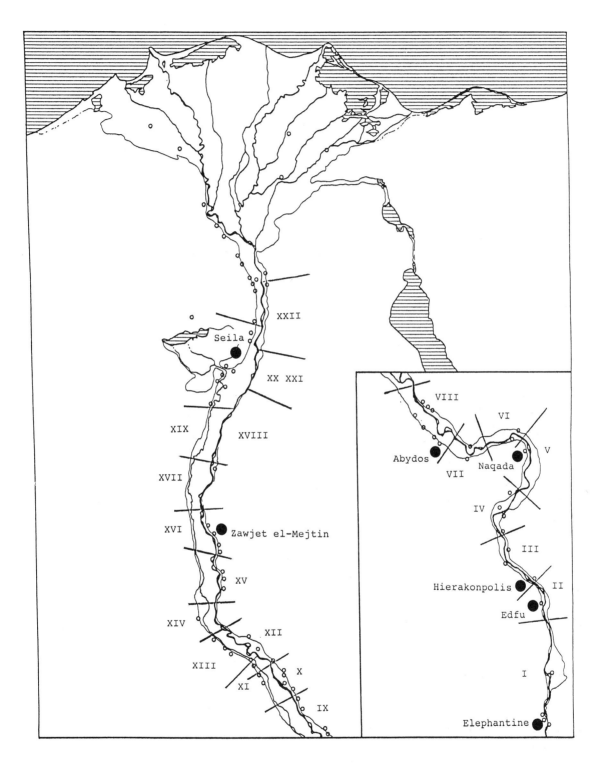

Figure 3 The distribution of the small step pyramids of the Third Dynasty across the country with approximate indication of nome boundaries

during the sed-festival, to the *wsḫt-ḥb-sd̠*, the 'court of the festival of the diadem.' As is well known, the *wsḫt*-sign normally shows an *ᶜḥ*-palace in one corner, so it seems logical to assume also the existence of a 'palace of the diadem festival'.

The coincidence with the key-terms encountered in the name of the complex at Elephantine is striking. This fact may be taken to indicate that the cult practised here was interpreted, as at the funerary pyramids, with reference to festivals of kingship. The role played by ritual palaces in the architecture of Djoser's complex at Saqqara, for instance, is well known; for the sacral rôle of *ᶜḥ*-palaces see Goelet 1982: 210ff.

It remains to seek the reasons why cults of this type should have been dispersed throughout the country. Two monuments of the Fourth Dynasty are informative for the relationship between the royal cult and the land. The first is the procession of funerary domains in the temple of the Bent Pyramid (Fakhry 1961: 17ff), which shows the royal estates nome by nome, bringing the provisions for the royal cult. Exactly the same idea is expressed by the nome-triads from the valley temple of Mycerinus at Giza (Reisner 1931: 109ff); here again we see the country (originally) nome by nome providing the material basis for the royal cult (contra Wood 1974; see Seidlmayer 1995: note 82). The inscriptions are explicit in this respect.

This symbolic expression relates very directly to reality, and the outstanding analysis of the Abusir papyri by Posener-Kriéger (1976, 1979) has shown that this reality, a system of villages and estates providing for the royal cult, was not just the economic background of individual temples, but, since it was run as a unified network by the administration of the palace, it functioned as the backbone of the economy of the state at large.

Let us look, with these matters in mind, at the distribution of the pyramids in the country. Most of them, those at Edfu, Hierakonpolis, Naqada and Abydos are situated near important early centres; but others, those at Elephantine, Zawjet el-Mejtin and Seila are not. Moreover, the pyramids near Edfu, Hierakonpolis and Abydos lie at a considerable distance from these places. Further, it is not clear why a cult of the king should be present at these particular sites.

Therefore, I would propose to assume that these pyramids were distributed, at least in principle, to the nomes, as the sequence of the three southernmost sites suggests. This idea implies, of course, that the known series of monuments is very incomplete, as had been assumed on other grounds already by Kaiser (Dreyer Kaiser 1980: 55 note 53) and Swelim (1983: 100). In fact, in their present state of preservation, these pyramids are not very conspicuous in the landscape, and two of them, those near Edfu (for a first mention see Legrain 1903: 222) and Abydos, were rediscovered recently only by chance. Further, on the west bank north of Asjût, any such monuments would have been covered by the well-known westward transgression of the alluvial land (Kaiser 1961: 24).

The advantage of this theory is that it offers an explanation of the dispersal of the pyramids throughout the country in terms attested as relevant in contemporary sources. They would represent a project of mapping the royal cult across the country; exactly as the representations in the temples do, but in a concrete, not in an abstract manner. Not that the ideological content expressed symbolically through these monuments is different (nor the economic structure implied), but it is merely expressed in an alternative form.

Possibly, the historical situation may provide a clue as to why this procedure could have been adopted in the late Third Dynasty. In fact, the procession of funerary domains in the temple of the Bent Pyramid is the first document to attest the existence of this economic system, which was to characterise the Old Kingdom, as systematically covering the whole land; the age of giant pyramids starting with Snofru bearing witness to its effectiveness and to the ever-growing economic burden imposed on the land by the state. The small step pyramids belong to a time when this system was being devised, as funerary domains founded by king Nebka (Borchardt 1907: 79 Abb. 54), who is probably identical with the Horus Z3-nḫt, and Huni (Urk. I, 2.12) prove.

Constructing these monuments throughout the country could have served to make explicit and intelligible the ideological background of the economic demands of the state on a local level. Further, working with organisational units of a smaller size, as was customary from the habits of the earlier palace-economy, could have been a first step in developing the later centralised system, which required, as the Abusir papyri clearly show, a considerable degree of administrative expertise. Both aspects were inevitably to lose relevance in the course of time, and maybe this is a reason why the scheme was abandoned already early in the reign of Snofru. But these considerations can hope only to reconstruct the structural logic of such an enterprise, not the conscious rationale held by the people responsible, which would have been phrased in rather different terms, but which remains, I fear, beyond the reach of the historian. I need hardly say that for Elephantine, this theory would explain splendidly both the historical and structural relationship existing between the pyramid and the estate in its neighbourhood.

This is, as I hasten to underline, interpretation, not plain fact; and therefore, hopefully to add to its plausibility, I would like to refer to a symmetrical historical case. As is well known, the system of funerary domains was to last for the whole of the Old Kingdom. Constantly expanding in size, this network needed administrative nodes throughout the country, and Jacquet-Gordon (1962: 81ff) demonstrated in her brilliant analysis of the names of the funerary domains, how, from the Fifth Dynasty onwards, it came to be centred more and more around the provincial temples. They had certainly been predestined to fill this rôle.

The resulting structure was portrayed in the decoration of the royal mortuary temples, as a relatively well-preserved scene in the funerary temple of Pepi II may serve to illustrate (Jequier 1940: Pl. 19). Here, at the upper end of the causeway, the king, enthroned, receives the gods of the country, heading an enormous procession of personifications of funerary domains; they bear names like $s^c n\underline{h}$ $B\exists stt\ Nfr-k\exists -R^C$ 'Bastet gives life to king Neferkare', emphasising that the benefactions are operated for the king by the gods.

The economic relationship between estates, temples and the state described in these scenes in an abstract manner, was to be given far more concrete expression in the reign of Pepi I, when $k\exists$-chapels were built systematically in the temples throughout the country. One, at Tell Basta, is preserved archaeologically (Habachi 1957b: 11ff); others, at Memphis, Zawyet el-Meitin, Asjût, Akhmim, Ombos and Elkâb, are known from the titularies of priests attached to them (Fischer 1958, 1964: 86-7). Most important is the testimony of the king's architect Nekhebu. He recounts in his famous autobiography (Dunham 1938) that he was charged 'to build the $k\exists$-houses of his majesty in Lower Egypt'. As already mentioned, statues of Pepi I discovered at Dendera and Hierakonpolis are probably also connected with this scheme.

The parallel to the older project seems obvious. Again a policy of mapping the royal cult throughout the country was followed. A glance at the historical situation is illuminating. Now, at the end of the Old Kingdom, when the importance of the temples and provincial towns was growing at the expense of the central institutions, it was again felt necessary to make the ideological background of the state's demands evident in the country, as it began to lose plausibility (similarly Fischer 1958: 332), as had been done at a time before it had acquired common acceptance.

The building of $k\exists$-houses by Pepi I was not an unique phenomenon. The systematic fashion in which it was carried out, however, seems to be quite extraordinary. Confining ourselves to real chapels for the cult of the king and excluding funerary domains named $k\exists$-houses, we can point at least to a $k\exists$-house of Teti at Tell Basta (El-Sawi 1979: 75-6) and a $k\exists$-house of Merenre, probably at Abydos (Fischer 1962, perhaps also Brovarski 1973). This material should not be viewed in isolation, however. Evidently, the royal $k\exists$-houses form part of the archaeological record which attests increased royal interest in the provincial temples during the late Old Kingdom.

Apart from a series of relatively minor votive gifts to the temples, only the naos of Pepi I from Elephantine and the relief slabs of Pepi II from Koptos mentioned above, undoubtedly derive from the furnishings of the temples themselves. Most of the inscribed architectural fragments, as well as the royal statues recovered from the temples, on the other hand, could stem from royal $k\exists$-houses. In fact, being connected ideologically to the royal cult, $k\exists$-houses would have been ideally suited to play a rôle as intermediaries in the transfer of the forms of monumental art to the provincial sanctuaries. In any case, the positive evidence referred to above entirely justifies O'Connor's (1992: 89ff) view that such chapels formed the dominant type of royal activity in the provincial temples. Therefore, it seems worthwhile to have a closer look at this phenomenon.

Comparing the $k\exists$-houses to the installations of the royal cult from the earlier Old Kingdom, important differences become apparent. No longer independent, the cult of the king is now attached to the temples of the local deities, and its installations lack typological exclusivity. In fact, *k3*-houses are also attested for members of the royal family (Goedicke 1967: 41-54) and even for non-royal persons (Balât, see above). Apart from this, however, the basic continuity between late Old Kingdom *k3*-houses and earlier forms of the official cult seems striking. As before, the key concept underlying the ideological expression of the unity of the land is the cult of the king. The configuration of the partners and the type of interaction between them, which is formulated symbolically in this ritual constellation, remained the same. Stressing the services the country provided for the king, the redistributive system was again presented as being mainly concerned with intake.

From this viewpoint, the increased royal activity in the provincial temples during the late Old Kingdom, which certainly reflects the developed economic and political importance of provincial towns in ideological terms, appears to be characterised nevertheless by a deep conservatism in thinking. Perhaps this could be taken as a symptom indicating the limited capability for development present in Old Kingdom kingship.

A short glance at the situation in the early Middle Kingdom makes this conclusion seem even more plausible. As the architectural history of the temple of Satet shows in an exemplary manner, and as architectural elements discovered re-used at many sites support on a broad basis, the kings of the Eleventh and Twelfth Dynasties did not only continue royal activity in the provincial temples along the lines marked out in the late Old Kingdom; rather they pursued it on an unprecedented scale and in an entirely systematic fashion.

Apart from this change in degree, a shift in focus seems no less clear and perhaps even more significant. *K3*-houses of the king are still attested, but the emphasis of royal activity is now clearly on building the temples themselves, where the king acts as a priest for the local gods, and this is exactly what the texts name as the *raison d'être* of kingship from the Middle Kingdom onwards (e.g. *pWestcar* 9.24-7).

Reading this pattern economically, the accent is now firmly on the 'giving' side of the redistributive system (compare Wilson 1951: 125, 1960: 132), a change in ideological attitude which may be interpreted to imply a profound re-interpretation of the relationship between the state and the country. Care for the local cults now figured among the basic tenets of the ruling doctrine, acknowledging the importance of the provincial communities. At the same time, this process of ideological assimilation claiming for the king decisive influence on the provincial cults, made them an important factor in the ideological and political *Gleichschaltung* of the country (Gomaa Müller-Wollermann Schenkel 1961: 5ff).

It comes as no surprise that this policy was inaugurated by the kings of the Eleventh Dynasty, whose social origins lay among the magnates of the First Intermediate Period, and who had acquired the fundamentals of their political thinking in the social, ideological and political milieu of the provincial towns in Upper Egypt. The Middle Kingdom, therefore, may be counted as a fourth phase in the sequence of stages in the relationship between the king and the provincial temples sketched above.

From the discussion it further emerges that this relationship should not be seen in isolation, but as part of a larger system embracing the royal funerary cult and also its derivations. The political significance of this system derives partly from the fact that, to an important degree, it *is* economic and administrative reality plain and simple. Moreover, aspects of the cultic constellation may be interpreted as a symbolic reflection of socio-economic relations, thus constituting a central sphere of ideological communication about these matters. In this respect, measures concerning the temples may be taken, apart from their immediate economic impact, as expressing basic attitudes which governed political action in general.

Concluding this synthesis, we should try to relate the development observed at Elephantine to the broader issue of the emergence of urbanisation in Egypt. Trigger (1972, 1985) argued persuasively in favour of a pluralistic approach. Since functioning as a structural node within a larger socio-economic system may be considered the hallmark of townhood, the development of towns must be highly dependent on their political, cultural and regional setting. In the case of Pharaonic Egypt, the range of possibilities can be defined by a pair of opposing alternatives.

Towns like Hierakonpolis developed as a result of autonomous socio-political evolution on a regional scale, as has been demonstrated by Hoffman et al. (1986). Bietak (1979: 106, 1986), on the other hand, stressed the importance of state enterprise in the foundation of towns, especially in Early Dynastic times. Planned settlements owing both their architectural layout and their social organisation entirely to outward imposition would come closest to a realisation of this model.

The case of Elephantine tends more towards the latter alternative. Clearly, the settlement gained its character as a town through the functions it took over on the national level, and the evidence for state interventions relating to the military, economic and ideological sectors during the Old Kingdom has been pointed out above.

It is equally clear, however, that the town of Elephantine was not wholly the product of acts of the central authorities. These tend to attract attention in spectacular and easily recognisable enterprises; the identity of the local community expresses itself in more subtle ways, and is revealed only through careful interpretation of the archaeological record. Settlement at the site preceded the first state activities; the local community retained the informal layout of the village and remained devoted to its temple as its ideological and organisational nucleus.

These traditional structures were not replaced through state intervention; quite to the contrary, *they* survived in the long run, assimilating new functions in the national context, while the state projects, designed in the first place to serve these functions, remained episodic. Clearly, individual aspects will have been conditioned by the specific situation at Elephantine, but the parallels quoted from other sites tend to show that the course of events documented here was not an isolated case.

In a preliminary attempt to generalise on these observations, one would suggest that towns developed through a dialectic process in the area of interaction between central organisation and local communities. This view would confirm the assumed relationship linking the development of urbanism to the emergence and later structural evolution of the state. As the beginnings of Pharaonic kingship were tied to the appearance of early capitals, the economic and political development of the Old Kingdom state caused a process of urbanisation on a country-wide scale, eventually leading to the situation known from the Middle Kingdom onwards, when provincial towns functioned as the backbone of Egypt's political and administrative organisation.

Acknowledgements

I am most grateful to the director of the excavation, Prof Dr W. Kaiser for his kind permission to draw on the material of the excavation, and in particular for several discussions and important comments which helped greatly in shaping the ideas presented here; responsibility for the views expressed, however, remains strictly my own.

I am much indebted as well to the colleagues involved in the excavations at Elephantine, especially Drs F. Andraschko, R. Avila, G. Dreyer and M. Ziermann, for their consent that I refer to the results of their work, along with my own. Drs Andraschko and Ziermann very kindly provided me with advance copies of their most recent excavation reports.

Further, I am obliged to Dr R. Müller-Wollermann for answering an inquiry concerning the dating of the priests of Elkab from the evidence of the Old Kingdom rock inscriptions, to Dr Nabil Swelim for communicating to me an unpublished newsletter concerning his excavations at Seila, and to the late Prof A.F. Shore for his kind permission to collate the Liverpool sealing impression of *Z3-nḫt* and to publish it here.

Last but not least my sincere thanks go to the editor for undertaking the arduous task of correcting my written English.

A Report on the Analysis of the Contents of a Cache of Jars from the Tomb of Djer

Margaret Serpico and Raymond White

During the winter of 1899-1900, Flinders Petrie undertook excavation of the First Dynasty royal cemetery at Abydos. In a north-west chamber of the tomb of king Djer, he uncovered a small cache of vessels which had apparently escaped earlier discovery, 'owing to the later brick stair having been built over them in the XVIIIth Dynasty, after the burning of the tomb' (Petrie 1901: 8-9, 46; Petrie 1902: 6). The group consisted of a calcite cylinder jar (fig.1, no. 11), four globular pottery jars of Egyptian manufacture (fig.1, nos. 9, 10, 13, and 14) and nine jars recognised by Petrie as foreign (fig.1, nos. 1-8). Although the group represented an exceptional example of a single, undisturbed deposit from a royal burial, the foreign vessels in the tomb were not unique. Similar imported jars were found not only elsewhere in this tomb and in other tombs at the cemetery, but also subsequently at a number of other Early Dynastic sites in Egypt (Adams and Porat: this volume).

Petrie's original suggestion that these foreign jars had been imported from the Aegean was rejected in light of the discovery of Palestinian vessels of corresponding shape or surface treatment (Helck 1962: 31-9; Hennessy 1967: 49-60; Amiran: 1969: 59, 62, 64-66; Adams and Porat: this volume). Based on these visual criteria, the imported jars have often been described as bottles, juglets and multiple handled vessels, or as red-polished, burnished, metallic or combed ware. Alternatively, the jugs and bottles are often known collectively as Abydos Ware. The Palestinian origin of some of the Egyptian examples was also confirmed by Hennessy and Millet's (1963: 10-17) spectrographic analysis of the fabric of the 'red burnished' pottery although, unfortunately, it is unclear from the report whether jars from the cache in the tomb of Djer were included in the study.

More recently, through geological analysis of a number of imported jars of this type found in Egypt, although again not from the Djer tomb, it has been possible to determine two sources for these jars, one in northern Israel or Lebanon around Mount Hermon, and the second slightly to the south near Lake Kinneret (Adams and Porat, this volume). Continuing this research, Adams and Porat have suggested that three jars from the Djer cache (see fig.1, nos. 3, 4 and 8) were of the more northern Canaanite origin (ibid.). Their observations on the possible correlations of fabric, geographical source and pre- and post-firing potmarks to the contents of the jars has heightened the importance of establishing the identity of the commodities transported in the vessels.

In the past, suggestions for the most likely contents of jars of these types have included oil, perfume and bitumen (Amiran 1969: 66, Hennessy 1967: 60, Kantor 1965: 15). Although Petrie did not mention the presence of ancient residues within the jars specifically, he did describe them as 'caked together by resins and burnt linen in the burning of the tomb' (Petrie 1901: 46). Hennessy, studying a number of jars from the cache held in the collection of the Ashmolean Museum, Oxford, noted that 'a number of the half and complete vessels of the "foreign ware" from the Tomb of Zer at Abydos contain thick deposits of a black material' (Hennessy 1967: 60).

In addition to the jars in the Ashmolean Museum, it has been possible to locate some of the remaining vessels in the collections of the British Museum and the Petrie Museum of Egyptian Archaeology at University College, London. Fortunately, the contents are preserved in these jars as well.

Visual examination of the exterior of the vessels revealed the presence of incised upright crosses (+) on the shoulders of Jars 2 and 5, in addition to the potmarks on Jars 3, 4, and 8 discussed by Adams and Porat (this volume). The crosses on both jars appear to be post-firing, but the mark on Jar 2 is partially obscured by surface residue. In addition, Jar 5 had a series of pre-firing incised lines across the base. Although the fabric has not been studied in detail, the cross potmarks on these vessels are consistent with those found on jars of northern Canaanite origin (Adams and Porat, this volume).

Given these factors, analysis of the contents of the imported jars could potentially provide new insights into trade during this period. The Djer group is particularly important because it includes jars of both Nile silt and foreign clays, making it possible to explore variations between the commodities

128

stored in Egyptian and imported vessels within a closed deposit. However, scientific analysis of the residues remaining in the jars from the Djer cache is greatly hampered by two factors. First, the ancient burning of the tomb has in some instances severely affected the contents of the jars. Second, although the group was mentioned by Petrie, details on the discovery were omitted which could affect the interpretation of the analytical results. Petrie noted that the jars were 'caked in linen-coated resin,' and residue is still visible on the exterior of most of the jars today. The various potential source(s) of these external residues must be considered as it is possible that they could have also contaminated the interior contents. Here, the lack of detailed information of the deposition of the jars is particularly unfortunate.

It was hoped that visual examination of the residues might provide some clues to the post-depositional history of the vessels. Inspection of the exterior surfaces of the jars with a 10x magnification hand lens indicated that in some cases, at least two types of residue appear to be present. Jars 1, 2, and 4 have a thin, patchy coating of black, slightly glossy material inside the mouth, extending onto the exterior rim and neck and sometimes over parts of the body. These residues could be the result of the ordinary use of the jar prior to burial.

In addition, some of the jars also have comparatively thick deposits of sand encrusted with residue on the exterior, which suggested that the jars had come into contact with more substantial quantities of residue, which had mixed with the sand and solidified. Two jars (4 and 7) have a distinct mass trapped between the handle and the body which at first glance looked like a lump of cloth soaked in residue, such as mentioned by Petrie, but on closer examination these masses proved to be a conglomeration of this hardened sand/residue mixture. Given the quantities of sand found adhering to the vessels, it would seem less likely that the jars had been completely or tightly wrapped in the linen.

While it is possible that this thicker residue was the result of a separate deposit poured over the jars collectively, as Petrie suggested, other sources, such as spillage, should be considered. From the position of the residues inside the jars, it does seem unlikely that the external conglomeration was the result of any spillage from the mouth of the vessels. In most cases, the contents form discrete deposits in the base. None of the jars are over half full and while in some instances, the contents are tipped, in only one case could the residue have reached the mouth. This exception is Jar 14, which is nearly empty except for one mass of residue on the side of the wall. Much of the neck and rim of this vessel has been reconstructed in modern plaster, and it is difficult to determine whether this restoration could have disturbed the contents. Although it appears that force from a sharp object perforated the walls of Jars 2 and 4 just below the shoulder, it seems unlikely that some of the contents could have leaked from these holes, as in both instances the main residue in the jar bases was tipped slightly away from the opening. Therefore, on the whole, it would seem that external residues were not caused by spillage of the main deposits from the mouth due to the position of the jars in the tomb.

In contrast, it is probable that some of the jars did break in the tomb. Not only does Petrie's drawing suggest that some jars were partially broken, but the base of Jar 6 is now in fragments and it is clear that the residue did extend over some of these breaks and onto the exterior surface of the base. Although the bases of Jars 1 and 12 have now been restored from fragments and the breaks cannot be studied, it does seem that residue also flowed over the break of the wall on the Jar 12. However, if most of the jars had been placed collectively on their bases, as the concentration of the internal residues suggest, then it would seem that only the lower part of the jars would be affected by the leakage. In fact, the deposition of the exterior residue is more comprehensive, often covering much of the upper body. It is possible that the jars had been stacked, with Jar 6 on top, which might account for the distinct rivulets of a blackened residue found on the upper exterior body of Jar 7 and on the upper interior of Jar 3.

Based on these observations, it seems that the external residues could be the result of the use of the jars prior to burial, overflow from broken jars and/or the addition of a separate fluid deposit poured over the vessels. Moreover, if the jars had been re-used before burial, the external residues could reflect this re-use. Due to high probability of cross-contamination suggested from this examination, priority turned to the jar contents.

It is possible that external residues had contaminated the contents in some cases. Therefore, samples of the internal contents were taken, where possible, from below the surface of the dense deposits concentrated in the base of the jar, not from areas near the mouth or from thin residues on the upper interior walls which could possibly be intrusive. As such, the samples of jar contents probably reflect only the final deposit of the dense residue in the base, making it difficult to address questions of re-use.

With the exception of Jar 5 (see below), all of the samples discussed here were taken with clean forceps and stored in glass vials with bakelite caps to reduce any modern contamination. Sample size was only a few milligrams, in no instance representing more than a minute proportion of the entire contents. In the past, contents were often largely or completely removed for study, but this is unnecessarily destructive. Although it is true that small sample size may adversely influence the results in heterogeneous mixtures, this can be overcome by taking multiple samples where indicated, as for Jar 4 (see below).

Some preliminary work on the samples was undertaken by Dr Gretchen Shearer. Based on the results of this analysis by Fourier Transform Infrared Spectroscopy (FT-IR), Jars 1, 3, 4, 5, 6, 7, 9, and 10 were selected for further analysis. For a comparable description of the experimental procedure used at this stage, see Shearer (1987: 254). Although the analysis focused on the jar contents, the results of FT-IR examination of samples taken from the exterior of the jars confirmed the complexity of these residues. In light of the difficulties concerning the possible variety of sources for these deposits, it is clear that extensive work would be necessary to distinguish between these residues, and even then, the results may not prove conclusive.

Thus, attention for the moment has turned to the jar contents. Further FT-IR analysis of the sub-group of jar contents was carried out by Mr White using a Nicolet 710 bench with a NicPlan infrared microscope. For a summary of the experimental procedure, see Mills and White (1994: 185-187) and Pilc and White (1995). Subsequent GC/MS analysis, again by Mr White, was carried out using a Kratos MS25 gas chromatography/mass spectrometry system. Following saponification of the samples, the reaction product was acidified, extracted with ether and evaporated to dryness. The residues were then leached with ether/methanol and gaseous diazomethone was passed through the solution. After concentration, the reaction product was examined by GC/MS. The chromatography conditions were as follows: 25m, wide-bore (0.53 mm) quartz capillary column with methyl silicone-equivalent bonded phase; on-column injection; helium carrier gas at 37cm s.s.$^{-1}$ linear velocity; temperature programming from 130°C to 290°C at 5° min s.s.$^{-1}$ The mass spectrometry conditions were as follows: EI mode, 70eV, source temperature 275°C, scanning at 1 s decade s.s.$^{-1}$ (Mills and White 1989: 40). The results of the analyses are summarised below. However, certain scientific aspects of the analyses will be discussed in greater detail in a future article.

Jar 1 (UC 17385) - As this red burnished bottle is largely complete, apart from the rim and small parts of the body, it was difficult to study the contents in detail visually (see fig.1, 1). The residue appeared to have a matte, uneven surface, which formed a thick coating (about 1.0cm) over most of the interior, becoming somewhat thicker at the base. There was no distinction between the appearance of the residues on the wall and base to suggest re-use. Although sand was visible on the surface of the interior contents, it was not apparent on the residue visible where a small area of the base was missing. Thus, it seems that the sand was intrusive and not deliberately mixed with the contents. Petrie commented on the intentional addition of mud to the contents of predynastic wavy-handled jars (Petrie 1896: 39), but this does not seem to have been the case here.

The sample was taken from the surface and below the thickened deposit towards the base in the interior of the jar. Beneath the grey, sandy surface, the sample had a mottled matte brown-orange to black appearance which indicated that it had not been completely charred. The residue was compact and fairly hard in texture, but there was no discernible odour to this, or any of the other samples.

Some evidence of fatty material was detected by the chemical analysis. The saponifiable fraction contained certain dicarboxylic acids, which represent the degraded fatty acids commonly found in aged lipids (vegetable oils or animals fats). Determination of the amounts of preserved dicarboxylic acids can be particularly useful in these analyses, as this information can sometimes help pinpoint the lipid source more specifically. While both saturated and unsaturated fatty acids are found in fresh oils and animal fats, vegetable oils usually contain more of the less stable unsaturated fatty acids. Over time, these unsaturated acids are more prone to polymerise and cross-link as well as degrade into

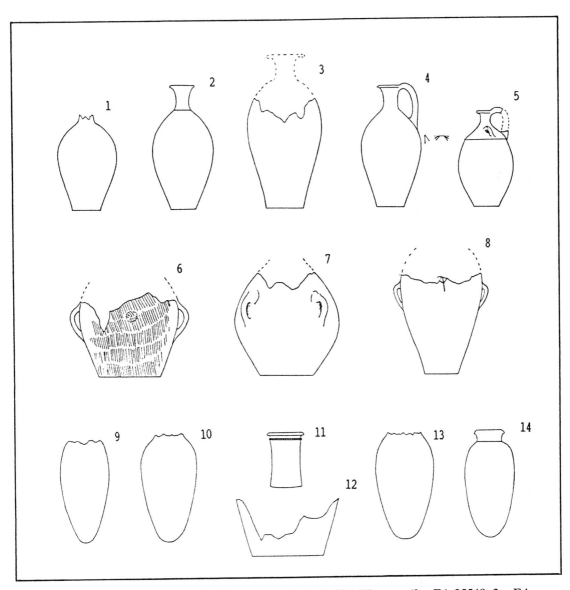

Figure 1 Jars from the Djer tomb. Four jars are in the British Museum (2 = EA 35548, 3 = EA 35549, 11 = EA 35546 and 13 = EA 35547). One jar is in the Petrie Museum, London (1 = UC 17385). The remainder are in the Ashmolean Museum, Oxford (4 = E3160, 5 = E3240, 6 = E4031, 7 = E3158, 8 = E4034, 9 = E4065, 10 = E4066, 12 = E4030 and 14 = E3159). After Petrie 1902: pl.viii. Scale 1:10.

dicarboxylic acids. The detection of abundant dicarboxylic acids, in this case as dimethyloctandioate and, to a lesser degree, dimethylazelate, suggested that degraded unsaturated fatty acids, more commonly associated with vegetable oils, were present.

As well as these degraded compounds, traces of the saturated fatty acids, palmitic and stearic acid, which are more stable and therefore more likely to remain detectable, were also noted. These saturated fatty acids are found in both animal and vegetable lipids but, significantly, the ratio of these acids is often higher in vegetable oils (usually nearer to 2.0) than in animal fats (usually nearer to 1.0) (Mills and White 1994: 171-2). The ratio of these acids in this sample was 1.7, which may also weigh in favour of an identification of the lipid source as a vegetable oil. While there was no evidence of animal sterols, such as cholesterol, to indicate the addition of an animal fat, a very minor component gave a mass spectrum resembling ß-sitosterol, a sterol found only in vegetable oils.

According to Lucas (1989, p. 331-6), the most common sources of vegetable oil available in pharaonic times would have been linseed (*Linum usitatissimum* L.), safflower (*Carthamus tinctorius* L.), balanos (*Balanites aegyptiaca* (L.) Del.), moringa (*Moringa peregrina* Fiori), castor (*Ricinus communis* L.), sesame (*Sesamum indicum* L.) and olive (*Olea europaea* L.). However, precise information on the distribution and profusion of these species in Egypt and the Near East during the First Dynasty is sometimes lacking. Much depends on the chance discovery of archaeobotanical remains of the various sources, taken in conjunction with the proposed centres of origin and subsequent paths of diffusion for those species.

Linseed, for example, seems to have been introduced into Egypt from the Near East sometime between 6000 and 5000 BC (Zohary and Hopf 1993: 123-4, Map 13), and seeds pre-dating the First Dynasty have been found at Merimde (ibid), Maadi (Kroll 1989: 132) and in the Fayum (Thompson and Gardner 1934: 49) to support this. In contrast, it appears that safflower, which probably originated in central Asia, did not reach the Near East or Egypt until after the Early Bronze Age (Germer 1989: 37-8; Zohary and Hopf 1993: 194).

Castor may have been available quite early as seeds, identified at the time by the Director of the Horticultural Section of the Egyptian Ministry of Agriculture, were found in one predynastic grave at Badari (Brunton and Thompson 1928: 38, 41). Similarly, balanos nuts were found in a predynastic grave at Genamieh (Keimer and Germer: 1984: 2) and were also in a burial (Grave 273) in the cemetery at Naqada (Petrie 1896: 54. The nuts are now in the Petrie Museum, U.C. 36097). Notably, the earliest secure occurrences of archaeobotanical remains of moringa appear to date to the Ptolemaic period (Keimer and Germer 1984: 27-8).

The possible date of introduction of sesame into the Near East and Egypt, probably from further east in Asia, is particularly problematic. With the exception of seeds from the tomb of Tutankhamun which were tentatively identified at the Royal Botanic Gardens, Kew, as sesame (Germer 1989: 41), the earliest confirmed identifications in the Near East thus far date to the first millennium (Zohary and Hopf 1993: 133), suggesting that the date for the introduction of sesame was much later than the Early Bronze Age. Petrie reported that some seeds, identified by Thiselton Dyer at Kew as sesame, were found in the predynastic cemeteries at Naqada and Ballas (Petrie 1896: 54), but this evidence is inconsistent with the proposed pattern of diffusion of sesame generally accepted today. As a number of the burials had been disturbed, it is possible that the seeds were a later contaminant. If so, this could also cast doubt on the identification of balanos at the site.

From archaeobotanical evidence, it is clear that olive trees grew in Palestine in the Early Bronze Age (for a summary of finds, see Stager 1985: 188), but olives do not seem to have been cultivated in Egypt until much later. Finds of olive stones are fairly common at New Kingdom sites, although Mary Anne Murray, archaeobotanist for the Egypt Exploration Society's expedition to Memphis, has noted particularly early examples of olive in Middle Kingdom levels at that site (Giddy and Jeffreys 1991: 5). In the absence of secure evidence of cultivation within Egypt, it is commonly assumed that olive oil would have been the principal oil export to Egypt during the Early Bronze Age. However, Zohary (1962: 146) has stated that linseed, balanos and moringa probably also grew in Palestine prior to the EBA. While it could be argued that it is unlikely that these oils would have been imported to Egypt on their own, they could have been used as the base in more complicated mixtures with resins, herbs or spices. Balanos and moringa oils might have been preferable to olive oil in some mixtures, as these oils do not carry a strong scent as olive does. Therefore, detection of balanos or moringa oil in an Egyptian sample would not necessarily indicate a locally produced oil. Only genus identification of olive in a sample would clearly point to an imported product.

Even where the archaeobotanical evidence indicates that certain oil-producing plants were available to the ancient Egyptians, botanical remains are not proof in themselves of an extensive oil industry within Egypt, as any or all of these sources might have been utilised for other purposes during the First Dynasty. Linseed, for example, could have been grown for flax, and balanos and moringa may have been used only as food. In this regard, analysis of jar residues could help establish the variety of oils in use in antiquity. Genus identification of vegetable oils could also help establish the intended use of the contents. If linseed or castor were present, for example, it would seem less likely that the oil was a food product, as linseed tends to turn rancid quite quickly and is prone to gel and solidify, and both are generally considered to have an unpleasant taste.

However, accurate genus identification of a vegetable oil is problematic. Vegetable oils usually contain similar fatty acids which vary only in proportion. The degradation of these fatty acids over time makes detection of these subtle variations in proportion much more difficult. At times, the proportions of the detectable degradation products can be used to narrow the likely sources, but the preservation of this sample was not sufficient to allow for such a distinction. Nonetheless, of these sources, it is possible to eliminate castor. In addition to the usual fatty acids, this oil has a very high proportion of ricinoleic acid, the degradation products of which were not found in the sample (Mills and White 1994: 33, table 3.2).

As well as the lipid component, some evidence of carbon, probably due to the burning, was detected in this sample by optical examination and combustion. However, it is clear that the lipid and carbonised components make up only a small proportion of the organic remains. Most of the sample, which was insoluble in ether/methanol, seems to derive from either inorganic or humic material. The FT-IR analysis indicated that the insoluble material was more likely humic. Usually, contact with the soil will result in humic matter, and initially it was thought that the sand mixed with the residue could have been the catalyst. Fine sand was found in other jars where no humic component was present, making it less likely as the cause. Alternatively, condensation between carbohydrates and proteins could cause this conversion, unfortunately leaving little trace of the original components. The presence of a peak at 1635cm $^{-1}$ in the FT-IR spectra, indicating a carbon double bonded with nitrogen, suggested that such a conversion had taken place. Although only weakly positive, the results of a furfural/aldehyde test also suggested that carbohydrates were present (Mills and White 1994: 78).

The carbohydrate component could be derived from a number of sources. Cellulose or lignin from plant fibres could be present, although no plant remains were visible to the eye in the sample. Other possible sources include saccharides found in honey or fruit, or starch. Finally, the carbohydrate could include polysaccharide gums. Possible sources of gums include shrubs of *Astragalus* spp., found in the Near East at this time, or *Acacia* spp. from Sudan and/or Egypt (Howes 1949: 1739). Although the best acacia gum is obtained from the Sudanese *Acacia senegal* Willd., lesser quality gums can be obtained from a number of species found in Egypt, including *Acacia nilotica* (L.) Willd. and *Acacia albida* Del. (Anderson 1978: 529-36; Täckholm 1974: 289-90; Howes 1949: 20). Charcoal specimens of both these species have been identified in predynastic hearths near Mahgar Canal in upper Egypt (Vermeersch et al. 1992: 170).

In order to try to determine the nature of the carbohydrate more specifically, the sample was spot tested with an iodine/potassium iodide reagent under a binocular microscope at 40x magnification. If the carbohydrate is derived from starch, the reagent will react to produce a blue stain (Mills and White 1994: 76). Despite the dark colour of the sample, it was possible to observe a weakly positive result to this test, suggesting that, at least in part, the source may have been starch. Grain crops such as barley (*Hordeum vulgare* L.) or emmer (*Triticum dicoccum* Schubl.), both present by early dynastic times, would be potential sources of starch (Zohary and Hopf 1993: 44, 64).

Thus, the humic component could have been caused by the condensation of protein and carbohydrate, the latter at least in part identified as starch. Given the degraded nature of the sample, it was not possible to determine whether the source of the protein was animal, including sources such as meat, eggs, milk or fish products, or possibly vegetable, derived from pulses such as lentil (*Lens culinaris*

Medic.) or pea (*Pisum sativum* L.), both of which would have been available in Egypt at that time (ibid: 93-4, 101). In addition, although generally present in lower quantities, cereals also contain protein (ibid: 14).

A combination of starch, cereal protein and simple sugars resulting from fermentation could, for example, suggest the presence of an ancient beer residue (Samuel 1994: 10-11), but, at present, there is no evidence to suggest that vegetable oils were added to ancient beer. It is possible that this combination of components reflects a re-use of the jar, at one time for oil storage and at another for beer. However, the sample was not taken from the wall of the vessel where re-use would have been more easily detectable, but from the main deposit in the base. While this would reduce the likelihood that the sample consists of two separate deposits, the possibility cannot be completely eliminated. Overall, this combination of ingredients suggests that the humic contents are probably a food mixture, and unlikely to have been a cosmetic. Although it is possible that edible gum was used in the mixture, gums are, for the most part, tasteless, and there is no immediately obvious reason for mixing a gum with the other components found in the jar.

However, for this and all samples, it is important to remember that chemical analysis will identify only the components that remain detectable over time. It is always possible that aromatic plant components had been added to scent or flavour the mixture, but as these components are volatile, their detection in ancient samples is rare. Moreover, for these jars, it is likely that the burning in the tomb would have driven off any remaining traces.

Jar 3 (BM EA 35549) - Only the lower part of this red-burnished vase, from the shoulder to the flat base, is preserved. Parts of the exterior surface show signs of burning. The residue in the base, which is black, somewhat glossy and friable with a fairly smooth surface, is slightly tipped and probably only about 3.0cm deep. Patches of a sandy residue remained on the interior walls and are again probably intrusive, but the coating of sand noted on the surface of the main deposit in the base of jar 1 was not visible on the base deposit of this jar. Interestingly, although most of the wall was fairly clean, there was a ring of residue about 3.0cm above the main deposit in the base, which suggests that some of the contents had been decanted anciently.

This sample contained no humic matter, but again, fatty acids dominated. In this instance, mainly palmitic and stearic acids were found. The comparatively high palmitate/stearate ratio of 2.2 would seem to favour a vegetable oil source. Again, dicarboxylic acids similar to those found in the sample from Jar 1 were detected but no sterols were found to establish the source conclusively. It is possible that this sample had been more affected by the burning of the tomb than the previous residue, and this could easily account for the absence of the sterols. The residue was, therefore, probably a vegetable oil, although, once again, castor is not likely as the source.

Jar 7 (Ash. E.3158) - Although badly damaged by fire, this bulbous four-handled jar had traces of vertical burnishing. In the areas less affected by burning, the thick coating of residue in the base was a dark brown colour, with a porous, irregular surface which extended partly up the sides of the interior.

The contents of this jar were similar to those found in the previous sample. The seven carbon (C_7) dicarboxylic ester predominates, followed by dimethylsuberate (C_8) and then dimethylazelate (C_9). The high proportion of degraded unsaturated fatty acids suggested that a vegetable oil was present, and the palmitate/stearate ratio of 1.8 supports this. Again, no sterols were detected, nor was there any indication of ricinoleic acid.

Jar 6 (Ash. E.4031) - This is roughly the lower half of a combed ware jar, now in fragments. Originally, the jar probably had four handles, (the join to the third handle is shown slightly misplaced in Petrie's drawing - see fig.1). Although the exterior of the vessel was partially burnt, the interior surface and contents were completely blackened. A thick coating of residue was found in the base, becoming thinner on the wall, with the upper areas nearly clean. The contents had a slightly glossier appearance than those previously analysed.

Nonetheless, dicarboxylic acid esters dominated the sample, and the palmitate/stearate ratio of about 2.3 also supports the presence of large quantities of vegetable oil. No sterols were detected. Like Jar 1, a peak at 1635cm $^{-1}$, possibly due to condensation of protein and carbohydrate, was present in the FT-IR spectrum. A furfural/aldehyde also test confirmed the presence of carbohydrates, but the results of a spot test with the iodine/potassium iodide reagent were negative, which would seem to indicate that the carbohydrate was not a starch, although the very black colour of the sample may have adversely affected the result.

It is particularly unfortunate that it is impossible to determine whether the oil component was original to the jar and not a later re-use. Stager (1985: 176) and Esse (1991: 119-24) both discussed the possible connection of combed ware jars and the olive oil industry in the Levant. Combed ware storage jars and large combed ware vats have been found in conjunction with mortars, possibly for grinding olives, at a few Early Bronze Age sites, such as Beth Yerah (Khirbet Kerak), (Esse 1991: 33, 123-4). For a summary of other sites, see Stager 1985: 176. However, olive stones are not always present in these industrial areas, nor has there been any systematic analysis of the contents of this type of pottery as yet to confirm this theory. Oil production may have begun as early as the Chalcolithic Period (Epstein 1993: 133-146).

Jar 5 (Ash. E.3240) - This jar has been recently restored and reconstructed from fragments and the mouth of the vessel is very small (about 1.5cm), making it impossible to study the contents visually. Normally, a sample from such a jar would be a poor choice for analysis, but as this is one of the jars least damaged by fire and, as the shape is of particular interest, an attempt was made to obtain a sample. A probe was inserted into a very restricted area of the base of the jar to try to loosen any remaining contents, which were then shaken from the mouth. Along with globules of modern plaster, many of which were loose in the jar, and small particles from the vessel wall, several minute (roughly 1.0 mm) red-brown, friable flakes, possibly the remains of the residue, were detected. However, blind samples such as this are always less reliable. Not only is it impossible to evaluate the likelihood of re-use, but the chances of contamination, particularly in this case from the modern plaster restoration, are quite high. Some information can be ascertained, but the results must be viewed with caution.

Analysis of the red-brown friable matter in the sample indicated that, in contrast to the other jars, the amount of dicarboxylic acid was quite low. The palmitate/stearate ratio was also much lower. This would seem to suggest that an animal fat, rather than a vegetable oil, was present, although no traces of sterols to confirm this could be found. Like the previous sample, this residue contained carbohydrates, possibly polysaccharides, but here in a slightly higher proportion. There was no evidence of humic matter.

Jar 9 (Ash. E.4065) - This is one of four jars in Nile silt clay. The jar was badly burned with only about 5.0cm of residue remaining in the base, although some patchy deposits of similar appearance still adhere to the wall. Because only the rim and neck are missing, it was not possible to examine the contents with a hand lens. To the eye, both the residues on the wall and in the base were black and friable with an open, porous surface. As such, the contents were distinctly different visually from the residues remaining in the imported jars which were on the whole more compact and glossy.

While some dicarboxylic acids were present in this sample, they did not dominate the chromatogram as in some of the other samples. Also, like the contents of Jar 5, the palmitate/stearate ratio was comparatively low. Therefore, although no sterols could be detected, it is more likely that the lipid present was an animal fat rather than a vegetable oil. There was no evidence of either humic or carbohydrate matter.

Jar 10 (Ash. E.4066) - The residue of a second Nile silt jar, which was also badly burned, looked similar to jar 9, but was somewhat more glossy. The contents were slightly tipped and formed a solid mass in the bottom of the jar, with a maximum depth of about 5.0cm. Like Jar 3, a ring of residue of similar appearance about 2-3cm above the main deposit suggests that some of the contents had been decanted.

Carbon was the dominant component, although some fatty acids were also found. These were predominately lower fatty acids, and this, combined with the absence of the dicarboxylic acids common to vegetable oils, would seem to indicate that the lipid was an animal fat. However, the palmitate/

stearate ratio was 1.7, which is higher than would be expected for a fat. The severe burning of the sample in antiquity may have affected the results. Some proteinaceous material was detected, although no humic matter or carbohydrates were observed.

Jar 4 (Ash. E.3160) - The contents of this one-handled jar were clearly not homogenous, and differed in appearance. A dry, compact deposit, about 4.0 - 5.0cm deep, and slightly tipped, was preserved at the bottom. The brown colour suggests that the contents were not completely burned. In addition, a black, glossy residue was found coating part of the upper interior wall. While this may represent contents from other vessels which had spilled into the jug, the density of the deposit suggests that the jar had, in fact, been re-used. If this were the case, then it would seem that the residue on the side of the vessel represents an earlier deposit.

In view of this distinction, two samples were taken from the contents of this jar, one of the residue in the base, the other from the deposit on the walls. The material from the wall, which was more glossy in appearance, again had a high proportion of dicarboxylic acids, predominately dimethylazelate (C_9) with lesser amounts of the C_7, C_8 and C_{10} esters. The palmitic and stearic ester content was about 50% of the dicarboxylic content but there was a low palmitate/stearate ratio. This suggests a predominately vegetable oil source, possible with some added animal fat. There was no evidence of humic matter or carbohydrates, and the results of a spot test with iodine/potassium iodide were negative.

Of interest were the detectable traces of dehydroabietic and 7-oxodehydroabietic acids. These acids are found in resins of the family Pinaceae (Mills and White 1977: 14-5). This family comprises the pine, cedar, and fir. Of these, fir (*Abies* spp.) can be eliminated as a source, as this resin contains quantities of the comparatively stable component abienol, the degradation products of which were not found in this sample. Often, it is possible to distinguish between pine and cedar resin by the detection of characteristic volatile components. However, due to their volatility, these compounds are often absent in ancient samples, and they were not detected here. It is very likely that the burning in the tomb would have driven off any trace. In addition to compounds suggesting a Pinaceae resin, a trace of the compound retene was also detected. The identification of retene would normally indicate the presence of a heated tar or pitch (Mills and White 1994: 65), but as the tomb had been burned in antiquity, it is equally possible that the retene was formed as a result of pyrolysis in the tomb.

Thus, cedar and pine remain as possible sources, although the extent to which cedar (*Cedrus libani* A. Richard) was available in antiquity has been widely debated (Meiggs: 1982: 405-9). Loret (1916: 47-51) argued against the ancient presence of widespread cedar forests in Lebanon and proposed that fir and pine were predominately used by the Egyptians. In addition, Lucas (1989: 319) dismissed cedar as a source of resin, claiming that the tree produces little resin. Loret's arguments, however, have been overturned for the most part by more recent research which indicates that there has been a significant reduction in cedar in Lebanon since antiquity. Studies of the relic stands indicate that cedar forests did extend along much of Lebanon (see fig.2) (Mikesell 1969: 10), generally at altitudes between 1500 and 1800m above sea level (Zohary 1973: 346). The possibility that cedar grew on Mount Hermon in antiquity is still debated, however (Mikesell 1969: 10-11).

Fragments of wood, identified by at the Royal Botanic Gardens, Kew, as cedar and pine, were found in a burial at Badari, suggesting that the Egyptians were familiar with the wood from predynastic times (Brunton and Thompson 1928: 62-3). Davies' recent review of botanical identifications of wood samples from ancient Egypt also confirms the prevalence of cedar wood (Davies 1995: 150, table 1). Although many of the earlier identifications of cedar resin need to be reconsidered in the light of more advanced analytical techniques, this resin has now been identified as the primary component in a small calcite cylinder jar of Middle Kingdom date from Kahun, now in the Petrie Museum (U.C. 7318) (Serpico, forthcoming). While not of contemporary date, these results suggest that cedar resin was at least occasionally available to the ancient Egyptians.

Although this information indicates that cedar could be the source of the resin in this jar, three pines, *Pinus brutia* Ten., *Pinus pinea* L. and *Pinus halepensis* Mill., are also found along the eastern Mediterranean coast and must be considered. Like cedar, it is often difficult to determine precisely the ancient distribution of these species. For example, *P. brutia* is highly invasive and *P. pinea* has often been planted for its edible nuts. Following Zohary (1973: 343-4), it appears that *P. brutia* and *P. pinea*

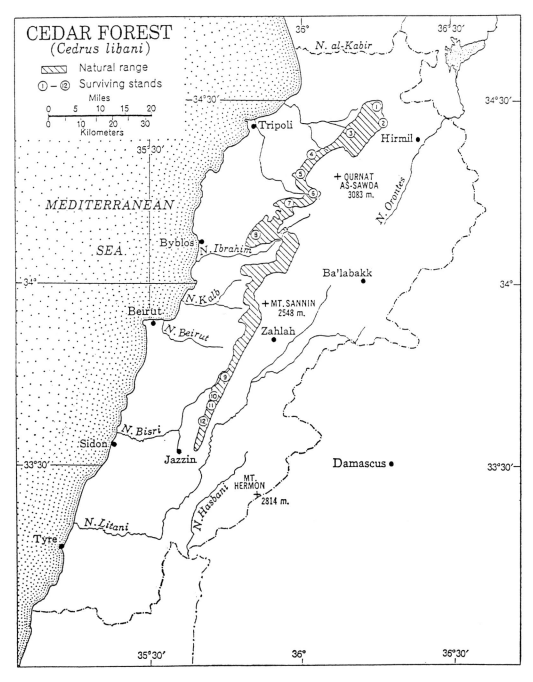

Figure 2 Map showing the natural range and surviving stands of cedar in Lebanon. After Mikesell 1969: fig.10.

extend only as far south as Lebanon. Like cedar, *P. brutia* is found along much of the length of central Lebanon, but generally at lower altitudes (ibid: 342-3; fig. 135). In contrast, *P. pinea*, which favours an altitude of no more than 500 m, is largely restricted to the area south of Beirut, but north of Sidon (ibid: 342,fig. 134, 344-5). There is, however, some evidence that it may have grown in coastal Israel as late as 1860 (ibid: 345).

The only pine known to extend into Israel and Jordan today is *Pinus halepensis* Mill. (ibid: 342, fig. 134). Fortunately, it is sometimes possible to distinguish *P. halepensis* chemically from *P. brutia* and *P. pinea,* as the former has a significantly higher ratio of sandaracopimaric acid to pimaric acid than the other two pines (White 1990: 81-88). The absence of sandaracopimaric acid in this sample would seem to make *P. halepensis* unlikely as the source. Thus, the evidence suggests that the resin was probably of Lebanese origin, derived from *Cedrus libani, Pinus pinea* or *Pinus brutia*.

The distribution of these species is particularly interesting when considered in conjunction with the proposed origin of the jar. Based on Adam's visual examination of the fabric, the jar has been grouped with those from sources in north-eastern Israel, around Mount Hermon, and in Lebanon (Adams and Porat, this volume). Although it is possible, in light of the likely Lebanese source of the resin, to suggest that the jar may also have been manufactured in Lebanon, it remains possible that the resin had been transported to the area of the manufacture of the jar. Evidence of such an exchange would have only been apparent if, for example, the clay had been exclusive to Israel and the resin restricted to Lebanon. However, the shape of the vessel is not conclusively that of a storage jar for bulk transport, such as Jars 6 or 7, which makes it difficult to determine whether jars of this type were more commonly used for raw materials or processed goods, or in fact, alternated between the two. The residue does appear to be a mixture of a lipid with some added *Pinaceae* resin, not a single raw commodity. Resins of this type would be soluble in a fluid lipid base, although, if the resin had solidified, some heating may have been necessary. The mixture could have been used as a cosmetic, although other usages cannot be discounted.

It is also apparent that the components detected in the residue in the base of the jar, probably from subsequent re-use, differ somewhat from the oil and resin mixture found on the walls of the vessel. Once again, some lipid component was present, although only in small quantities. Unfortunately, the sterols could not be characterised, but the palmitate/stearate ratio was 1.9, which suggested that the lipid was a vegetable oil.

In addition to carbon, humic material, probably the result of protein and carbohydrate condensation, was present, and the FT-IR spectrum again revealed a significant peak at 1635cm[-1] to confirm this. The results of a furfural/aldehyde test indicated that polysaccharides were present, and there was a weakly positive reaction to spot testing with iodine. Therefore, this residue would seem to consist predominately of humic matter, originally polysaccharides, including starch, and protein, as well as a small amount of vegetable oil. This sample would seem to be similar to that found in jar 1 and again appears to be more consistent with a food product.

To summarise, results to date indicate that all samples contained lipid matter, derived either from vegetable oils or animal fats. While, with the exception of Jar 5, most of the imported pottery appear to have contained vegetable oils, the two Egyptian jars analysed (Jars 9 and 10) may have held animal fats, one with added proteinaceous matter. Jar 5 possibly contained an animal fat, but the analysis of the contents of this vessel was problematic and must be considered with caution. Nonetheless, the possible distinction in the source of the lipid components between Egyptian and foreign jars deserves further consideration. The slight distinction between the contents of the two Egyptian jars suggests that the shape was not exclusively linked to a particular commodity. Although it is usually assumed that the Egyptians were producing oil at this time, the results might lead some to question the extent to which locally made oils were available. Clarification of this issue would require much more analytical work. The overlap of distribution of oil sources in Egypt and the Levant, as well as the problems in genus identifications of these oils would make the task more difficult. In addition, it is unclear whether these lipids were original to the jar and not the result of re-use.

In two examples (Jars 3 and 7), only vegetable oils were detected. Although the identity of the oil is unknown, castor oil was eliminated as a likely source, and in fact, none of the samples appear to have contained this oil. Without further information, it is impossible to determine the intended use of the oil in these two jars, possibly in food preparation or cosmetically.

The residues from the remaining jars (1, 4, 5 and 6) were more complex. While the results of the analysis of the residue from Jar 5 deserve caution, it does appear that the components identified in these jars are generally more consistent with food mixtures. It is also particularly unfortunate that the sample from Jar 5 is unreliable, as it would have offered an interesting comparison with the contents of Jar 4. Nonetheless, the evidence of re-use in Jar 4 suggests that other jars could also have been re-used and indicates that, on the whole, the residues analysed here may be secondary. Further work comparing samples from the walls of the vessels to those from the base would be necessary to address this problem. Despite the possibility of re-use, the overall diversity of the mixtures suggests that the vessels were not systematically filled from a single source at the time of burial. This fact may make it more likely that the contents relate to the use or re-use of the jars prior to interment.

Without more information on the original discovery of the group, interpretation of the exterior residues is very difficult. Although it is likely that these residues resulted from a deposit poured collectively over the group, there is also a high probability that some of the exterior residues derive from ordinary use of the jars prior to burial, or from breakage of one of the jars after deposition. Thus, the possibility of cross-contamination cannot be eliminated, especially as the burning may have caused the residues to become more fluid. The FT-IR analysis suggested that these external residues were mixtures, and given the complexity of the internal residues, the possibility of accurate assessment of the origin of the external samples is greatly reduced.

In conclusion, although the number of jars examined here was too small to provide firm links between contents and shape, fabric or potmark, the results may be useful, nonetheless, for further studies. While only Jar 4 had contents which were indisputably imported, these results provide important secure evidence, not only of coniferous resin trade in the period, but also on one commodity transported in these characteristic one-handled jars. In the future, continued chemical analysis of jar residues, targeting vessels of similar shape and/or origin could help to resolve questions concerning the relationship between jar shape and commodity, or between the commodities found in jars of different geographical origin. Finally, in light of the recent discussions on the significance of potmarks, comparison of the contents to those found in jars with similar potmarks may at long last help resolve the purpose of these enigmatic signs.

Acknowledgements

We would like to thank Mr W.V. Davies, Keeper of the Department of Egyptian Antiquities at the British Museum for inviting us to contribute this paper. For permission to study and sample material from the jars, we are also grateful to Dr A.J. Spencer, Assistant Keeper in the same Department, Dr Helen Whitehouse, Assistant Curator of the Department of Antiquities at the Ashmolean Museum, Oxford, and Mrs Barbara Adams, Curator of the Petrie Museum at University College London.

The incised *serekh*-signs of Dynasties 0-1

Part I: complete vessels

Edwin C.M. van den Brink

Introduction

Since the last comprehensive treatment, more than a decade ago, of *serekh* signs incised on pottery storage jars of the proto- and early dynastic periods (Kaiser & Dreyer 1982, 260ff.), this writer has collected data on many more examples raising the total number in the known corpus from 52 to 110.[1] Therefore, we take this opportunity to discuss them as a complement to our initial survey of 'Thinite' potmarks (cf. van den Brink 1992b, 267).

Offered here is the first part of a revised, chronological arrangement of the incised *serekh* signs which differs in various details from that suggested by Kaiser (op.cit., 262ff.), who arranged them into a chronological framework consisting of three consecutive 'horizons', ('Horizonte A,B and C'[2]). These were predicated on the recognition of a sequential development, in three distinctive stages, of cylindrical jars.[3]

Following a progression (accelerated during Naqada IIIa2; cf. Pumpenmeier 1993, 47, note 47) of cylindrical jars decorated with a continuous band ('umlaufendes Dekorband') of vestigial, wavy line or rope impression around the upper part, to jars lacking this decoration, Kaiser was able to demonstrate clear-cut chronological implications at the earlier (i.e. Horizon A) and later (i.e. Horizon C) extremes of the range of their appearance.[4] Between these extremes, however, remains an ill-defined area (i.e. Horizon B) which allows for interpretation,[5] dependent upon relative frequencies of decorated and plain types of cylindrical jars appearing together within tombs or cemeteries.

We do not question here the general validity of Kaiser's relative chronological Horizon schema - which in any case is of minor importance in his subdivision of Naqada Stufe III. We do question, however, his reliance on the sequential development of the cylindrical jars as a relative dating criterion for the various incised *serekh* signs.

There are also additional problems with Kaiser's proposed dating of these *serekhs*. He considered the typology of the *serekh* incised storage jars as of only secondary importance and therefore never treated this aspect in his own right, although he did deal with the various distinctive features of the jars in a general way (cf. Kaiser & Dreyer 1982, fig. 15; Kaiser 1964, fig. 1). Since these characteristics are of primary importance in the dating of the *serekhs* themselves, it is to a discussion of these aspects, in detail (see below), that we must turn. Following that discussion, based on a typological presentation of the complete preserved storage jars incised with *serekh* signs,[6] we will compare our findings with those of Kaiser's Horizons A-C, and conclude with a brief summary of our views on the chronology of these jars. At the end of this paper the reader will find an appendix, tabulating additional contextual data concerning each of the jars at issue.

The typology of pottery storage jars incised with *serekh* signs (Pls. 24-32, Figs. 1-3, Table 1)

To date 24 complete vessels, incised prior to firing, with various kinds of *serekh* signs have been found. These vessels make up a corpus which is listed here with each vessel given an identifying number (nos. 1-24) used as a reference throughout this paper:

1. ABUSIR EL-MELEQ T. 1021 (Berlin 19330)[7]   Pl. 24a, Fig.1,3 (Scharff 1926, 20, <u>zu</u> nr. 28; 35, 162-163); height: ca. 46,2cm

2. ABUSIR EL-MELEQ T. 1144 (Berlin 19331)   Fig. 1,1 (Scharff 1926, 20, nr. 28; 35; 162-163[8], pl.11, no. 28); height: ca. 49,5cm

3. 'RAFIAH' (Israel Museum 69.31.367)	Pl. 24b-c; Fig. 1,2 (Amiran 1970, 88, pl.1[9]; 1974); height: ca. 58cm
4. 'RAFIAH'	Fig. 1,4 (Gophna 1970, 54[10]; cf. also Kaiser & Dreyer, op. cit. 269); height: ca.56cm
5. EL-BEDA (Ismailia Mus. no.1928)	Pl. 25a, Fig. 1,5 (Cledat 1914[11], pl. 13; cf. also Weill 1961, 293-294); height: ca.58cm
6. TURAH SS (Ezbet Lüthy)	for *serekh*, see Table 1, no. 6 (Junker 1912, 47[12], fig. 57: 5); height: —
7. TURAH T. 16.g.9 (KHM.Wien ÄS.6808)	Pl. 25b-d, Fig. 1,6 (Junker 1912, 46ff[13], 63) height:—
8. TURAH T. 19.g.1	(for *serekh*, see Table 1, no.8) (Junker 1912, 46ff., 63); (height:—)
9. TARKHAN T. 1702 (U.C. 16084)	Pl. 26a, Fig. 2,7 (Petrie 1914, 10[14], pls. 6, 1702 and 30, 74b); height: ca. 60cm
10.TARKHAN T. 1100	Fig. 2,8 (Petrie 1914, 10, pls. 6, 1100; 30, 74g); height: ca. 52,2cm
11. MAO T. 1210.21	Pl. 26b, Fig. 2,9 (Kroeper 1988, fig. 94) height: ca.55,5cm
12. MAO T. 520. 3	Pl. 27a-b, Fig. 2,10 (Kroeper 1988, fig. 140); height: ca.50cm
13. MAO T. 160.1	Pl. 28a-b, Fig. 2,11 (Wildung 1982, fig. 32; Kroeper 1988, fig. 95); height: ca. 61cm
14. ABYDOS, T. B 1	Fig. 3,19 (Petrie 1900, pl. 40, 8); height: ca. 84cm
15. HELWAN T. 1627 H. 2	Fig. 3,16 (Saad 1947, pl. LX [left] and fig. 11); height: ca.57cm
16. HELWAN T. 1651 H. 2	Fig. 3,17 (Saad 1947, pl. LX [right] and fig. 12); height: ca. 61cm
16a. ABYDOS, T. B 7/9	Pl. 29a, Fig. 2,15a (Kaiser & Dreyer op. cit., pl. 58, d); (M110; fragment)
16b. ABYDOS, T. B 19	Pl. 29b, Fig. 2,15b[15] (M118; fragment)
17. MMA 61.122	Pl. 30a, Fig. 2,13 (Fischer 1963, pl. 6a[16]); height: ca. 68,5cm
18. TURAH T. 15. g. 2 (KHM Wien ÄS 6805)	Fig. 2,14a (Junker 1912, pp. 32, 63; fig. 57, Marke 1 [17]); height:—
19. TURAH T. 17.l.7.a	Fig. 2,14b (Junker 1912, pp. 32, 74[18]; fig. 57, Marke 2); height:—
20. MAO T. 44. 3	Pl. 30b-c, Fig. 2,12 (Wildung 1982, fig. 33; Kroeper 1988, fig. 141); height: ca. 57cm
21. EZBET EL-TELL (reg. no. 182)	Fig. 3,18 (Leclant & Clerc 1986, 244, 17, Pl. XI, 7[19]); Bakr 1988, 52, pl. 1a); height:—
22. ABYDOS T. B 1 (U.C. 16089)	Pl. 31a-b, Fig. 3,20 (Petrie 1900, 4) (height: ca.99cm)
23. TARKHAN T. 414 (U.C. 16083)	Pl. 32a-b, Fig. 3,21) (Petrie et al. 1913, 9[20], pl. XXXI, 68; pl. LVI, 76b); height: ca. 97cm
24. ABU ROASH T. 402	for *serekh*, see Table 1, no. 24 (Klasens 1959, 41); height: ca. 86,5cm[21]

The majority of these jars derive from burial contexts in Lower Egypt and chance finds in North Sinai[22]. It was possible, using characteristics such as the presence or absence of certain types of rudimentary handles or details concerning the mouths or rims of vessels, to place these jars into four different categories, each with chronological significance (see Table 1 for an overview of the distribution of the incised *serekh* signs according to these groups). Their chronological ordering will be discussed below.

Type I: Elongated jars with <u>pushed-up,</u> vestigial, wavy handles and simple, rolled rim (nos. 1-3; Figs 1, 1-3; Pls. 24a-c)

This type of jar is distinguished by its simple, rolled rim and its short but well articulated neck. In common with jars of Type II (see below), it has a 'scalloped design on the shoulder, consisting of a series of curved ridges made by the thumb' (Amiran 1970, 90). The Abusir el-Meleq jar Tomb 1021 (here no. 1) forms in this respect an exception: the discontinuous handles of this jar consist of short, thumb-impressed, bands <u>applied</u> to the shoulder of the jar (cf. pl. 24a, fig.1,3).

The few *serekh* bearing jars of Type I have often been compared with, and considered to be parallels

Table 1: Overview of the distribution of *serekh* signs according to jar typology

TYPES	ABUSIR EL-MELEQ	'RAFIAH'	EL-BEDA	TURAH	TARKHAN	EASTERN NILE DELTA	MINSHAT ABU OMAR	HELWAN	ABYDOS	EZ. EL-TELL	ABU ROASH
I	1, 2	3									
IIa		4	5	6							
IIb				7, 8	9, 10						
III				18, 19		17	11, 12, 13, 20	15, 16	16a, 16b, 14	21	
IVa					23				22		

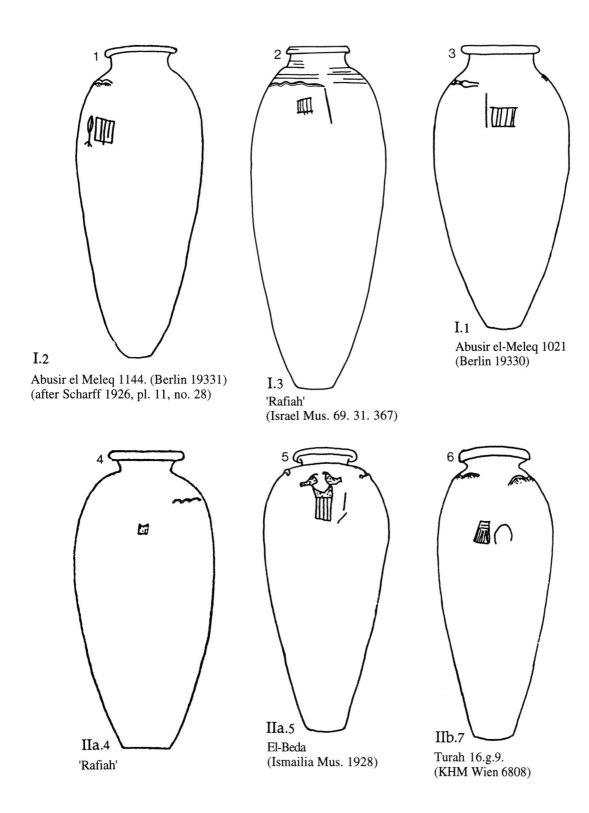

I.2

Abusir el Meleq 1144. (Berlin 19331)
(after Scharff 1926, pl. 11, no. 28)

I.3
'Rafiah'
(Israel Mus. 69. 31. 367)

I.1
Abusir el-Meleq 1021
(Berlin 19330)

IIa.4
'Rafiah'

IIa.5
El-Beda
(Ismailia Mus. 1928)

IIb.7
Turah 16.g.9.
(KHM Wien 6808)

NB The numbers at the bottom of each jar give the vessel Type (Roman numerals)
followed by the individual jar reference number used throughout this paper

Figure 1

of the *serekh* bearing el-Beda jar, belonging to Type II (cf. below, no. 5, pl. 25a, fig. 1,5). Type II jars, however, have a pronounced and flaring rim which is also found in Type III jars, although the last completely lack a neck (cf. for instance no. 11, pl. 26b, fig. 2,9). Thus, although each type has its particular constellation of characteristics, individual traits are often shared between them.

With the height varying between ca. 46,2 cm and 58 cm, these jars are the smallest of the four types discussed here. The *serekhs* of this group are – as can be expected on chronological grounds (see below, Chronological considerations)[23] – anonymous, lacking separate 'name compartments' and all are accompanied with an additional sign c.q. potmark (twice applied to the left [nos. 1 and 2], once applied to the right of the *serekh* [no. 3]).

Type II:
This type is made up of two sub-types which have minor decorative variations.

Type IIa:
Elongated jars with *two*, <u>pushed-up</u>, vestigial, wavy handles, short neck and flaring rim (nos. 4-6; Figs. 1,4-1,5; Pl. 25a)

Type IIb:
Elongated jars with *four*, <u>pushed-up</u>, vestigial, wavy handles, short neck and flaring rim (nos. 7-10; Figs. 1,6; 2,7-8; Pls. 25b-d; 26a)

The main characteristics of these jars are the handles which consist of either two or four discontinuous bands of three, low-relief, pushed-up scallops at regular intervals around the shoulder. They are described by Kaiser (op. cit., 264) as 'grosse Weinkrüge mit zwei und vierfachen Wellendekor'[24] – a description so general, that it is applied by him as a common denominator for jars pertaining to our Types I and III as well. They coincide with Junker's Turah Types Ia and I, respectively (Junker 1912, 31ff.[25]), and are equated by Petrie et al. (1913, pl. 68) to his Type 75s (ibid. pl. 55).

Seven *serekh* bearing vessels can be attributed to this group. Their lengths vary only from 52,2 to 60 cm, indicating the standardization of this type. They all derive from Lower Egypt or Northern Sinai. The type group includes at least four, or possibly five different rulers (cf. Table 1), viz. 'Double Falcon' (2x) *Nj-Ḥr* (2x), *Ḥ3.t-Ḥr* (1x), unidentified (1x; here no. 10, fig. 2,8; read by Kaiser as Narmer; see below, Comparison with Kaiser's Horizons A-C) and a sixth 'anonymous' *serekh*. With the exception of the last example (no. 4, fig. 1,4), all the *serekhs* are accompanied by an additional sign or potmark, three of which are applied to the right of the *serekh* (nos. 4, 7 and 8) and two of which appear on the left (nos. 6 and 9), while one (no. 10) is incised below the *serekh*.

Type III: Tall, elongated jars with flaring rim and <u>impressed</u>, crescentic decoration on the shoulder (nos. 11-21; Figs. 2,9-2,15; 3,16-3,21; Pls. 26b-30c)

The three most characteristic features of this type are the very pronounced and flaring rim, the virtual absence of a neck and the <u>impressed</u>, crescent-shaped marks on the shoulders of the jars. The crescentic marks (e.g. pls. 27a-b, 29a-b, 30b) can be contrasted with the <u>pushed-up</u> scallops of Types I (e.g. pl. 24c) and II (e.g. pls. 25a, 26a), of which they are considered to be degenerate, and therefore slightly later, forms.

This type coincides with Junker's Turah Type II (1912, p. 32[26], fig. 37, TII), and with Petrie's 74j (Petrie et al. 1913, pl. 54). Although this type was subdivided by Junker on the basis of the presence of either two (his Type II) or four (his Type IIa) 'Wellenlinien', we have refrained from any subdivision of this group on that particular basis, because 'These crescent-shaped impressions usually appear in three groups of these crescent shapes. In a few cases a scallop pattern runs continuously around the shoulder; exceptionally 1x4 plus 1x3 plus 1x2 arrangements occur on the same vessel. The execution of the pattern shows a great variety so that almost no two are exactly alike' (Kroeper 1986/7, figs. 60-69).

Eleven complete, *serekh*-bearing storage jars and two fragments, distinctive enough to be identi-

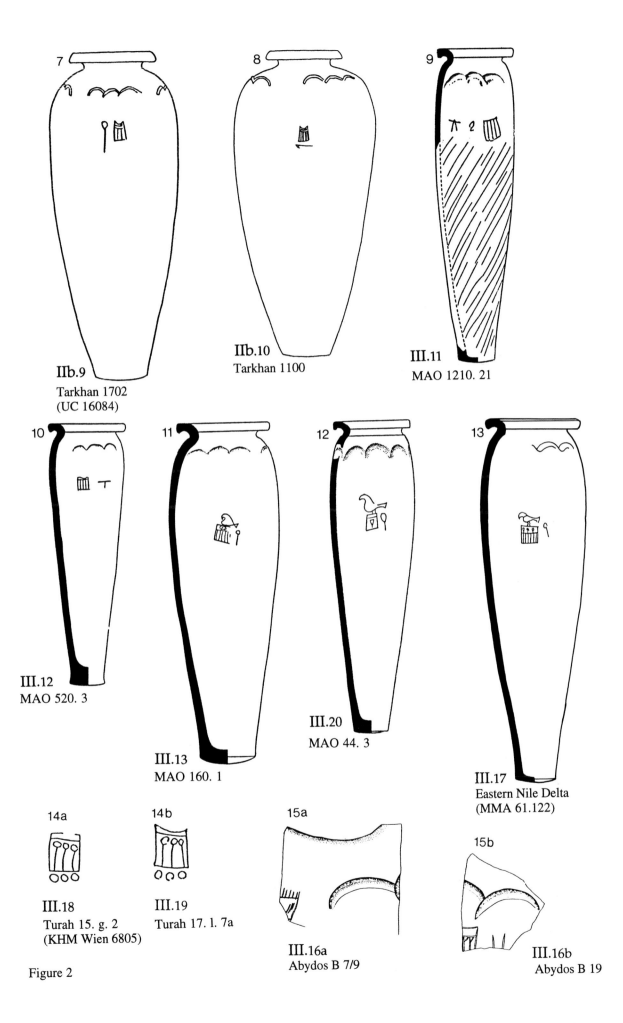

7

IIb.9
Tarkhan 1702
(UC 16084)

8

IIb.10
Tarkhan 1100

9

III.11
MAO 1210. 21

10

III.12
MAO 520. 3

11

III.13
MAO 160. 1

12

III.20
MAO 44. 3

13

III.17
Eastern Nile Delta
(MMA 61.122)

14a

III.18
Turah 15. g. 2
(KHM Wien 6805)

14b

III.19
Turah 17. 1. 7a

15a

III.16a
Abydos B 7/9

15b

III.16b
Abydos B 19

Figure 2

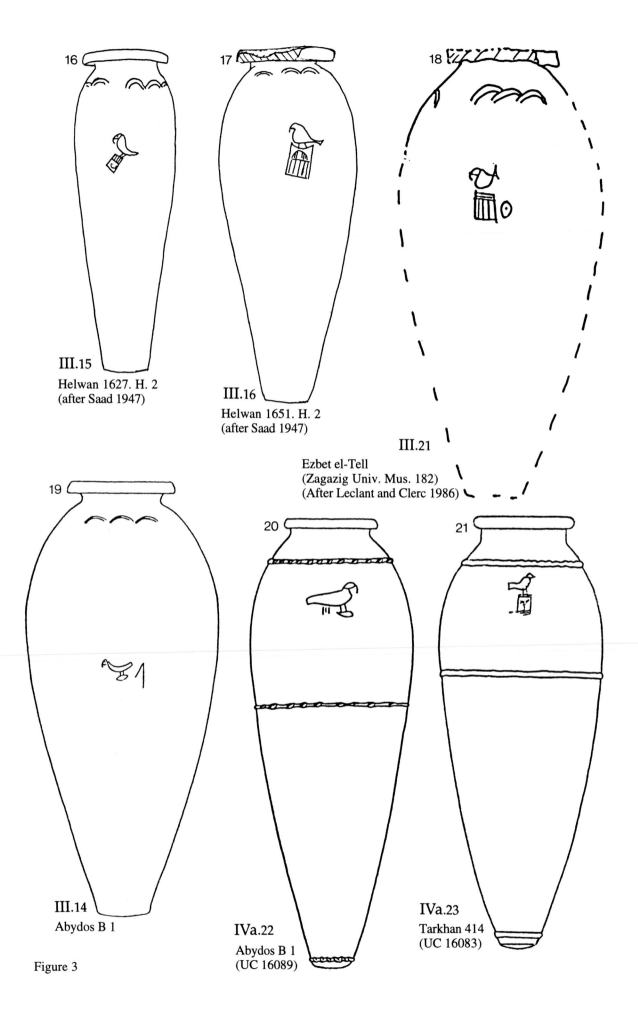

III.15
Helwan 1627. H. 2
(after Saad 1947)

III.16
Helwan 1651. H. 2
(after Saad 1947)

III.21
Ezbet el-Tell
(Zagazig Univ. Mus. 182)
(After Leclant and Clerc 1986)

III.14
Abydos B 1

IVa.22
Abydos B 1
(UC 16089)

IVa.23
Tarkhan 414
(UC 16083)

Figure 3

fied as parts of similar vessels, also bearing *serekhs* have been found to date; Nos. 11-13 and 15-20 all derive from Lower Egyptian contexts, while nos. 14, 16a and 16b derive from Abydos, Cemetery B, in Upper Egypt.

The height of the vessels belonging to this group, with the exception of the two outsized examples from Abydos (Tomb B1; ca. 84 cm) and Ezbet el-Tell (reg. no. 182; see above nos. 14 and 21)[27] varies between ca. 50 - 68,5 cm.

Additional observations on the details of the *serekhs* on vessels of this particular type strengthen the coherency of this group. In all cases where a *serekh* is surmounted by a falcon on Type III jars, the bird is facing left (cf. Table 1), an apparent convention which may have been less faithfully adhered to from the reign of 'Iry-Hor' onwards, although this is not sure: Falcons facing both to the left and right bearing this king's name are known. The majority of them are facing to the right (one preserved on a Type IVa jar [see below, no. 22]; seven preserved on fragments[28] too small to be of typological value). In two cases they are facing to the left[29] (one preserved on a Type III jar [no. 14]; the other preserved on a fragment too small to be of typological value). We could perhaps assume that the seven fragments with falcons facing to the right originally appeared on jars belonging to Type IVa (as does the only complete preserved example on a Type IVa jar), whereas the one fragment with falcon facing to the left would have originally appeared on a Type III jar. If so, then this phenomenon can be explained not as an abandonment of a certain convention, but as the introduction of a new type of jar (Type IVa) during the reign of 'Iry-Hor'. This might eventually be verified in the future with additional finds of complete jars incised with the name of 'Iry-Hor'.

The two examples preserved on complete jars where a falcon surmounts the *serekh* of 'Horus Ka' (nos. 15-16; cf. also Table 1), adhere to the pre-'Iry-Hor'-Type IVa principle: as all the other falcons incised on Type III jars they are facing to the left. Thus far *serekh* signs of 'Horus Ka' have not been found incised on a Type IVa jar, although theoretically they could occur on them, provided that the generally accepted, relative position of Horus 'Ka' within Dynasty 0, succeeding 'Iry-Hor', is correct.

It is of interest to note that even the examples attributed to 'Horus Narmer' still seem to conform to this convention. The falcon appearing above Narmer's *serekh* incised on a Type III jar (see above, no. 20; fig. 2,12, pl. 30b-c) faces to the left, whereas the one appearing on a Type IVa jar (see below, no. 23; fig. 3,21, pl. 32a-b) faces to the right. On the same grounds it could, perhaps, be argued that the 'Narmer' *serekh* fragment found at Tel Arad (Amiran 1974), surmounted by a falcon facing to the right, had been incised on a Type IVa jar. This conclusion was reached along a totally different line of reasoning, long before by Amiran (1976), and is confirmed by the considerable diameter of the jar. The *serekh* fragment found in Zawayit el-Ariyan, with a falcon facing left[30], perhaps appeared on a Type III jar.

Further corroborative evidence for the validity of this typology is found in certain signs accompanying *serekhs*. With a unique exception where a *ḥḏ*-like sign appears to the left of the *serekh* on an (earlier) jar of Type IIb from Tarkhan Tomb 1702 (see above, no. 9; pl. 26a, fig. 2,7), these *ḥḏ* signs always appear to the right of the *serekh*, restricted, furthermore, to Type III jars only (cf. Table 1).

The group as a whole contains at least five, and possibly six different names of rulers, three of which ('Iry-Hor', 'Horus Ka' and 'Horus Narmer') whose tombs have been identified in Cemetery B, at Umm el-Qaab (Abydos). Two *serekhs* belong to two different, yet unidentified, rulers (nos. 13 and 17-19) whose origin ought perhaps to be sought for in Lower Egypt.

As for the reading of the *serekh* sign on jar no. 13, attributed with great incertitude to 'Horus Scorpion'[31], we have suggested elsewhere a reading of 'Horus (Crocodile) the Subduer' (van den Brink, forthcoming).

Based on a certain similarity of *serekh* signs of nos. 17-19, with M8 of Gardiner's (1969) sign list, we suggest that there may be a connection between the ruler indicated by these three *serekhs* and the captive prisoner, surmounted by a falcon which holds him by a rope attached to the nose (see recto of the Narmer palette; cf. Asselberghs 1961, pl. 94; for the reading of this 'composite' sign, cf. Fairservis 1991, 10-11; cf. also Helck 1987, 98, who proposes to read the captive's name as w'š [?]).

Type IV
This type is made up of four sub-types which have minor decorative variations.

Type IVa: Tall jars with three, applied, continuous bands of rope decoration around the shoulder, waist and the base (nos. 22-24; Figs. 3,20-3,21, Pls. 31-32)

The most characteristic feature of this type of tall jar with tapering body is a rope decoration applied in three continuous bands around the body of the jar[32] at the shoulder, waist and the base. Described by Kaiser (op. cit., 264) as 'grosse Weinkrüge mit dreifachen Schnurdekor' this type coincides with Junker's Turah Type VIII (Junker 1912, 33[33]), and Petrie's 76b (Petrie et al. 1913, pl. 68). Sizes of the vessels vary between ca. 86,5 cm. to 99 cm.

Only three examples of this type of jar are known to bear incised *serekh* signs.[34] These are the latest attested cases. One belongs to 'Iry-Hor' (no. 22), one to 'Horus Narmer' (no. 23) and one remains anonymous (no. 24). This last, on the basis of an ink inscription on a cylindrical jar found in the same tomb, has been attributed to 'Horus Aha' (Klasens 1959, 41).

Types IV b-d: Tall jars with three[35], two, one or no continuous, plain band(s) applied around the tapering body

They coincide with Junker's Turah Types IX-XI (Junker 1912, 33[36]), and Petrie's 76d, 76l and 75m (Petrie et al. 1913, pl. 68) respectively. These types do not bear incised *serekhs* in the strict sense[37] and are, therefore, beyond the scope of this paper.

Comparison with Kaiser's Horizons A-C division

Of the 52 *serekhs* collected by Kaiser (op. cit., figs. 14-16), 20 are on complete vessels, while the remaining 32 are preserved on fragments too small to be indicative of any particular pottery type and are therefore are not germane to the discussion here (cf. above, note 6). The typology of these complete jars was considered as only of secondary importance by Kaiser, and was never treated in its own right, although various, distinctive features of the jars at issue were noted by him in a general manner.[38] The way he presented the incised *serekh* signs in his 1982 publication, <u>visually</u> divorced from the actual jars on which they were incised, further hampers the reader's possibility of checking his schema, because of the lack of this primary data.

The following tables, two and three, give an overview of Kaiser's distribution of the complete vessels in Horizons A-C, as compared to our own typological division[39] into four distinct types:

Table 2: Distribution of the various incised *serekh* signs over Horizons A-C in comparison to the four jar types on which they appear.

Horiz. A	Type		Horiz. B	Type		Horiz. C	Type	
2*	IIa	(5)***	19	IVa	(22)	48	IVa	(24)
4	IIa	(6)	21	III	(14)			
6	IIb	(9)	23	III	(16)			
7	IIb	(8)	24	III	(15)			
8	IIb	(7)	34	III	(13)			
9	I	(1)	35	IVa	(23)			
10	I	(2)	38	III	(20)			
—40	III	(17)	39	IIb	(10)			
11	III	(18)	44	III	(19)			
16,1*	IIa	(4)						
16,2**	I	(3)						

*   Unless stated otherwise, all arabic numbers in this table refer to Kaiser & Dreyer 1982, Fig. 14. Latin numbers refer to Types I-IV.

**   This number refers to Kaiser & Dreyer 1982, fig. 16, nos. 1-2.

*** Numbers in brackets are the identifying numbers (1-24), used throughout this paper, in reference to the jars at issue.

148

Table 3: Total numbers of Horizons A-C incised *serekh* signs according to jar types

Group	I	IIa-b	III	IVa
Horizon A	3	6	2	
Horizon B		1	6	2
Horizon C				1

It can be concluded from Table 3 that:

1) <u>Different</u> types of jars are attributed by Kaiser to <u>one</u> and the <u>same</u> horizon. Jars of Types I, II and III are attributed to Horizon A, while jars of Types II, III, and IVa are assigned to Horizon B.

Discussion:
Based on relevant data, for example from the Turah cemetery and the B-cemetery, Umm el-Qaab, at Abydos (see below), it is clear that the division into four types presented here does not represent a simple, linear cum- chronological sequence. Rather the types overlap at some points. Jars belonging to different types (with the exception of Type I jars), viz. Types II, III and IVa, have been found together in one and the same tomb in the following instances:

a) Turah Tomb 19. g. 1: Junker's (1912, 65) Type I (our Type IIb, no. 8) found together with his Type IIa (our Type III) and his Type LXIV (cylindrical jar with continuous rope decoration).
b) Turah Tomb 16. i. 3: Junker's (1912, 69) Type I (our Type II) found together with his Type VIII (our Type IVa) and Types LIV-LV and CX.
c) Abydos, Tomb B 1: (Petrie 1900; pls. 39, 2 and 40, 8); Petrie's (1953) Type 75q (here attributed to Type III) found together with the latter's Type 76a (our Type IVa).

From this one has to conclude that Kaiser's attribution of different types of jars, incised with *serekh* signs, to one and the same Horizon is, in general, acceptable.

2) Jars of the <u>same</u> type, in one case with identical *serekh* signs, are found within <u>different</u> Horizons. Type II jars are assigned to Horizons A and B, while jars of Type III, and jars of Type IVa, are each assigned to Horizons B and C.

Discussion:
The assignment of identical jars to different Horizons is less than convincing. Kaiser places the jar incised with a *serekh*, from Tarkhan Tomb 1100 (cf. above, no. 10), in the latter part of Horizon B. Although not explicitly stated, this is probably because of the location of the tomb, within the Tarkhan cemetery and/or, his reading of this particular *serekh* (Kaiser & Dreyer op. cit., fig. 14, no. 39) as belonging to 'Horus Narmer'.

However, this jar belongs to our Type II which makes up Kaiser's Horizon A. It is thus separated by at least four rulers[41] from the earliest, identified 'Horus Narmer' examples, appearing on jars belonging to Type III (which makes up his Horizon B). This seems to exclude[42] the possibility of attributing this particular vessel to 'Narmer'. Therefore, another reading of the name contained within this *serekh*, should be looked for.

A second example wherein Kaiser's schema fails to convince us, concerns his attribution of two identical *serekhs*, found on identical jars (Junker 1912, 46)[43], in the same cemetery, to two separate Horizons (Kaiser & Dreyer op. cit., fig. 14, nos. 11 of Horizon A[44] and 44 of Horizons B or C[45]; here nos. 18 and 19, respectively). Although again the reason for this is not stated by Kaiser, we assume that this division is based on an evaluation of the spatial distribution of the two tombs within the cemetery of Turah.[46] Moreover, his recent attribution (Kaiser 1990, 288, note 5) to Horizon A of a third, identi-

149

cal Type III jar with a *serekh* (MMA 61.122; here no. 17), clearly related to the two Turah *serekhs* mentioned above (nos. 18-19), seems incorrect. The type of jar on which all three *serekhs* appear is not the same as those ascribed by him to his Horizon A (dominated by Type II jars) but is in fact our Type III (which dominates Kaiser's Horizon B) and, therefore, should be placed, typologically, within Horizon B.

3) No typological distinctions seem to have been made by Kaiser between jars of groups I and II, all of which (with one exception, viz. the jar found in Tarkhan Tomb 1100 [here no. 10], attributed to Horizon B) are attributed to Horizon A.

Discussion:
We will argue below (Chronological considerations) that Type I jars are slightly earlier (i.e. Naqada IIIa2/b1) than the other jars attributed by Kaiser to Horizon A (Naqada IIIb1-2), and should therefore be separated from them.

If the conclusions under 1-3) of the discussion are accepted, we could correct Table 3 accordingly:

Table 4: A suggestion for correcting Kaiser's attribution of total numbers of *serekh* signs according to our typology

Group	I	IIa-b	III	IVa
(Naqada IIIa2/b1)	3			
Horizon A		8		
Horizon B			7	2
Horizon C				1

This would further strengthen the following observations:

4) Horizon A is made up by jars of Type II
5) Horizon B is made up by jars of Type III

The chronology of the jars incised with *serekh* signs (cf. Table 5)

A detailed discussion of the internal chronology of the four jar types will have to wait until after the presentation and contextual analysis - in Part II (van den Brink, in preparation) - of the remaining *serekh* signs, preserved on jar <u>fragments</u>. Therefore, we will confine ourselves here, to some general observations concerning the chronology of the four types.

Type I
This type, not found in the Turah cemeteries, is, however, present in the cemetery at Abusir el-Meleq and represents the earliest examples, on which *serekh* signs have been <u>incised</u>. Typologically they are related to Petrie's (1953, pl. 8) 44c and 44f, examples of which (without *serekh* signs) have been found in e.g. Tarkhan Tombs 315 (SD77) and 38 (SD78). Like Tomb 1021 at Abusir el-Meleq, which yielded a *serekh* incised example of Type I (no. 1), these two tombs contained, 'Arkadenzylinder' without net-painting, which are type-dated to Naqada IIIa2-b1 (Pumpenmeier 1993, 49; cf. also Table 5).
The early chronological position of Type I seems also confirmed by the *serekhs* found on them. They are all anonymous and conform to the earliest, and equally anonymous *serekh*-signs found to date, inscribed in <u>ink</u> on <u>cylindrical</u> jars, deriving from near contemporary contexts in Tombs U-s

Table 5 Contextual, typo-chronological overview of jar types I-IV

Brink Type	Junker Type	Petrie Type	Emery Type	Kaiser Horiz.	Turah Cem.	MAO grave group	cylindr. jars	Naqada Stufe	Cem. U	incised serekhs (complete jars)	
										(only anonymous, ink inscribed serekhs)	
							W50/51	IIIa2	U/j[1], U/k		
											ca. 3200 BC
							mit umlauf. Dekorb.				
											ca. 3150 BC
I	---	(44c,f)	---	A	---	---	" " esp. Arkadenzyl. Netzzylinder	IIIa2-b1	U/s(119),U/i[2] U/f, g, h[3]	1-3:	anonymous
											ca. 3100 BC
IIa-b	Ia, I	75s	---	A	S	---	W71-85[4]	IIIb1(/2)	U/t,y[5]	4:	anonymous
										5-6:	'Double Falcon'
										7-8:	Nj̓-Hr
										9:	Ḥ3.t-Ḥr
										10:	unidentified (prev. 'Narmer')
III	II, IIa	74j		B	S	3 b-c	mit/ohne Zierring	IIIb2-c1		11-12:	anonymous
										13:	'Horus Crocodile' (?)
										14:	'Iry-Hor'
										15-16:	'Horus Ka'
										17-19:	unidentified (W'š?)
										20-21(?)	'Horus Narmer'
											ca. 3000 BC
IVa	VIII	76a-b	A6	C	S	4	mit/ohne Zierring[6]	IIIb2-c2		22:	'Irj-Hor'
										23:	'Horus Narmer'
										24:	anonymous (reign of 'Aha')
											ca. 2900 BC
IVb	IX	76d	A7a-b	C	N	4	ohne Zierring	IIIc2		(in Saqqara: Djer-Djet[7])	
IVc	X	76l-m	A8	-	N	4	....[8]	IIIc2-3		(in Saqqara: Djer/Djet - Qa-a)	
IVd	XI	75n-o	A3	-	N	4		IIIc2-3		(in Saqqara: Djer-Adjib)	

---

1   'Mit dem Grab U/j erreicht die Zylindergefässentwickelung die Stufe des umlaufenden Dekorbandes, das aus einem flachen mit dem Finger vertikal oder schräg flache Dellen gedrückt oder geschoben sind.' (Pumpenmeier 1993, 47).

2   'U/i (.....) nur noch Zylinder mit umlaufenden Dekorband aktuell (.....), und letzteres zeigt in vielen Fällen keine Fingerdellen, sondern eine Folge gratig-linearer Arkaden' (Pumpenmeier 1993, 47).

3   'in der Gruppe U-f, g, h (...), wo auch die Reihe der mit einem Netzmuster bemalter Zylindergefässes deutlich einsetzt.' (Pumpenmeier 1993,48).

4   '(.....) Zylindergefässen und Fragmente mit linearem Dekorband (W71-85) sicher in die Stufe IIIb.' (Pumpenmeier 1993, 49).

5   'im Bereich von U-t hat sich die letzt genannte Gruppe von Zylindern [Netzzylinder] zu den 'klassischen' späten Zylindern entwickelt (.....). Die Dekorbänder sind sehr schmal, zumeist eine Reihe von mit dem Fingernagel oder einem Stöckchen hochgeschobenen Bögen, Kordelimpressionen oder eine blosse geritzte Linie.' (Pumpenmeier 1993, 48).

6   '(.....) wobei letztere an Zahl stetig zunehmen (.....).' (Kaiser & Dreyer 1982, 264).

7   cf. Hendrickx in this volume, Table 7.

8   'Der nächste, hier nicht mehr interessierende Einschnitt in der Entwicklung der Zylindergefässe (.....) liegt bei Udimu' (Kaiser & Dreyer 1982, 264, note 195a). A strong reduction in size of the plain cylindrical jars is apparent, cf. Petrie 1953, 50t.

(Naqada IIIa2/b1; Dreyer 1990, 59, figs. 3a-b) and U-t ost/1 (Naqada IIIb1; Pumpenmeier 1993, 46, fig. 9) in cemetery U, Umm el-Qaab, at Abydos.

Another jar, related to Type I, without a *serekh*, was recently found in cemetery U at Abydos, in Tomb U-i süd/1 dated to the Naqada Stufe IIIa2, although later than the by now well-known tomb U-j (Pumpenmeier 1993, 49[47]).

Another Type I related jar, identical to those discussed above, but again without incised *serekh*, was found in Hierakonpolis Tomb 11 which on the basis of accompanying finds[48] can also be dated to Naqada IIIa2. Concerning these particular, Type I related '(.....) thin walled, tall, late forms of wavy handled jars (Proto Corpus 44f), which have a sandy body coated with a vertically burnished, cream slip' (Friedman and Adams 1992, 331; fig. 13 a-b), the writers mention that 'E. Oren reported finding jars of a very similar ware in his north Sinai survey and in his opinion they were locally made there, but of hybrid Egyptian/Canaanite manufacture' (Friedman and Adams, op. cit.). This last observation can now be corroborated by the recent find of an anonymous *serekh*, preserved on the upper part of a related, locally made, storage jar of Egyptianised style from Palmahim Quarry, stratum 2 in central Israel, found in an Early Bronze Ib context (cf. Braun et al., in preparation).

Type IIa-b

Examples of Type I jars (absent at Turah) and Type II jars (present in the S cemetery of Turah) have, to our knowledge, not be found together in a single context and a direct synchronism between the two types, therefore, can not be established. The stylistic parallel between the incised Palmahim *serekh* fragment mentioned above (with punctured 'name compartment'), found on the one hand on a storage jar related to Type I, and the incised 'Double Falcon' *serekhs* found on Type II jars at el-Beda and Turah on the other hand, seems to indicate that both groups are chronologically close to each other.

Type III

The impressed, crescentic decoration, so typical for this type, is considered a further degeneration of the pushed-up, vestigial, wavy handles, typical on Types I and II and, therefore, should be at least slightly later. On the other hand, we have to recall the early (?) occurrence of a Type III jar together with a Type II jar in Turah, Tomb 19. g. 1 (no. 8, see above).

At Minshat Abu Omar, jars of this type derive from both grave groups 3b and 3c. The distinction between these two grave groups is based, not on a differentiation of the Type III jars (which are all quite similar), but on the presence in the former, and absence in the latter group, of *decorated* cylindrical jars. This observation seems to strengthen our opinion, already expressed above, that the cylindrical jar *per se* is not a good chronological marker with respect to the *serekh* incised storage jars at issue. Typologically identical jars, incised with *serekhs*, appear in graves with cylindrical jars of different (i.e. decorated and undecorated) types.

Other, Type III related jars, without *serekh* signs, have been found e.g. at Hierakonpolis Locality 29A (Friedman and Adams 1992, 327-8, note 8; fig. 8, c) and Tell el-Fara'in/Buto Schicht IV (Köhler 1992, 12, fig. 1).

Type IVa

This type of jar, in the Turah cemetery notably restricted to the earlier, viz. S- part, appears from the reign of 'Iry-Hor' until at least the reign of 'Horus Djet' (cf. Hendrickx, in this volume, Table 7). The latest jar incised with an (anonymous) *serekh* belonging to this group derives from Abu Roash, Tomb 402, which has been ascribed to 'Horus Aha'. Its dating is based on the accompanying find of a cylindrical jar with the *serekh* and name of 'Horus Aha' (cf. Klasens 1959, 4), written in ink on it.

Type IV b-d

In Turah these sub-types are found only in the later, viz. N- part of the cemetery. For the chronological range of these particular jars, cf. Hendrickx, op. cit., Table 7. Type IVc appears around the reigns of 'Horus Djet' / 'Horus Den'.[49]

Examples of Types IVb-d can appear together in a single tomb context, as for instance at Tell Ibrahim Awad, Area B, sq. 210/160, Tomb 1 (van den Brink 1988b, figs. 14-15; 1992c, 51). In this respect it is, perhaps, of interest to note that another, related type (Type IVe, Petrie's [1913, pl. 55] 75u-v), apparently absent in the Turah cemeteries, was found in the same tomb (van den Brink 1988b, fig. 14, nos. 64-65, 69).

Conclusions

We have tried to point out and to explain several inconsistencies in Kaiser's Horizon schema. Our observations refute his reliance on the sequential development of the morphology of, and the type of decoration employed on, cylindrical jars, as a criterion for the relative dating of *serekh* signs incised on tall, storage jars mostly dating from Dynasty 0. We have, instead, proposed a four-fold typology of the corpus of twenty-four complete jars under discussion. This offers a firmer basis for discussing the order and chronology of the rulers represented by the *serekhs*. Such an ordering is urgently needed because of recent discoveries, foremost in Cemetery U at Umm el-Qa'ab, Abydos. These indicate that the time limits for the protohistoric, Dynasty 0 period, have to be stretched more and more.

In terms of relative chronology the jars at issue cover the period from Naqada IIIa2/b1 to Naqada IIIc2, a time span of about 200 years (cf. Table 5). The recognition of Type I, as a separate group, predating the jars of notably Types II and III, and nearly contemporary with several tomb assemblages from Cemetery U at Umm el-Qaab, Abydos (cf. Table 5) is a major development of the present study. It is, of course, of special pertinence to what is coming to light concerning Egyptian-Canaanite inter-action, especially concerning jars of Type I.

The twenty-four *serekhs* include seven anonymous *serekhs*, two ascribed to 'Double Falcon', two to '*Nj-Ḥr*', one to '*Ḥ3.t-Ḥr*', two to 'Iry-Hor', two to 'Horus Ka'[50], four to two unidentified rulers, one to 'Horus (Crocodile) the Subduer' and three to 'Horus Narmer'. We have attempted to identify various *serekh* signs, and the rulers they represent, with other known records of the period, including the ceremonial slate palettes. Included are the *serekhs* with 'Double Falcon', nos. 5 and 6, associated with the so-called City palette and nos. 17-19 (W'š ?), associated with the Narmer palette. The *serekh* incised on jar no. 13 has been tentatively ascribed elsewhere (van den Brink, forthcoming) to 'Horus (Crocodile) the Subduer', a ruler recently identified by G. Dreyer (1992b). Further, we believe that there is a good chronological basis for refuting the reading of the *serekh* incised on jar no. 10 as 'Narmer', although we cannot offer an alternative reading.

Addendum

Karla Kroeper has kindly informed me about two unpublished storage jars, recently excavated in the Early Dynastic cemetery at Minshat Abu Omar and numbered MAO T. 1640.13 and MAO T.1800.7. They both have an incised *serekh* with empty name compartment. The *serekh* on MAO T.1800.7 has a curvilinear top; the other is straight. Both *serekhs* are surmounted by falcons, which, in the case of MAO T.1800.7 is facing left. On jar MAO T.1640.13, on the basis of the photographs kindly provided by Karla Kroeper, it is not clear to me in which direction to falcon is facing. It would appear that the latter *serekh* has been applied post-firing, and is, therefore, much less clear than all the others found in Minshat Abu Omar. Both jars belong to Type III, discussed above.

Acknowledgements

We owe a debt of gratitude to the following persons and institutions for providing us with photographs and drawings of relevant, and sometimes still unpublished, material and for giving permission to reproduce them here: B. Adams, Petrie Museum of Egyptian Archaeology, University College, London (pls. 26a, 31a-b, 32a-b); R. Amiran, the Israel Museum, Jerusalem (pl. 24b-c); D. Arnold, The Metropolitan Museum of Art, New York (pl. 30a); G. Dreyer, German Archaeological Institute, Cairo (pl. 29a-b); K. Kroeper and D. Wildung, Münchner Ostdelta Expedition (pl. 26b, 27a-b, 28a-b, 30b-c); H. Satzinger, Kunsthistorisches Museum, Wien (pl. 25b-d); D. Wildung, Staatliche Museen Preussischer Kulturbesitz, Ägyptisches Museum (pl. 24a).
Eliot Braun most kindly and patiently perused the typescript.

APPENDIX

Summary of contextual data concerning the jars according to types

Below we have listed the accompanying grave goods for each of the twenty-four jars according to types, as far as may be ascertained from publications.

Type I

1. ABUSIR EL-MELEQ T. 1144.   SCHARFF 1926, 162-163: <u>1 grosser Wellenhenkeltopf mit eingeritzter Marke</u>[51], 1 gewöhnlicher Wellenhenkeltopf[52], 1 Napf, 9 gewöhnliche Töpfe (z.T. sehr gross).

2. ABUSIR EL-MELEQ T.1021.   Scharff 1926, 150/151: 7 Wellenhenkeltöpfe (3 mit Netzmuster bemalt[53], <u>1 sehr gross und mit Marke</u>), 1 gewöhnlicher Topf.

3. 'RAFIAH'   —

Type IIa

4. 'RAFIAH'   —
5. EL-BEDA   —
6. TURAH SS (Ezb. Lüthy)   —

Type IIB

7. TURAH T. 16. g.2   Junker 1912: 64, no. 64   <u>1xI (75s)*</u>   1xXIIX(sic!)   3xLXIV(47p)[54] CIV (3f/16n) o.a.

8. TURAH T. 19. g. 1   Junker 1912: 65, no. 89   <u>1xI (75s)</u>   1xIIa (74j)   1xLXIV(47p)

9. TARKHAN T. 1702   Petrie 1914: pl. 40   pottery: 14y 491[55] 60r 70m <u>74g</u> slate: 57h, 86m + coffin

10. TARKHAN T. 1100   Petrie 1914, pl. 38   pottery: 491" 50de 60n <u>74b</u> 91n + coffin

Type III

11. MAO T. 1210. 21   Kroeper 1988, fig. 94: MAO grave group 3b; idem. 1989a, pl. 23, no. 1; idem. pers. comm.: 18x <u>III</u> (only one with *serekh*); 4 cylindrical jars, all with engraved 'Schnurornament'; 4 bowls; stone vessels; jewellery

12. MAO T. 520. 3   Kroeper 1988, fig. 140 : MAO grave group 3c; idem. pers. comm. 2x <u>III</u> (1 with, 1 without *serekh*); 3 plain cylindrical jars

13. MAO T. 160. 1   Kroeper 1988, fig. 95; MAO grave group 3b, i.e. with cylindrical jars with continuous rope decoration[56]; idem. pers. comm. 4x <u>III</u> (only one with *serekh*); 3 cylindrical jars (1 plain, 2 with engraved line decoration)

14. ABYDOS T. B 1   Petrie 1902; Kaiser & Dreyer 1982, 235-241

15. HELWAN T. 1627 H.2   —

16. HELWAN T. 1651 H.2   —

16a. ABYDOS T. B 7/9   Petrie 1902: Kaiser & Dreyer 1982, 235-241

16b. ABYDOS T.B 19   Petrie 1902; Kaiser & Dreyer 1982, 235-241

17. MMA 61. 122   —

18. TURAH T. 15. g. 2.   Junker 1912, 63, no. 54: 1xI/II (75s/74j) 1xII (74j) 3xLXV (48)[57]

19. TURAH T. 17. l. 7a   Junker 1912, 74, no. 313: 1xII (74j) Reste von LXVI (50d)[58] u.ä

20. MAO T. 44. 3   Kroeper 1988, fig. 141: MAO grave group 3c, i.e. with plain cylindrical jars[59]; idem pers. comm. 5x <u>III</u> (only one with *serekh*, the other four with somewhat wider shoulders; 5 plain cylindrical jars; palette; stone vessels; copper; jewellery

21. EZBET EL-TELL reg. no. 182 Bakr 1988, 52: Sq. C.IV-b.6

Type IVa

22. ABYDOS T. B1	Petrie 1902; Kaiser & Dreyer 1982, 235-241
23. TARKHAN T.414 (UC 16083)	Petrie et al. 1913, pl. 41. pottery: 3dg5 48s[60] 49l 50de 60d 70n 72g <u>76bc</u> stone vessels: 8e,o 5it(?) + copper chisel + seal impression
24. ABU ROASH T. 402 (Aha)	Klasens 1959, 41ff. pottery: 2x<u>A6</u> (76b) 7xF11 (plain cyl. jar) 1xH2 1xK3 1xL7 1xL10 1xR2 1xW12 1xY1 stone vessels: 1xB10 1xC11 1xT10 + rectangular slate palette

* Numbers in brackets refer to Petrie et al. (1913).

Some chronological observations can be made on the presence of cylindrical jars, which are so pivotal to Kaiser's Horizon-schema:

Jars of <u>Type I</u> are found with net-painted, cylindrical jars, one of which, according to a drawing published by Kaiser (1964, fig. 1 A.M. 1021) at least is an 'Arkadenzylinder'[61], together with an unpainted example with a continuous band of rope decoration.

Jars of <u>Type II</u> were often found with cylindrical jars with continuous bands of rope-decoration. A single, late type of the net-painted cylindrical jar is also present.

Most jars of <u>Type III</u> were found together with undecorated cylindrical jars, although decorated cylindrical jars (inferred from esp. Minshat Abu Omar grave group 3b-c materials) are known in the same contexts. The same observation is valid for jars of <u>Type IVa</u> ; both decorated and plain cylindrical jars appear with this type in the same tomb contexts.

Notes

1   The biggest increase is in incised *serekh* signs preserved on pottery fragments. To Kaiser's (op. cit.) initial corpus of 52 *serekh* signs, which included 20 *serekh* signs preserved on complete jars and 32 preserved on pottery fragments- only four additional complete jars with incised *serekhs* can be added, as opposed to 56 additional *serekh* signs preserved on pottery fragments. For two more complete jars see above, Addendum.

2   Henceforth Horizon(s) A-C. Hor. A: before 'Iry-Hor', Hor. B from 'Iry-Hor' until 'Horus Narmer', Hor. C from 'Horus Aha' onwards (Kaiser op.cit.); Note, however, the apparent changes made by Kaiser himself (1990, fig. 1): Horizon C no longer is referred to and, more significantly, Horizon A seems to extend, in the new schema, <u>into</u> the reign of 'Iry-Hor'.

3   '(.....) vor allem auf der Grundlage der Zylindergefässe, <u>eine Abfolge von drei deutlich getrennten</u> <u>Horizonten</u> zu erkennen (.....)' (Kaiser op. cit., 264).

4   'Horizont A: Zylindergefässe mit Zierring' (Kaiser & Dreyer, op. cit., 264) and 'Horizont C: Zylindergefässe ohne Zierring' (ibid.) respectively.

5   'Horizont B: Zylindergefässe mit und ohne Zierring nebeneinander, wobei letztere an Zahl stetig zunehmen' (Kaiser & Dreyer, op. cit., 264).

6   The by far more numerous group of *serekh* signs preserved on pottery fragments -a not insubstantial part of which derives from Early Bronze Ib contexts in southern Israel- will be treated in part II of this study (van den Brink, in preparation).

7   In this list 'T.' stands for Tomb.

8   Aus Grab 1144. H. 49, 5 cm. Grosses Vorratsgefäss aus mittelfeinen Ton, rot gestrichen (.....). Es hat 2 ganz kleine Wellenansätze auf der Schulter und am Bauch eine Topfmarke. (.....) Ähnlich: Berlin19330 (ebenfalls mit Topfmarke) und 19927.'

9   'Our jar (.....) characterized by an elongated body (.....) with a short neck (.....), a heavy rail rim and a small base (.....). Further characteristic is the hard brown-reddish texture and well-smoothed surface (.....)'; for the provenance of this jar cf. below, note 10.

10   'The jar, 56 cm. high, is of dark-brown fabric. Two wavy patterns representing degenerated ledge-handles are on its shoulder, while on its body is a graffito which was scratched on before the vessel was fired. The graffito represents a schematized Egyptian *serekh* sign.' Since then it was learned that this jar and the previous jar (no. 3) did not derive from Rafiah but from a site in Wadi el-Arish (Ram Gophna, pers. comm.).

11   'c'est la jarre au galbe pur, a forte panse, au col court et tropu, aux anses ondulées [anses tri-arquées] et modelées à la partie le plus renflée(.....).' The remaining three *serekh* signs from this site are preserved on mere

fragments and, therefore, are not germane to the discussion here. cf. Cledat (1914, 116) : '(.....) dans le lot se trouvait une vase entier [here no. 5], admirable de conservation, avec les *fragments* gravés de trois autres'.

12   'Fund aus 1903; Fruchtland der Ezbet Lüthy' [i.e. south of S-cemetery] (.....); Typ Ia mit Wellenlinien nur an zwei Seiten. 1. Lüthy mit Marke 5, erhöhte Wellenlinien'.

13   'Typ I (.....) 1) 16. g. 9 mit Zeichen 4. Erhöhte Wellenlinien. 2) 19.g.1 ebenso. - Also nur in *S* belegt.'

14   'Two large jars were found, of very fine clay, and beautifully made as to solidity, regularity, and smoothness. As both bore royal names (pl. VI, 2, 3) marked before baking, it seems that such jars were produced at the royal pottery (see forms in pl. XXX, 74 b.g.; and see copies in pl. XX, 1, 2).' Concerning the jar from Tarkhan Tomb 1702, B.Adams kindly informed us that the jar is made of Nile silt and that it shows traces of a cream slip on its exterior.

15   Unpublished fragment. With kind permission of G. Dreyer.

16   'Reddish buff ware, slip showing diagonal marks left by fingers in smoothing surface.'

17   'Typ II (.....) 1. 15. g. 2 mit Marke 1. Wellenlinien ringsum etwas erhöht'. Although registered in the Kunsthistorisches Museum Wien under inv. nr. ÄS 6805, its present whereabouts are unfortunately unknown (by kind communication of H. Satzinger).

18   '(.....) [Marke] 2. Grab 17. l. 7a. Typ II'.

19   At present it is kept in the Zagazig University Museum. According to the excavator it was found together with several other wine jars in a settlement context, away from the actual cemetery (M. I. Bakr, pers. comm.).

20   'This grave was one of the largest, and the most important historically as it contained the large jar of king Nar-mer (XXXI, 68), and the sealings with his name and the variant Nar-mer-tha (II, 1-4).'

21   Based on the measurement of Klasens's drawing of the type jar: A6.

22   The jars at issue derive from: Minshat Abu Omar (4 tombs), Turah (5 tombs), Tarkhan (3 tombs), Helwan (2 tombs), Abusir el-Meleq (2 tombs), Abydos (2 tombs), Abu Roash (1 tomb), Ezbet el-Tell (1 jar); from 'Rafiah' (2 jars), el-Beda (1 jar), and Fischer's MMA jar the exact context is unknown.

23   The earliest *serekh* signs found to date (NB. ink inscribed on cylindrical jars), in Cemetery U at Abydos, viz. tombs U-s (Naqada IIIa2/b1; Dreyer et al. 1990, 59, figs. 3a-b) and U-t ost/1 (Naqada IIIb; Pumpenmeier 1993, fig. 9, U-t ost/1) - which are near contemporary to those incised on jars of Type I- are 'anonymous'.

24   Perhaps better to read 'Wellenansätze'? (after Scharff 1926; cf. above, note 8).

25   'Typ I: Feiner Ton, bis kurz unter die Wellenlinien leicht poliert; gedrungenes Format mit ziemlich breiter Basis. Wellenlinien an den vier Seiten. Typ Ia mit Wellenlinien nur an zwei Seiten.'

26   'Typ II. Material wie Typ I [cf. above, note 25], langes Format mit sehr breitem Rand, wiederum nur bis zum oberem Teil -unterhalb der Wellenlinien- poliert (.....). Typ IIa. Wellenlinien nur an zwei Seiten (.....). Auch Typ II ist nur in *S* vertreten.'

27   These two vessels share the impressed, crescentic decoration on the shoulder as well as the type of rim with the other vessels belonging to this type group; because of their outstanding size, the two jars are considered here to be transitional to Type IVa (/e; see further below).

28   cf. Kaiser, op. cit., fig. 14, nos. 19 and 13, 18 and 20 respectively.

29   cf. Kaiser, op. cit., fig. 14, nos. 21 and 22 respectively.

30   Although this *serekh* is accepted without comment by Kaiser as belonging to 'Horus Narmer' (Kaiser & Dreyer, op. cit., fig, 14, no. 37), a *caveat* is necessary here: if only the upper part of this fragment had been preserved (i.e. falcon without the *serekh*) probably no-one would have hesitated to attribute it to 'Iry-Hor'. *Vice versa* it is theoretically conceivable that some of the preserved 'Iry-Hor' fragments (especially if found outside the immediate context of 'Iry-Hor's' own tomb at Umm el-Qa'ab) may be incomplete and could belong to the same ruler as attested for on the Zawayit el-Aryan fragment.

31   e.g. Wildung-Kroeper 1985, 75: 'Beide Horusnamen sind nicht volkommen klar geschrieben, so dass die Lesungen 'Horus Narmer' und 'Horus Skorpion' unsicher bleiben'; Kaiser & Dreyer, 1982, Abb. 15, Anm. u: 'Der Bezug von Grab 160 in Minshat Abu Omar auf Skorpion ist andererseitz nicht gänzlich sicher'.

32   'The applied bands are an imitation of the rope supports that were necessary in the construction of such a large vessel, and they may actually cover the joins between sections' (Bourriau 1981, 50, no. 81).

33   'Typ VIII. Rand wie Typ VII, Format schmäler (.....) mit drei ganz erhabenen Reifen, die eine geflochtene Schnur nachahmen. Feiner Ton, bis zum oberen Ring leicht poliert, aber weniger gute Arbeit als Type Iff.'

34   There is apparent, at about this time, the disappearance of *serekh* signs incised on jars and an ever increasing application of cylinder seals on mud cones used as stoppers for storage jars: 'Die Serech-Marken auf den grossen Krügen werden offentsichlich bereits unter Aha selten -wohl nicht ohne Zusammenhang mit der nun in grossem Umfang einsetzenden Siegelung der Krugverschlüsse.' (Kaiser & Dreyer op. cit., 264, note 195a). Although something of the original function of the *serekh* signs may be inferred from this causal relationship, it is difficult to explain why so relatively few vessels, in comparison to the total number found, bear *serekhs*. It is notable that both incised *serekhs* on storage jars and ink inscribed *serekhs* on cylindrical jars are few in number

while many more vessels with seal-bearing stoppers are known.

35 For the differentiation between Types IVa and IVb, cf. note 33 and 36.

36 'Typ IX [here Type IVb]. Weiterentwickelung von Typ VIII; die Format wird schmäler, der Rand oben enger (Torpedoformat). Die Ringe werden meist durch eine erhabene Linie angedeutet; der Mittelring tritt nur ganz schwach hervor. Das Material ist gröber, die Flächen sind nachlässiger gearbeitet. Die oberflächliche Politur geht nur bis zum oberen Ring.'

'Typ X [here Type IVc] unterscheidet sich von IX nur dadurch, dass er die beiden mittleren Ringe nicht besitzt (.....).'

'Typ XI [here Type IVd]. Weiterbildung von Typ VII; ohne jeden Ring. Material wie die vorhergehenden Typen.'

37 Mention should be made, however, of a particular combination of *serekh* signs, usually within 'enclosures' (e.g. Saad, 1951, pl. 71, nos. 3-4), appearing on jars of Types IV c-d, mainly attributable to the reign of 'Horus Semerkhet' (cf. e.g. Petrie 1900, pls. 44-46; 1953, pl. 23, 76h; cf. also Kroeper 1988, pl. 13; for additional references cf. van den Brink 1992a, 267, 2, note 11).

38 The following distinctions were recognized in the group of 'grosse Krüge': 2 W (zweifaches Wellendekor), 4W (vierfaches Wellendekor), Wr (Wellendekor rundum), Sr (Schnurringe), O (ohne Wellen- bzw. Schnurdekor)' [Kaiser & Dreyer op. cit., fig. 15; cf. also Kaiser 1964, fig. 1].

39 Included in this paper, but not in Kaiser's 1982 presentation, and therefore not appearing in these two tables, are : MAO Tomb 1210-21, MAO Tomb 520-3 and Ezbet el-Tell reg. no. 182 (nos. 11, 12 and 21 in this study, respectively).

40 cf. Kaiser 1990, 288, note 5.

41 These are 'Iry-Hor', 'Horus Ka', 'Horus Crocodile'(?) and 'Horus ?' (unidentified; here no. 17).

42 On should keep in mind, however, that at least in two cases jars of Types II and III, c.q. III and IVa were found together in one and the same tomb (see above).

43 1. Grab 15. g. 2 Typ II; 2. Grab 7. 1. 7a Typ II.'

44 i.e. Turah Tomb 15. g. 2 (our no. 18); cf. Kaiser & Dreyer op. cit., 265, note 198: 'Horizont A: (.....) sowie eventuel 11'.

45 i.e. Turah Tomb 17. 1. 7a (our no. 19); cf. Kaiser & Dreyer op.cit., 265, note 198: 'Horizont B oder C: nach dem Keramikbefund des Grabes die Marke 44 (....).'

46 Bear in mind the chronological distinctions between the 'Südfriedhof, Übergangslinie and Nordfriedhof' (Junker1912) at this site.

47 'über das Arkadenbanddekor in die Zeitstufe IIIa2 zu stellen, aber später als U/j.'

48 They include: 'cyl. jar (W60g); net-painted jars (W62 and 46D2); comma-painted jar (D26d); W-handled jar (44f); conical jar (54g); bowl (R26A); jars (L36a +n); jars (63b), and 'hes' jars (74v)' (Friedman and Adams 1992, 331).

49 'etwa zur gleichen Zeit [viz. around the reigns of 'Horus Djet' /'Horus Den'] erscheinen die ersten grossen Krüge mit nur einem Schnurring (.....)' (Kaiser 1964, 95-96, note 4).

50 The incised *serekh* preserved on fragment no. 16a, likewise incised on a Type III jar, can be attributed to the same king; we don't have a suggestion as to whom belongs the, only partly preserved, incised *serekh* on the second fragment reproduced here, viz. no. 16b.

51 The examples underlined in this list are those of jars incised with a *serekh* sign.

52 cf. Kaiser 1964, fig. 1, Ältere Serech-gruppe, cylindrical jars A.M. 1021 and A.M. 1144.

53 Based on Kaiser 1964, 94, Abb1, A.M.1021, one example at least concerns a net-painted 'Arkaden-zylinder' (Petrie 1953, ca. 46d).

54 cf. Junker 1912, 39: 'Type LXIV. Nur in S häufig belegt. Feiner heller Ton mit feiner Glasur, festgebrannt; (.....) Die Form ist rein Zylindrisch, der Rand kaum ausladend; der Ring besteht aus kleinen Wellenlinien verschiedener Ausführung, oder aus kleinen schrägen Strichen (.....). Bei einigen wird das untere Ende breiter.'

55 Cylindrical jar, net-painted, but with continuous 'plain line' instead of 'Arkaden' pattern.

56 Zylindergefässen mit und ohne Zierring (Kaiser & Dreyer op. cit., 267, note u ; Abb. 15).

57 i.e. plain cylindrical jar; 'wie LXIV [cf. above, note 54], jedoch verbreitert sich der Krug am oberen Ende Kelchartig' (Junker 1912, 39).

58 i.e. plain cylindrical jar, 'Dieselbe Form [as Typ LXV], aber ohne Ring'. (Junker 1912, 39).

59 Zylindergefässen (mit ? und) ohne Zierring; grosse Krüge ohne Wellen bzw. Schnurdekor' (Kaiser & Dreyer op. cit., Abb. 15).

60 i.e. cylindrical jar with cord impression.

61 For a most recent discussion of the development of the cylindrical jar, cf. Pumpenmeier 1993, 44-49; cf. also above, Table 5.

References

Adams, B. 1974a. *Ancient Hierakonpolis.* Warminster.

Adams, B. 1974b. *Ancient Hierakonpolis Supplement.* Warminster.

Adams, B. 1982. 'Artifacts (from Locality 6)', in: Hoffman, M.A. (ed.) 1982a: 56-58.

Adams, B. 1987. *The Fort Cemetery at Hierakonpolis.* London.

Adams, B. 1992. 'Two More Lions from Upper Egypt: Hierakonpolis and Koptos', in: Friedman & Adams (eds) 1992: 69-76.

Adams, B. 1993a. 'Hierakonpolis 1992', in: *Bulletin de Liason du Groupe International d'Étude de la Céramique Égyptienne,* XVII: 35-6.

Adams, B. 1993b. 'Potmark Forgery: A Serekh of Semerkhet from Abydos', in: *Discussions in Egyptology,* 25: 1-12.

Adams, B. 1995. *Ancient Nekhen.* New Malden.

Adams, B. & Friedman, R. 1992. 'Imports and Influences in the Predynastic and Protodynastic Settlement and Funerary Assemblages at Hierakonpolis', in: van den Brink, E.C.M. (ed.) 1992a: 317-338.

Adams, W.Y. 1977. *Nubia, Corridor to Africa,* London.

Altenmüller, H. 1974. 'Djebaut', in: *LÄ* 1: 1098-1099.

Amélineau, E. 1899a. *Les nouvelles fouilles d'Abydos* I. (1895-1896). Paris.

Amélineau, E. 1899b. *Le tombeau d'Osiris.* Paris.

Amélineau, E. 1902. *Les nouvelles fouilles d'Abydos* II. (1896-1897). Paris.

Amélineau, E. 1904. *Les nouvelles fouilles d'Abydos* III. (1897-1898). Paris.

Amiran, R. 1968. 'Two Canaanite Vessels Excavated in Egypt with Egyptian Signatures', in: *IEJ* 18, no 4: 241-243.

Amiran, R. 1969. *Ancient Pottery of the Holy Land from its Beginnings in the Neolithic Period to the End of the Iron Age.* Jerusalem

Amiran, R. 1970. 'An Egyptian First Dynasty Jar', in: *The Israel Museum News* 8: 89ff.

Amiran, R. 1974. 'An Egyptian Jar Fragment with the Name of Narmer from Arad', in: *IEJ* 24: 4-12.

Amiran, R. 1976. 'The Narmer Jar Fragment from Arad: an Addendum', in: *IEJ* 26: 44-46.

Anderson, D.M.W. 1978. 'Chemotaxonomic aspects of the chemistry of *Acacia* gum exudates', in: *Kew Bulletin* 32: 529-536.

Arnold, D. 1974. *Der Tempel des Königs Mentuhotep von Deir el-Bahari.* Mainz.

Arnold, D. 1982a. 'Per-nu', in: *LÄ* 4: 932-933.

Arnold, D. 1982b. 'Per-wer II', in: *LÄ* 4: 934-935.

Arnold, D. 1991. *Building in Egypt, Pharaonic Stone Masonry.* New York .

Asselberghs, H. 1961. *Chaos en beheersing; Documenten uit aeneolitisch Egypte.* Leiden.

Ayrton, E.R. & Loat, W.L.S. 1911. *The Pre-dynastic Cemetery at El-Mahasna.* London.

Baer, K. 1960. *Rank and Title in the Old Kingdom,* Chicago.

Bakr, M. I. 1988. 'The New Excavations at Ezbet el-Tell, Kufur Nigm; the First Season (1984)', in: van den Brink (ed.) 1988a: 49-62.

Balcz, H. 1934. 'Die Gefässdarstellungen des Alten Reiches', in: *MDAIK* 5: 45-94.

Barta, W. 1973. 'Zum altägyptischen Namen des Königs Aches', in: *MDAIK* 29: 1-4.

Baumgartel, E.J. 1955. *The Cultures of Prehistoric Egypt* I. (2nd. rev. ed.). London.

Baumgartel, E.J. 1970a. 'Predynastic Egypt' (2nd rev. edn) in: *The Cambridge Ancient History,* vol. I, chap. IXa. London.

Baumgartel, E.J. 1970b. *Petrie's Naqada Excavation: A Supplement*. London.

Ben-Tor, A. 1975. 'Two Burial Caves of the Proto-Urban Period at Azor', in: *Qedem* I: 1-53.

Ben-Tor, A. 1982. 'The Relations between Egypt and the Land of Canaan during the Third Millennium BC', in: *IEJ* 33: 3-17.

Bietak, M. 1975. *Tell el-Dab'a II, Der Fundort im Rahmen einer archäologisch-geographischen Untersuchung über das ägyptische Ostdelta*. Vienna.

Bietak, M. 1979. 'Egyptology and the Urban Setting', in: Weeks, K. (ed.) *Egyptology and the Social Sciences*: 95-144. Cairo.

Bietak, M. 1981. 'Das Stadtproblem im Alten Ägypten', in: *150 Jahre DAI, Kolloquium Berlin 1979*: 68-78. Mainz.

Bietak, M. 1986. 'La naissance de la notion de ville dans l'Égypte Ancienne - un acte politique?', in: *CRIPEL* 8: 29-35.

Bietak, M. 1993. Review of T. Säve-Söderbergh, 'Middle Nubian Sites ...', in: *Bi.Or.* 50: 385-91.

Bisson de la Roque, F. 1937. *Tôd (1934 à 1936)*. Cairo.

Black, J. (ed.) 1987. *Recent Advances in the Conservation and Analysis of Artifacts, (Jubilee Conservation Conference, University of London, Institute of Archaeology, July 6-10, 1987)*: 253-256. Whitstable.

Boehmer, R.M., Dreyer, G. & Kromer, B. 1993. 'Einige frühzeitliche 14C-Datierungen aus Abydos und Uruk', in: *MDAIK* 49, 63-68.

Boessneck, J. & von den Driesch, A. 1982. *Studien an subfossilen Tierknochen aus Ägypten*. Munich.

Boessneck, J., von den Driesch, A. & Eissa, A. 1992. 'Eine Eselsbestattung der 1. Dynastie in Abusir', in: *MDAIK* 48: 1-10.

Bonnet, H. 1928. *Ein frühgeschichtliches Gräberfeld bei Abusir*. Leipzig.

Borchardt, L. 1907. *Das Grabdenkmal des Königs Ne-user-re^C*. Leipzig.

Bothmer, B.V. 1974. 'The Karnak Statue of Ny-user-ra', in: *MDAIK* 30: 165-70.

Bouriant, U. 1885. 'Les tombeaux d'Hierakonpolis', in *Étude archéologiques, linguistiques et historiques dédiée à M. de Dr. C. Leemans*: 37-40. Leiden.

Bourriau, B. 1981. *Umm el-Ga'ab. Pottery from the Nile Valley before the Arab Conquest*. Cambridge.

Braun, E., van den Brink, E.C.M., Gophna, R. & Goren, Y. 'New Evidence for Egyptian Connections during the Late Early Bronze Age I, from the Soreq-Basin in South-Central Israel', in: Wolff, S. (ed.) *Douglas Esse Memorial Volume* (in preparation).

Brewer, D. 1987. 'A Report on the Aquatic Fauna from HK-29A', in: Hoffman, M.A. (ed.) 1987: 45-47. South Carolina.

Brewer, D. & Friedman, R. 1989. *Fish and Fishing in Ancient Egypt*. Warminster.

Brovarski, E.J. 1982. 'Naga (Nag')-ed-Dêr', in: *LÄ* 4: 296-317. Wiesbaden.

Brovarski, E.J. 1973. 'An Unpublished Stele of the First Intermediate Period', in: JNES 32: 453-65.

Brunner, H. 1952-3. 'El Qatta', in: *AfO* 16: 160-1.

Brunton, G. 1927. *Qau and Badari,* I. London

Brunton, G. 1937. *Mostagedda and the Tasian Culture*. London.

Brunton, G. 1948. *Matmar*. London.

Brunton, G. & Caton-Thompson, G. 1928. *The Badarian Civilization and the Predynastic Remains near Badari*. London.

Burleigh, R. 1983. 'Two Radiocarbon Dates for Freshwater Shells from Hierakonpolis: Archaeological and Geological Interpretations', in: *Journal of Archaeological Science* 10: 361-67.

Case, H. & Payne, J.-Crowfoot. 1962. 'Tomb 100: the Decorated Tomb at Hierakonpolis', in: *JEA* 48: 9-18.

Caton-Thompson, G. & Garner, E. W. 1934. *The Desert Fayum*. Plates. London

Cledat, M.J. 1914. 'Les vases de el-Beda', in: *ASAE* 13: 115-121.

Cleyet-Merle, J.-J. & Vallet, F. 1982. Égypte. in: Beck, F., Cleyet-Merle, J.-J. et alii. *Archéologie comparée. Catalogue sommaire des collections du musée de Saint-Germain en Laye*, 1: 68-165. Paris.

Crubezy, E. (ed.) 1992. 'Paléo-ethnologie funéraire et paléobiologie', in: *Archéo-Nil* n°2.

d'Amicone, E. 1988. 'Le site archéologique de Gebeleyn', in: Donadoni-Roveri, A.M. (ed.), *La civilisation des égyptiens. Les croyances religieuses*: 38-43. Turin.

Daressy, G. 1905. 'Un édifice archaique à Nezlet Batran', in: *ASAE* 6: 99-106.

Daumas, F. 1953. 'Le trône d'une statuette de Pépi Ier trouvé à Dendara', in: *BIFAO* 52: 163-72.

Daumas, F. 1973. 'Derechef Pépi Ier à Dendera', in: *RdÉ* 25: 7-20.

Davies, N. de G. 1902. *The Rock Tombs of Deir el Gebrawi* I. London.

Davies, W.V. 1995. 'Ancient Egyptian Timber Imports: an Analysis of Wooden Coffins in the British Museum', in: Davies & Schofield (eds) 1995: 146-156.

Davies, W.V. & Schofield, L. (eds) 1995. *Egypt, the Aegean and the Levant, Interconnections in the Second Millennium BC*.

de Morgan, H. 1909. 'L'Égypte primitive', *Revue de l'Ecole d'Anthropologie de Paris*: 128-140, 263-281.

de Morgan, H. 1912. 'Report on Excavations made in Upper Egypt during the Winter 1907-1908' in: *ASAE* 12 (1912): 25-50.

de Morgan, J. 1897. *Recherches sur les origines de l'Égypte II. Ethnographie préhistorique et tombeau royal de Negadah*. Paris.

de Morgan, J. et al. 1894. *Catalogue des Monuments et Inscriptions de l'Égypte antique*, I.1. Vienna.

Debono, F. 1951. 'Expedition archéologique royale au désert oriental (Keft Kosseir): Rapport préliminaire sur la campagne 1949', in: *ASAE* 51: 59-110.

Debono, F. 1971. 'Recherches préhistoriques dans la région d'Esna (4 Mars-2 Avril 1968)', in: *BIFAO* 69, 245-261.

Dreyer, G. 1981. Ein frühdynastisches Königsfigürchen aus Elephantine, in: *MDAIK* 37: 123-4.

Dreyer, G. 1986. *Elephantine 8: Der Tempel der Satet, Die Funde der Frühzeit und des Alten Reiches*. Mainz.

Dreyer, G. 1987. 'Drei archaisch-hieratische Gefäßaufschriften mit Jahresnamen aus Elephantine', in: Dreyer, G. & Osing, J. (eds) *Form und Maß, Fs. G. Fecht*: 98-109. Wiesbaden.

Dreyer, G. 1990. 'Umm el-Qaab: Nachuntersuchungen im frühzeitlichen Königsfriedhof. 3./4. Vorbericht', in: *MDAIK* 46 (1990): 53-90.

Dreyer, G. 1991. 'Zur Rekonstruktion der Oberauten der Königsgräber der 1. Dynastie in Abydos', in: *MDAIK* 46: 93-104.

Dreyer, G. 1992a. 'Recent Discoveries in the U-Cemetery at Abydos', in: van den Brink (ed.) 1992a: 293-300.

Dreyer, G. 1992b. 'Horus Krokodil, ein Gegenkönig der Dynastie 0', in: Friedman & Adams (eds) 1992: 259-63.

Dreyer, G. 1993. 'Umm el-Qaab. Nachuntersuchungen im frühzeitlichen Königsfriedhof. 5./6. Vorbericht', in: *MDAIK* 49: 23-62.

Dreyer, G. & Kaiser, W. 1980. 'Zu den kleinen Stufenpyramiden Ober- und Mittelägyptens', in: *MDAIK* 36: 43-59.

Dreyer, G. & Swelim, N. 1982. 'Die kleine Stufenpyramide von Abydos-Süd (Sinki), Grabungsbericht', in: *MDAIK* 38: 83-93.

Duday, H., Courtaud, P., Crubezy, E., Sellier, P. & Tillier, A.M. 1990. 'L'anthropologie 'de terrain': reconnaissance et interprétation des gestes funéraires', in: *Bull. et Mém. de la Société d'Anthropologie de Paris,* n.s., t.2, n°3-4: 29-50.

Dunham, D. 1938. 'The Biographical Inscriptions of Nekhebu in Boston and Cairo', in: *JEA* 24: 1-8.

Dunham, D. 1978. *Zawiyet el-Aryan. The Cemeteries Adjacent to the Layer Pyramid*. Boston.

Ehrich, R.W. (ed.) 1954. *Chronologies in Old World Archaeology.* Chicago.

el-Banna, A. 1990. 'Une nécropole inédite d'époque archaique découvertée, près de Hélouan, au Sud du Caire', in: *GM* 117-8: 7-54.

el-Hadidi, M.N. 1982. 'The Predynastic Flora of the Hierakonpolis region', in: Hoffman, M.A. (ed.) 1982a: 102-115.

el-Hagg Ragab, A.M. 1992. 'A Report on the Excavations of the Egyptian Antiquities Organization (E.A.O.) at Beni 'Amir and el-Masha'la in the Eastern Nile Delta', in: van den Brink (ed.) 1992a: 207-13.

el-Hangary, S.M. 1992. 'The Excavations of the Egyptian Antiquities Organization at Ezbet Hassan Dawud (Wadi Tumilat), Season 1990', in: van den Brink (ed.) 1992a: 215-6.

el-Khouly, A. 1968. 'A Preliminary Report on the Excavations at Tura, 1963-64', in: *ASAE* 60.1: 73-6.

el-Sawi, A. 1979. *Excavations at Tell Basta, Report of Seasons 1967-1971 and Catalogue of Finds.* Prague.

el-Sayed, A. 1977. 'A Prehistoric Cemetery in the Abydos Area', in: *MDAIK* 35: 249-301.

Elias, J. 1986. *Observations on the Excavations at Hierakonpolis Locality 29A.* Unpublished field report.

Emery, W.B. 1938. *Excavations at Saqqara: The Tomb of Hemaka.* Cairo.

Emery, W.B. 1939. *Excavations at Saqqara (1937-38). Hor-Aha.* Cairo.

Emery, W.B. 1949. *Great Tombs of the First Dynasty*, I. Cairo.

Emery, W.B. 1954. *Great Tombs of the First Dynasty*, II. London.

Emery, W.B. 1958. *Great Tombs of the First Dynasty*, III. London.

Engelbach, R. & Gunn, B. 1923. *Harageh.* London.

Epstein, C. 1993. 'Oil Production in the Golan Heights during the Chalcolithic Period', in: *Tel Aviv* 20 (2): 133-146.

Esse, D.L. 1991. *Subsistence, Trade, and Social Change in Early Bronze Age Palestine*, Chicago.

Fairservis, W.A. 1986. *Excavation of the Archaic Remains East of the Niched Gate, Season of 1981. (The Hierakonpolis Project Occasional Papers in Anthropology III).* Poughkeepsie, N.Y.

Fairservis, W.A. 1991. 'A Revised View of the Na'rmr Palette', in: *JARCE* 28, 1-20.

Fakhry, A. 1961. *The Monuments of Sneferu at Dahshur II, The Valley Temple, pt. 1, The Temple Reliefs.* Cairo.

Fischer, H.G. 1958. review of Habachi 1957(b), in: *AJA* 62: 330-3.

Fischer, H.G. 1962. 'The Cult and Nome of the Goddess Bat', in: *JARCE* 1: 7-23.

Fischer, H.G. 1963. 'A First Dynasty Wine Jar from the Eastern Delta', in: *JARCE* 2: 44-47.

Fischer, H.G. 1964. *Inscriptions from the Coptite Nome Dynasties VI-XI.* Rome.

Fischer, H.G. 1968. *Dendera in the Third Millennium B.C., Down to the Theban Domination.* New York.

Fischer, H.G. 1993. 'Another Pithemorphic Vessel of the Sixth Dynasty', in: *JARCE* 30: 1-9.

Fisher, C.S. 1913. 'The Harvard University Museum of Fine Arts Egyptian Expedition. Work of 1912 at Gizeh and Mesheikh', in: *BMFA* 11, no. 62: 19-22.

Frankfort, H. 1930. 'The Cemeteries of Abydos: Work of the Season 1925-1926, II. Tombs', in: *JEA* 16: 213-9.

Freed, R.E. 1974. 'Cemetery at Naqa el-Hai (Qena)', in: *NARCE* 91: 28.

Friedman, R. 1987. 'Description and Qualitative Analysis of the HK-29A Ceramic Assemblage', in Hoffman, M.A. (ed.) 1987: 68-185.

Friedman, R. 1990. 'Hierakonpolis, Locality 29A', in: *Bulletin de Liason*, XIV: 18-25.

Friedman, R. 1981. *Spatial Distribution in a Predynastic Cemetery: Naga ed Dêr 7000.* Berkeley. (unpubl. M.A. thesis).

Friedman, R. 1994. *Predynastic Settlement Ceramics of Upper Egypt: A Comparative Study of the Ceramics of Hemamieh, Naqada and Hierakonpolis.* Ph.D. dissertation. Berkeley.

Friedman, R. & Adams, B. 1992. (eds) *The Followers of Horus: Studies Dedicated to Michael Allen Hoffman 1944-1990.* Oxford.

Galassi, G. 1955. *L'arte del più antico Egitto nel Museo di Torino*. Rome.

Gardiner, A.H. 1944. 'Horus the Behdetite', in: *JEA* 30: 23-116.

Gardiner, A.H. 1957. *Egyptian Grammar*. 3rd edn Oxford.

Gardiner, A.H. 1969. *Middle Egyptian Grammar*. Reprint of the 3rd edition. London-Oxford.

Gardiner, A.H. 1947. *Ancient Egyptian Onomastica I*. Oxford.

Garstang, J. 1903. *Mahâsna and Bêt Khallâf*. London.

Garstang, J. 1907. 'Excavations at Hierakonpolis, at Esna and in Nubia', in: *ASAE* 8: 132-148.

Germer, R. 1986. 'Zeder', in: *LÄ* 6: 1357-8.

Germer, R. 1989. *Die Pflanzenmaterialien aus dem Grab des Tutanchamun*, Hildesheim.

Giddy, L.L. & Jeffreys, D.G. 1991. 'Memphis, 1990', in *JEA* 77, 1-6.

Goedicke, H. 1956. 'The Pharaoh Ny-Swth', in: *ZÄS* 81: 18-24.

Goedicke, H. 1967. *Königliche Dokumente aus dem Alten Reich*. Wiesbaden.

Goedicke, H. 1979. 'Cult-Temple and "State" during the Old Kingdom in Egypt', in: Lipinski, E. (ed.) *State and Temple Economy in the Ancient Near East*: 113-32.

Goelet, O. Jr. 1982. *Two aspects of the Royal Palace in the Egyptian Old Kingdom*. Diss. Columbia University.

Gomaà, F., Müller-Wollermann, R. & Schenkel, W. 1961. *Mittelägypten zwischen Samalut und dem Gabal Abu-Sir, Beiträge zur historischen Topographie der pharaonischen Zeit*. Wiesbaden.

Gophna, R. 1970. 'A Protodynastic Egyptian Jar from Rafiah', in: *Museum Haaretz Tel Aviv Bulletin*, no. 12, 53-54.

Gophna, R. 1987. 'Egyptian Trading Posts in Southern Canaan at the Dawn of the Archaic Period', in: Rainey, A.F. (ed.), *Egypt, Israel, Sinai*: 13-21. Tel Aviv.

Habachi, L. 1957a. 'A Group of Unpublished Old and Middle Kingdom Graffiti on Elephantine', in: *Fs. H. Junker,* in: *WZKM* 54: 55-71.

Habachi. L. 1957b. *Tell Basta, SASAE* 22. Cairo.

Hamroush, H.A. 1987. 'A Preliminary Report on the Geoarchaeological Setting of Locality HK-29A in the Low Desert Region at Hierakonpolis', in: Hoffman, M.A. (ed.) 1987: 22-31.

Hansen, D.P. 1967. 'The Excavations at Tell el Rub'a', in: *JARCE* 6: 16.

Harlan, J.F. 1985. *Predynastic Settlement Patterns: A View from Hierakonpolis*. Ph.D. dissertation, Washington University, St. Louis, Missouri.

Harlan, J.F. 1992. 'Wadi and Desert Settlement at Predynastic Hierakonpolis', in Friedman, R. & Adams, B. (eds) 1992: 14-18.

Hassan, F.A. 1980. 'Radiocarbon Chronology of Archaic Egypt', in: *JNES* 39: 203-7.

Hassan, F.A. 1984a. 'The Beginnings of Civilisation at Hierakonpolis' (review of *The Predynastic of Hierakonpolis*), in: *Quarterly Review of Archaeology*: 13-15.

Hassan, F.A. 1984b. 'Radiocarbon Chronology of Predynastic Naqada Settlements, Egypt', in: *Current Anthropology* 25: 681-3.

Hassan, F.A. 1985. 'Radiocarbon Chronology of Neolithic and Predynastic Sites in Upper Egypt and the Delta', in: *The African Archaeological Review* 3: 95-116.

Hassan, F.A. 1988. 'The Predynastic of Egypt', in: *Journal of World Prehistory* 2: 135-86.

Hassan, F.A. & Robinson, S.W. 1987. 'High-Precision Radiocarbon Chronometry of Ancient Egypt and Comparisons with Nubia, Palestine and Mesopotamia', in: *Antiquity* 61: 119-35.

Hawass, Z. 1980. 'Archaic Graves, Recently Found at North Abu Roash', in: *MDAIK* 36: 229-44.

Hayes, W.C. 1953. *Scepter of Egypt* I. New York.

Helck, W. 1962. *Die Beziehungen Ägyptens zu vorderasien im 3. und 2. Jahrtausend v. Chr.* Wiesbaden.

Helck, W. 1974. *Die altägyptischen Gaue*. Wiesbaden.

Helck, W. 1990. *Thinitische Töpfmarken*. Wiesbaden.

Hendrickx, S. 1984. 'The Late Predynastic cemetery at Elkab (Upper Egypt)', in: Krzyzaniak, L. and Kobusiewicz, M. (eds) *Origin and Early Development of Food Producing Cultures in Northeastern Africa*: 225-230. Polish Academy of Sciences, Poznan.

Hendrickx, S. 1986. 'Predynastische objecten uit Naqada and Diospolis Parva (Boven Egypte)', in: *BMRAH* 57, 2: 31-44.

Hendrickx, S. 1989. *De grafvelden der Naqada-cultuur in Zuid-Egypte, met bijzondere aandacht voor het Naqada III grafveld te Elkab. Interne chronologie en sociale differentiatie.* Leuven, (unpubl. Ph.D. thesis).

Hendrickx, S. 1994. *Elkab V. The Naqada III Cemetery.* Brussels.

Hendrickx, S. 1995. *Analytical Bibliography of the Prehistory and the Early Dynastic Period of Egypt and Northern Sudan. Egyptian Prehistory Monographs* 1. Leuven.

Hendrickx, S. & Midant-Reynes, B. 1988. 'Preliminary Report on the Predynastic Living Site Maghara 2 (Upper Egypt)', in: *Orientalia Lovaniensia Periodica* 19: 5-16.

Hennessey, J. 1967. *The Foreign Relations of Palestine during the Early Bronze Age.* London.

Hennessey, J.B. and Millett, A. 1963. 'Spectrographic Analysis of the Foreign Pottery from the Royal Tombs of Abydos and Early Bronze Age Pottery of Palestine', in *Archaeometry* 6, 10-17.

Hoffman, M.A. 1980. 'A Rectangular Amratian House from Hierakonpolis and Its Significance for Predynastic Research', in: *JNES* 39: 119-137.

Hoffman, M.A. (ed.) 1982a. *The Predynastic of Hierakonpolis, an Interim Report, Egyptian Studies Association* 1, Cairo.

Hoffman, M.A. 1982b. 'Settlement Patterns and Settlement Systems', in: Hoffman M.A. (ed.) 1982a: 122-138.

Hoffman, M.A. 1982c. 'Excavations at Locality 29', in: Hoffman M.A. (ed.) 1982a: 7-13.

Hoffman, M.A. 1983. 'Where Nations Began', in: *Science* 83, no.4: 42-51.

Hoffman, M.A. 1985. *Report to the EAO on Predynastic Research at Hierakonpolis in 1985.* Unpublished report.

Hoffman, M.A. (ed.) 1987. *A Final Report to the National Endowment for the Humanities on Predynastic Research at Hierakonpolis, 1985-86.* Columbia, South Carolina.

Hoffman, M.A. 1989 'An Introduction to the Predynastic Period in Egypt', in: *Terra* (Natural History Museum of Los Angeles County) 27 (5-6): 34-43.

Hoffman, M., Hamroush, H.A. & Allen, R.O. 1986. 'A Model of Urban Development for the Hierakonpolis Region from Predynastic through Old Kingdom Times', in: *JARCE* 23: 175-87.

Hoffman, M.A. and H. Barakat. 1987. 'A Preliminary Report on the Floral Remains from HK-29A' in: Hoffman, M.A. (ed.) 1987: 40-41.

Hollmann, A. 1990. *Säugetierknochenfunde aus Elephantine in Oberägypten (8. bis 16. Grabungskampagne, 1978-1987),* Diss. Munich.

Holmes, D.L. 1987. 'A Preliminary Report on the Chipped Stone Assemblage from HK-29A', in: Hoffman, M.A. (ed.) 1987: 196-212.

Holmes, D.L. 1989. *The Predynastic Lithic Industries of Upper Egypt. A Comparative Study of the Lithic Traditions of Badari, Naqada and Hierakonpolis.* Oxford.

Holmes, D.L. 1992a. 'Chipped Stone-working Craftsmen, Hierakonpolis and the Rise of Civilization in Egypt', in: Friedman & Adams (eds) 1992: 37-44.

Holmes, D.L. 1992b. 'The Evidence and Nature of Contacts between Upper and Lower Egypt during the Predynastic: A View from Upper Egypt', in: Van den Brink (ed.) 1992a: 301-16.

Howes, F.N. 1949. *Vegetable Gums and Resins,* Chronica Botanica Co., Waltham, MA.

Jacquet-Gordon, H. 1962. *Les noms des domaines funéraires sous l'ancien empire égyptien.* Cairo.

Jéquier, G. 1906. 'Les Temples Primitifs et La Persistance des Types Archaiques dans l'Architecture Religieuse', in: *BIFAO* 6: 24-41.

Jéquier, G. 1940. *Le monument funéraire de Pepi II, tome III, les approches du temple.* Cairo.

Junker, H. 1912. *Bericht über die Grabungen der Kaiserlichen Akademie der Wissenschaften in Wien, auf dem Friedhof in Turah, Winter 1909-1910.* Vienna.

Junker, H. 1919. *Bericht über die Grabungen von der Akadamie der Wissenschaften in Wien, auf den Friedhöfen von El-Kubanieh-Sud, 1910-1911.* Vienna.

Junker, H. 1920. *Bericht über die Grabungen ... auf den Friedhöfen von el-Kubanieh Nord.* Vienna.

Junker, H. 1930. 'Vorläufiger Bericht über die zweite Grabung der Akademie der Wissenschaften in Wien auf der vorgeschichtlichen Siedlung Merimde Beni-Salâme vom 7 Februar bis 8 April 1930', *Vorgelegt in der Sitzung der phil.-hist.Klasse* (Wien), 14 Mai 1930.

Kadish, G.E. 1970. 'An Inscription from an Early Egyptian Fortress', in: *JNES* 29: 99-102.

Kaiser, W. 1956a. 'Zu den Sonnenheiligtümern der 5. Dyn.', in: *MDAIK* 14: 104-16.

Kaiser, W. 1956b. 'Stand und Probleme der Ägyptische Vorgeschichtsforschung', in: *ZÄS* 81: 87-109.

Kaiser, W. 1957. 'Zur Inneren Chronologie der Naqadakultur', in: *Archaeologica Geographica* 61: 67-77.

Kaiser, W. 1961. 'Bericht über eine archäologische-geologische Felduntersuchung in Ober- und Mittelägypten', in: *MDAIK* 17: 1-53.

Kaiser, W. 1964. 'Einige Bemerkungen zur Ägyptischen Frühzeit III', in: *ZÄS* 91: 86-125.

Kaiser, W. 1982. 'Zur Reihe der gesamtägyptischen Könige vor Aha', in: Kaiser & Dreyer 1982: 260-269.

Kaiser, W. 1987. 'Zum Friedhof der Naqada-kultur von Minshat Abu Omar' in: *ASAE* 71: 119-26.

Kaiser, W. 1990. 'Zur Entstehung des gesamtägyptisches Staates', in: *MDAIK* 46: 287-299.

Kaiser, W. & Dreyer, G. 1982. 'Umm el-Qaab. Nachuntersuchungen im frühzeitlichen Königsfriedhof. 2. Vorbericht', in: *MDAIK* 38: 211-70.

Kaiser, W. & Grossman, P. 1979. 'Umm el-Qaab. Nachuntersuchungen im frühzeitlichen Königsfriedhof. 1. Vorbericht', in: *MDAIK* 35: 155-64.

Kaiser, W. et al. 1970 (& following years as below). *Stadt und Tempel von Elephantine, 1.-22. Grabungsbericht,* in: *MDAIK* 26, (1970): 87-139, *MDAIK* 27, (1971): 181-201, *MDAIK* 28, (1973): 157-200, *MDAIK* 30, (1974): 65-90, *MDAIK* 31, (1975): 39-84, *MDAIK* 32, (1976): 67-112, *MDAIK* 33, (1977): 63-100, *MDAIK* 36, (1980): 245-91, *MDAIK* 38, (1982): 271-345, *MDAIK* 40, (1984): 169-205, *MDAIK* 43, (1987): 75-114, *MDAIK* 44, (1988): 135-82, *MDAIK* 46, (1990): 185-249, *MDAIK* 49, (1993): 133-87, *MDAIK* 51, (1995): 99-187.

Kantor, H.J. 1944. 'The Final Phase of Predynastic Culture, Gerzean or Semainean', in: *JNES* 3: 110-36.

Kantor, H.J. 1965. 'The Relative Chronology of Egypt and Its Foreign Correlations before the Late Bronze Age', in: Ehrich, K. (ed.) *Chronologies in Old World Archaeology*: 1-46. Chicago.

Kaplony, P. 1962. 'Gottespalast und Göttersfestungen in der ägyptischen Frühzeit', in: *ZÄS* 88: 5-16.

Kaplony, P. 1963. *Die Inschriften der Ägyptischen Frühzeit* I-III. Weisbaden.

Kaplony, P. 1965. 'Eine Schminkpalette von König Skorpion aus Abu Umuris', in: *Orientalia* 34: 132-67.

Katzmann, L. 1990. *Tierknochenfunde aus Elephantine in Oberägypten (Grabungsjahre 1976 bis 1986/87), Vögel, Reptilien, Fische und Mollusken.* Diss. Munich.

Keimer, L. & Germer, R. 1984. *Die Gartenpflanzen im alten Agypten*, Band II. Mainz.

Kemp, B.J. 1963. 'Excavations at Hierakonpolis Fort, 1905: A Preliminary Note', in: *JEA* 49: 24-8.

Kemp, B.J. 1972. 'Temple and Town in Ancient Egypt', in: Ucko, P., Tringham, R. & Dimbleby, G. (eds) *Man, Settlement and Urbanism*: 657-680. London.

Kemp, B.J. 1973. 'Photographs of the Decorated Tomb at Hierakonpolis', in: *JEA* 59: 36-43.

Kemp, B.J. 1977. 'The Early Development of Towns in Egypt', in: *Antiquity* 51: 185-200.

Kemp, B.J. 1982. 'Automatic Analysis of Predynastic Cemeteries: A New Method for an Old Problem', in: *JEA* 68: 5-15.

Kemp, B.J. 1989. *Ancient Egypt, Anatomy of a Civilization.* London.

Kendall, D.G. 1963. 'A Statistical Approach to Flinders Petrie's Sequence Dating', in: *Bull. Int. Statist. Inst.* 40: 657-80.

Klasens, A. 1957. 'The Excavations of the Leiden Museum of Antiquities at Abu-Roash: Report of the First Season: 1957. Part I', in: *OMRO* 38: 58-68.

Klasens, A. 1958a. 'The Excavations of the Leiden Museum of Antiquities at Abu-Roash: Report of the First Season: 1957. Part II', in: *OMRO* 39: 20-31.

Klasens, A. 1958b. 'The Excavations of the Leiden Museum of Antiquities at Abu-Roash: Report of the Second Season 1958. Part I', in: *OMRO* 39: 32-55.

Klasens, A. 1959. 'The Excavations of the Leiden Museum of Antiquities at Abu-Roash: Report of the Second Season 1958. Part II', in: *OMRO* 40: 41-61.

Klasens, A. 1960. 'The Excavations of the Leiden Museum of Antiquities at Abu-Roash: Report of the Third Season 1959. Part I', in: *OMRO* 41: 69-94.

Klasens, A. 1961. 'The Excavations of the Leiden Museum of Antiquities at Abu Roash: Report of the Third Season: 1959, Part II, Cemetery M', in: *OMRO* 42: 108-128.

Klemm R. & Klemm, D. 1993. *Steine und Steinbrüche im Alten Ägypten.* Berlin.

Köhler, E. Ch. 1992. 'The Pre- and Early Dynastic Pottery of Tell el-Fara'in/Buto', in: van den Brink (ed.) 1992a: 11-22.

Kroeper, K. 1986/87. 'The Ceramics of the Pre/Early Dynastic Cemetery of Minshat Abu Omar', in: *Bulletin of the Egyptological Seminar* 8: 73 - 94.

Kroeper, K. 1988. 'The Excavations of the Munich East-Delta Expedition in Minshat Abu Omar', in: van den Brink (ed.) 1988a: 11-46.

Kroeper, K. 1989a. 'Latest Findings from Minshat Abu Omar', in: Schoske, Sylvia (ed.) *Akten des vierten Internationalen Ägyptologen-Kongresses München 1985*, Band 2. Hamburg: 217-228, Taf. 21-24.

Kroeper, K. 1989b. 'Palestinian Ceramic Imports in Pre- and Protohistoric Egypt', in: De Miroschedji, P. (ed.) *L'urbanisation de la Palestine à l'âge du Bronze ancien, Actes du Colloque d'Emmaüs, 20-25 octobre 1986, Jerusalem*: 407-421. Oxford.

Kroeper, K. 1992. 'Tombs of the Elite in Minshat Abu Omar', in: van den Brink (ed.) 1992a: 127-150.

Kroeper, K. & Krzyzaniak, L. 1992. 'Two Ivory Boxes from Early Dynastic Graves at Minshat Abu Omar', in: Friedman & Adams (eds) 1992: 207-214.

Kroeper, K. & Wildung, D. 1985. *Minshat Abu Omar. Münchner Ostdelta-Expedition. Vorbericht 1978-1984.* Munich.

Kroeper, K. & Wildung, D. 1994. *Minshat Abu Omar: Ein vor- frühgeschichtliche Friedhof im Nildelta,* I, *gräber 1-114.* Mainz.

Kroll, H. 1989. 'Die Pflanzenfunde von Maadi', in Rizkhana, I. and Seeher, J., *Maadi III: The Non-Lithic Small Finds and the Structural Remains of the Predynastic Settlement,* 129-36. Mainz.

Kromer, K. 1973. 'Ausgrabungen in Ägypten', in: *Antike Welt* 4, 3 (1973): 31-4.

Krzyzaniak, L. 1989. 'Recent Archaeological Evidence on the Earliest Settlement in the Eastern Nile Delta', in: Krzyzaniak, L. & Kobusiewicz, M. (eds) *Late Prehistory of the Nile Basin and the Sahara*: 267-85. Poznan.

Krzyzaniak, L. 1991. *Antiquity* 65, Nr. 248, Sept. 1991, p. 529, fig. 11,3.

Krzyzaniak, L. 1992. 'Again on the Earliest Settlement at Minshat Abu Omar', in: van den Brink (ed.) 1992a: 151-156.

Lansing, A. 1935. 'The Museum's Excavations at Hierakonpolis', in: *BMMA Supplement*: 37-45.

Lauer, J-P. 1936. *La Pyramid à degrés. L'architecture.* Cairo.

Lauer, J-P. 1948. *Études complémentaires sur les monuments du roi Zoser à Saqqarah.* Cairo.

Lauer, J-P. 1954. 'L'apport historique des récentes découvertes du Service des Antiquités de l'Égypte dans la nécropole memphite', in: *CRAIBL* 1954: 368-79.

Lauer, J-P. 1962a. *Histoire Monumentale des Pyramides d'Égypte,* I. Cairo.

Lauer, J-P. 1962b. 'Sur l'âge et l'attribution possible de l'excavation monumentale de Zaouiêt el-Aryân', in: *RdÉ* 14: 21-36.

Lauer, J-P. 1985. 'A propos de l'invention de la pierre de taille par Imhotep pour la demeure d'éternité du roi Djoser', in: *Fs. G. Mokhtar*: 61-7. Cairo.

Leclant, J. 1950. 'Compte rendu des fouilles et travaux menés en Égypte durant la campagne 1948-1950. Lisière occidentale du Delta', in: *Orientalia* 19: 494-5.

Leclant, J. 1952. 'Fouilles et travaux en Égypte, 1950-1951. Lisière occidental du Delta (El Qatta)', in: *Orientalia* 21: 247.

Leclant, J. 1953. 'Fouilles et travaux en Égypte, 1951-1952. El Qatta', in: *Orientalia* 22: 98-9.

Leclant, J. 1954. 'Fouilles et travaux en Égypte, 1952-1953. El Qatta', in: *Orientalia* 23: 74.

Leclant, J. 1961. 'Fouilles et travaux en Égypte, 1957-1960. Tourah', in: *Orientalia* 30: 104.

Leclant, J. 1968. 'Fouilles et travaux en Égypte et au Soudan, 1966-1967. Hélouan', in: *Orientalia* 37: 107.

Leclant, J. 1973a. 'Fouilles et travaux en Égypte et au Soudan, 1971-1972. Naqadah', in: *Orientalia* 42: 406.

Leclant, J. 1973b. 'Fouilles et travaux en Égypte et au Soudan, 1971-1972. Tourah', in: *Orientalia* 42: 403.

Leclant, J. 1974. 'Fouilles et travaux en Égypte et au Soudan, 1972-1973. Naqada', in: *Orientalia* 43: 187.

Leclant, J. 1978. 'Fouilles et travaux en Égypte et au Soudan, 1976-1977. Tourah', in: *Orientalia* 47: 274.

Leclant, J. 1979. 'Fouilles et travaux en Égypte et au Soudan, 1977-1978. Tourah', in: *Orientalia* 48: 353-4.

Leclant, J. 1980. 'Fouilles et travaux en Égypte et au Soudan, 1978-1979. Tourah', in: *Orientalia* 49: 368.

Leclant, J. 1982. 'Fouilles et travaux en Égypte et au Soudan, 1980-1981. Naqada', in: *Orientalia* 51: 447.

Leclant, J. & Clerc, G. 1986. 'Fouilles et travaux en Égypte et au Soudan, 1984-1985', in: *Orientalia* 55: 236-319.

Leclant, J. & Clerc, G. 1992. 'Fouilles et travaux en Égypte et au Soudan, 1990-1991. Abousir', in: *Orientalia* 61: 242.

Leclant, J. & Clerc, G. 1994. 'Fouilles et travaux en Égypte et au Soudan, .. el Adwa, Edfu', in: *Orientalia* 62: 427.

Legge, G.F. 1913. 'New Light on Sequence-Dating', in: *PSBA* 35: 101-13.

Legrain, G. 1903. 'Le Shatt er Rigal (Sabah Rigaleh)', in: *ASAE* 4: 220-3.

Lesko, L.H. 1988. 'Seila 1981', in: *JARCE* 25: 215-35.

Logan, T. 1990. 'The Origins of the Jmy-wt Fetish', in: *JARCE* 27: 61- 69.

Loret, V. 1916. 'Quelques notes sur l'arbre <u>ach</u>', in *ASAE* XVI, pp. 33-51.

Lucas, A. 1989. *Ancient Egyptian Materials and Industries*, rev. by J. R. Harris, London.

Lupton, C. 1981. 'The Other Egypt. In Search of the First Pharaohs', in: *Lore (Milwaukee Public Museum)* 31, no.3: 2-21.

Lupton, C. 1982. 'Tombs and Features', in: Hoffman, M.A. (ed.) 1982a: 50-56.

Lythgoe, A.M. 1907. 'An Offering Stand of King Khafra', in: *BMMA* 2: 180-1.

Lythgoe, A.M. & Dunham, D. 1965. *The Predynastic Cemetery N7000. Naqa-ed-Der*. Part IV. Berkeley.

Mace, A.C. 1909. *The Early Dynastic Cemeteries at Naqa-ed-Der*. Part II. Leipzig.

Macramallah, R. 1940. *Un cimetière archaïque de la classe moyenne du peuple à Saqqarah*. Cairo.

Maher, R. 1977. 'Preliminary Report on an Excavation at Nag el Hagg Zeidan', in: *CdE* 52: 203-6.

Maragioglio, V. & Rinaldi, C.A. 1963. *L'architettura delle piramidi menfite,* II. Turin.

Marro, G. 1920. 'Les nécropoles égyptiennes et les fouilles de la mission archéologique Italienne', in: *Annales de l'Université de Grenoble* 33,2: 399-442.

Marro, G. 1929. 'L'esplorazione della necropoli di Gebelen. Dai lavori della Missione Archaeologica Italiana in Egitto', in: *Atti della Societa Italiana per il Progresso delle Scienze*, Torino, 15-22 Settembre 1928: 592-636. Pavia.

Maspero, G. M. 1912. 'Amélineau et ses fouilles d'Abydos 1895-1899', in: *Etudes de mythologie et d'archéologie égyptiennes*, vol. 6: 153-82. Paris.

McArdle, J. 1982. 'Preliminary Report on the Predynastic Fauna of the Hierakonpolis Project', in: Hoffman, M.A. (ed.) 1982a: 116-121.

McArdle, J. 1987. 'Preliminary Report on the Mammalian Fauna from HK-29A', in: Hoffman, M.A. (ed.) 1987: 42-44.

McArdle, J. 1992. 'Preliminary Observations on the Mammalian Fauna from Predynastic Localities at Hierakonpolis', in: Friedman & Adams (eds) 1992: 53-56.

Meiggs, R. 1982. *Trees and Timber in the Ancient Mediterranean World*. Oxford.

Midant-Reynes, B., Buchez, N., Hesse, A. & Lechevalier, C. 1990. 'Le site prédynastique d'Adaima. Rapport préliminaire de la campagne de fouilles 1989', in: *BIFAO* 90: 247-58, pl.I-VIII.

Midant-Reynes, B., Buchez, N., Crubezy, E., Janin, T. 1991. 'Le site prédynastique d'Adaïma. Rapport préliminaire de la deuxième campagne' (avec une annexe de C. de Vartavan), in: *BIFAO* 91: 231-247, pls. 63-70.

Midant-Reynes, B., Buchez, N., Crubezy, E., Janin, T. & Hendrickx, S. 1992. 'Le site prédynastique d'Adaima. Rapport préliminaire de la troisième campagne de fouille', in: *BIFAO* 92: 133-46, 7 fig.

Midant-Reynes, B., Buchez, N., Hesse, A., Lechevalier, C. 1993a. Adaïma: Ramassage raisonné de surface, actes du colloque: 'L'arte e l'ambiente del Sahara preistorico: Dati e interpretazione', *Memorie della Societa Italiana di Scienze Naturali e del Museo Civico di Storia Naturale di Milano,* vol. XXVI, Fascicolo II: 359-363. Milan.

Midant-Reynes, B., Crubezy, E., Janin, T. & van Neer, W. 1993b. 'Le site prédynastique d'Adaïma. Rapport préliminaire de la quatrième campagne de fouille', in: *BIFAO* 93: 349-70.

Midant-Reynes, B, Buchez, N, Crubezy, E. & Janin, T. 1994. 'Le site prédynastique d'Adaïma. Rapport de la cinquième campagne de fouille', in: *BIFAO* 94: 329-48.

Mikesell, M.W. 1969. 'The Deforestation of Mount Lebanon', in: *The Geographical Review*, vol. LIX, no. 1, Jan., 1-28.

Millet, N. 1990. 'The Narmer Macehead and Related Objects', in: *JARCE* 27: 53-59.

Mills, J. & White, R. 1977. 'Natural Resins of Art and Archaeology: Their Sources, Chemistry, and Identification', in: *Studies in Conservation*, vol. 22: 12-31.

Mills, J. & White, R. 1989. 'The Identity of the Resins from the Late Bronze Age Shipwreck at Ulu Burun (Kas)', in: *Archaeometry* 31: 37-44.

Mills, J. & White, R. 1994. *Organic Chemistry of Museum Objects*. London.

Mond, R. & Myers, O.H. 1937. *Cemeteries of Armant* I. London.

Mond, R. & Myers, O.H. 1940. *Temples of Armant*. London.

Monnet-Saleh, J. 1983. 'Les Représentations de Temples sur Plate-formes à Pieux, de la Poterie Gerzéenne d'Egypte', in: *BIFAO* 83: 263-296.

Monnet-Saleh, J. 1987. 'Remarques sur les Representations de la Peinture d'Hierakonpolis (Tombe No. 100)', in: *JEA* 73: 51-58.

Montet, P. 1938. 'Tombeaux de la Ire et de la IVe dynasties à Abou-Roach', in: *Kemi* 7: 11-69.

Montet, P. 1946. 'Tombeaux de la Ire et de la IVe dynasties à Abou-Roach, deuxième partie: inventaire des objets', in: *Kemi* 8: 157-227.

Mortensen, B. 1991. *Change in the Settlement Pattern and Population in the Beginning of the Historical Period,* in: *Ägypten und Levante* 2: 11-37.

Müller, H.W. 1966. *Bericht über im März/April 1966 in das Östliche Nildelta unternommene Erkundungsfahrten*, Bayrische Akademie der Wissenschaften Philosophisch-historische Klasse, Sitzungsberichte, Heft 8, Munich.

Müller-Wollermann, R. 1991. 'Präliminierungen zur ägyptischen Stadt', in: *ZÄS* 118: 48-54.

N.N. 1952. 'El-Qatta. Fouilles du Service des Antiquités, 1951-1952', in: *CdE* 27: 350-1.

Naville, E. 1898. *The Temple of Deir el-Bahari III*. London.

Naville, E., Peet, T.E., Hall, H.R. & Haddon, K. 1914. *The Cemeteries of Abydos*, I. London.

Needler, W. 1984. *Predynastic and Archaic Egypt in the Brooklyn Museum*. Brooklyn.

Nordström, H.A. 1972. *Neolithic and A-Group Sites*. Uppsala.

Nordström, H.A. 1986. 'Ton', in: *LÄ* 6: 629-34. Wiesbaden.

O'Connor, D. 1989 'New Funerary Enclosures (Talberzirke) of the Early Dynastic Period at Abydos', in: *JARCE* 26: 51-86.

O'Connor, D. 1992. 'The Status of Early Egyptian Temples: An Alternative Theory', in: Friedman & Adams (eds) 1992: 83-98.

Omlin, J. A. 1973. *Der Papyrus 55001 und seine satirisch-erotischen Zeichnungen und Inschriften.* Turin.

Oren, E.D. 1973. 'The Overland Route between Egypt and Canaan in the Early Bronze Age', in: *IEJ* 23: 198-205.

Oren, E.D. 1989. 'Early Bronze Age Settlement in Northern Sinai: A Model for Egypto-Canaanite Interconnections', in: De Miroschedji, P. (ed.) *L'urbanisation de la Palestine à l'âge du Bronze ancien. Actes du Colloque d'Emmaus:* 389-405. Oxford.

Oren, E.D. & Yekutieli, Y. 1992. 'Taur Ikhbeineh: Earliest Evidence for Egyptian Interconnections', in: van den Brink (ed.) 1992a: 361-364.

Patch, D.C. 1991. *The Origin and Early Development of Urbanism in Ancient Egypt: A Regional Study.* Ph.D. thesis. University of Pennsylvania.

Payne, J.C. 1973. 'Tomb 100. The Decorated Tomb at Hierakonpolis Confirmed', in: *JEA* 59: 31-5.

Payne, J.C. 1987. 'Appendix to Naqada Excavations Supplement', in: *JEA* 73: 181-90.

Payne, J.C. 1990. 'The Chronology of Predynastic Egyptian Decorated Ware', in: *Eretz-Israel* 21: 77-82.

Payne, J.C. 1992. 'Predynastic Chronology at Naqada', in: Friedman & Adams (eds) 1992: 185-92.

Payne, J.C. 1993. *Catalogue of the Predynastic Egyptian Collection in the Ashmolean Museum.* Oxford.

Peet, T.E. 1914. *The Cemeteries of Abydos*, II. London.

Petrie, W.M.F. & Quibell, J.E. 1896. *Naqada and Ballas*. London.

Petrie, W.M.F. 1896. *Koptos*. London.

Petrie, W.M.F. 1899. 'Sequences in Prehistoric Remains', in: *JRAI* 29: 295-301.

Petrie, W.M.F. 1900. *The Royal Tombs of the First Dynasty*, I. London.

Petrie, W.M.F. 1901. *The Royal Tombs of the Earliest Dynasties*, II. London.

Petrie, W.M.F. 1902. *Abydos,* I. London.

Petrie, W.M.F. 1903. *Abydos,* II. London.

Petrie, W.M.F. 1914. *Tarkhan*, II. London.

Petrie, W.M.F. 1920. *Prehistoric Egypt*. London.

Petrie, W.M.F. 1921. *Corpus of Prehistoric Pottery and Palettes*. London.

Petrie, W.M.F. 1923. *Lahun*, II. London.

Petrie, W.M.F. 1953. *Ceremonial Slate Palettes and Corpus of Protodynastic Pottery*. London.

Petrie, W.M.F. & Mace, A.C. 1901. *Diospolis Parva. The Cemeteries of Abadiyeh and Hu. 1898-1899*. London.

Petrie, W.M.F., Wainwright, G.A. & Mackay, E. 1912. *The Labyrinth, Gerzeh and Mazguneh.* London.

Petrie, W.M.F., Wainwright, G.A. & Gardiner, A. 1913. *Tarkhan I and Memphis V*. London.

Pilc, J. & White, R. 1995. 'Application of FT-IR Microscopy to the Analysis of Paint Binders in Easel Paintings', in *National Gallery Technical Bulletin*, 16 (in press).

Piotrovski, B.B. 1967. 'The Early Dynastic Settlement of Khor Daoud and Wadi-Allaki: The Ancient Route to the Gold Mines', in: *Fouilles en Nubie* (1961-1963): 127-40. Cairo.

Podzorski, P.V. 1988. 'Predynastic Egyptian Seals of Known Provenience in the R.H. Lowie Museum of Anthropology', in: *JNES*, 47: 259-68.

Podzorski, P.V. 1990. *Their Bones shall not Perish. An Examination of Predynastic Human Skeletal Remains from Naga-ed-Dêr in Egypt.* New Malden.

Porat, N. 1989. *Composition of Pottery - Application to the Study of the Interrelations between Canaan and Egypt during the 3rd Millenium B.C.* Unpublished Ph.D. thesis, Hebrew University of Jerusalem.

Porta, G. 1989. *L'Architettura Egizia Delle Origini in Legno e Materiali Leggeri.* Milan.

Posener-Kriéger, P. 1976. *Les archives du temple funéraire de Néferirkarê Kakai*. Cairo.

Posener-Kriéger, P. 1979. 'Les papyrus d'Abousir et l'économie des temples funéraires de l'Ancien Empire', in: Lipinski, E. (ed.) *State and Temple Economy in the Ancient Near East*: 133-51. Leuven.

Puglisi, S.M. 1967. 'Missione per ricerche preistoriche in Egitto', in: *Origini* 1: 301-12.

Pumpenmeier, F. 1993. 'Keramik des Friedhofes U', in: Dreyer 1993: 39-49.

Quibell, J.E. 1898. *El Kab*. London

Quibell, J.E. 1900. *Hierakonpolis*, I. London.

Quibell, J.E. 1905. *Catalogue général des antiquités égyptiennes. nos. 11.001-12.000 et 14.001-14.754. Archaic Objects*. Cairo.

Quibell, J.E. & Green, F.W. 1902. *Hierakonpolis*, II. London.

Radwan, A. 1991. 'Ein Treppengrab der 1. Dynastie aus Abusir', in: *MDAIK* 47: 305-8.

Randall-McIver, D. & Mace, A.C. 1902. *El Amrah and Abydos, 1899-1901*. London.

Redford, D.B. 1981. 'The Acquisition of Foreign Goods and Services in the Old Kingdom', in: *Scripta Mediterranea* 2: 5-16.

Redford, D.B. 1986. 'Egypt and Western Asia in the Old Kingdom', in: *JARCE* 23: 125-43.

Reisner, G.A. 1900-1901. 'Work of the University of California at El-Ahaiwah and Naga-ed-Dêr', in: *EEF Archaeological Report 1900-1901*: 23-5. London.

Reisner, G.A. 1908. *The Early Dynastic Cemeteries at Naqa-ed-Der*. Part I. Leipzig.

Reisner, G.A. 1931. *Mycerinus, The Temples of the Third Pyramid at Giza*. Cambridge (Mass.)

Reisner, G.A. & Firth, C.M. 1910-27. *Archaeological Survey of Nubia*: Reports for 1907-8, 1908-9, 1909-10, 1910-1. Cairo.

Renouf, P. le Page 1887. 'Inscriptions at Küm el-ahmar', in: *PBSA* 10: 73-78.

Ricke, H. 1944. *Bemerkungen zur Agyptischen Baukunst des Alten Reichs*. Zurich.

Rizkana, I. & Seeher, J. 1987. *Maadi I: The Pottery of the Predynastic Settlement*. Mainz.

Rizkana, I. & Seeher, J. 1988. *Maadi II: The Lithic Industries of the Predynastic settlement*. Mainz.

Rizkana, I. & Seeher, J. 1989. *Maadi III: The non-Lithic Finds and the Structural Remains of the Predynastic Settlement*. Mainz.

Rösing, F.W. 1970. 'Prädynastische Menschenreste von der Nilinsel Elephantine vor Aswân (Ägypten)', in: *Homo* 21: 210-20.

Rowe, A. 1938. 'Provisional Notes on the Old Kingdom Inscriptions from the Diorite Quarries', in: *ASAE* 38: 391-6.

Saad, Z.Y. 1947. *Royal Excavations at Saqqara and Helwan (1941-1945)*. Cairo.

Saad, Z.Y. 1951. *Royal Excavations at Saqqara and Helwan (1945-1947)*. Cairo.

Saad, Z.Y. 1969. *The Excavations at Helwan: Art and Civilization in the First and Second Egyptian Dynasties*. Oklahoma.

Samuel, D. 1994. 'A New Look at Bread and Beer', in: *Egyptian Archaeology* 4: 9-11.

Sauneron, S. 1974. 'Les travaux de l'Institut Français d'Archéologie Orientale en 1973-1974. Adaima', in: *BIFAO* 74: 186-95.

Schäfer, H. 1902. *Ein Bruchstück altägyptischer Annalen*. Berlin.

Scharff, A. 1926. *Die archaeologischen Ergebnisse des vorgeschichtlichen Gräberfeldes von Abusir el-Meleq*. Leipzig.

Scharff, A. 1931. *Die Altertümer der Vor- und Frühzeit Ägyptens, I. Werkzeuge, Waffen, Gefässe*. Berlin.

Seidlmayer, S.J. 1988. 'Funerärer Aufwand und soziale Ungleichheit. Eine methodische Anmerkung zum Problem der Rekonstruktion der gesellschaftlichen Gliederung aus Friedhofsfunden', in: *GM* 104: 25-51.

Seidlmayer, S.J. 1990. *Gräberfelder aus dem Übergang vom Alten zum Mittleren Reich. Studien zur Archäologie der Ersten Zwischenzeit. Studien zur Archäologie und Geschichte Altägyptens* 1. Heidelberg.

Seidlmayer, S.J. 1992. 'Beispiele nubischer Keramik aus Kontexten des hohen Alten Reiches aus Elephantine', in: *Gs. P. Behrens, Afrikanistische Arbeitspapiere Sondernummer 1991,* 337-50. Köln.

Seidlmayer, S.J. 1995. 'Die staatliche Anlage der 3. Dyn. in der Nordweststadt von Elephantine, Archäologische und historische Probleme', in: Bietak, M. (ed.), *Haus und Palast im Alten Ägypten,* Internationales Symposium 8 bis 11 April 1992 in Kairo, Untersuchungen der Zweigsteele Kairo des ÖAI, Vienna (forthcoming).

Seidlmayer, S.J. *Elephantine 12: Ausgrabung in der Nordweststadt von Elephantine 1979-1982* (forthcoming). Mainz.

Serpico, M. 'Chemical Analysis of Coniferous Resins from ancient Egypt using Gas Chromatography/Mass Spectrometry (GC/MS)' to appear in: *Proceedings of the Seventh International Congress of Egyptologists* (forthcoming).

Sethe, K. 1917. 'Ein ägyptisches Denkmal des Alten Reichs von der Insel Kythera mit dem Namen des Sonnenheiligtums des Königs Userkaf', in: *ZÄS* 53: 55-58.

Sethe, K. 1933. *Urkunden des Alten Reiches,* I. Leipzig.

Shearer, G.L. 1987. 'Use of Diffuse Reflectance Fourier Transform Infrared Spectroscopy in Art and Archaeological Conservation', in Black, J. (ed.) 1987: 253-256.

Shehata, R.Z.A. 1989. 'Status Report on the Predynastic Cemetery of Khozam', in: *VA* 6: 165-6.

Sliwa, J. 1992. 'On the Meaning of the so-called Sinusoidal Walls in Egypt during the Middle Kingdom', in: *Intellectual Heritage of Egypt (Studia Aegyptiaca* XIV), Budapest: 523-526.

Smith, H.S. 1966. 'The Nubian B-Group', in: *Kush* 14: 69-124.

Smith, H.S. 1991. 'The Development of the 'A-Group' Culture in Northern Lower Nubia', in: Davies, W.V. (ed.), *Egypt and Africa: Nubia from Prehistory to Islam*: 92-111. London.

Smith, W.S. 1946. *A History of Egyptian Sculpture and Painting in the Old Kingdom,* Boston.

Soukiassian, G. Wuttman, M. & Schaad, D. 1990. 'La ville d'Ayn-Asil à Dakhla, État des recherches', in: *BIFAO* 90: 347-58.

Sourouzian, H. 1988. 'Standing Royal Colossi of the Middle Kingdom Reused by Ramesses II', in: *MDAIK* 44: 229-54.

Spencer, A.J. 1979. *Brick Architecture in Ancient Egypt.* Warminster.

Spencer, A.J. 1980. *Catalogue of Egyptian Antiquities in the British Museum,* V. *Early Dynastic Objects.* London.

Stager, L.E. 1985. 'The First fruits of Civilization', in Tubb, J. N. (ed.) 1985: 172-188.

Stewart, H.M. 1979. *Egyptian Stelae, Reliefs and Paintings from the Petrie Collection II.* Warminster.

Swelim, N. 1983. *Some Problems on the History of the Third Dynasty, Archaeological and Historical Studies* 7. Alexandria.

Swelim, N. 1987. *The BYU Expedition to Seila, The Pyramid of Seila, Season 1987,* unpublished newsletter.

Tackholm, V. 1974. *Students' Flora of Egypt.* Beirut.

Trad, M. 1992. 'The Sequence of Artist's Strokes on a Sherd from Hierakonpolis', in Friedman & Adams (eds) 1992: 65-8.

Trigger, B. 1972. 'Determinants of Urban Growth in Pre-Industrial Societies', in: Ucko, P.J., Tringham, R. & Dimbleby, G.W. (eds.) *Man, Settlement and Urbanism*: 575-99. London.

Trigger, B. 1985. 'The Evolution of Pre-Industrial Cities: A Multilinear Perspective', in: *Mélanges offerts à Jean Vercoutter*: 343-53.

Tubb, J. N. 1985. (ed.) *Palestine in the Bronze and Iron Ages: Papers in Honour of Olga Tufnell.* London.

Tutundzic, S.P. 1992. 'Meaning and Use of the Term 'Predynastic' in Egyptian Archaeology', in: *Sesto congresso internazionale de egittologia. Atti.* Vol. I: 605-11. Turin.

Uphill, E.P. 1988. *Egyptian Towns and Cities.* Princes Risborough.

171

Valbelle, D. 1981. *Satis et Anoukis*. Mainz.

Valloggia, M. 1980. 'Deux objets thériomorphes découverts dans le Mastaba V de Balat', in: *Livre du Centenaire*: 104: 143-51.

van den Brink, E.C.M. (ed.) 1988a. *The Archaeology of the Nile Delta; Problems and Priorities*. Proceedings of the Seminar held in Cairo, 19-22 October 1986, on the occasion of the fifteenth anniversary of the Netherlands Institute of Archaeology and Arabic Studies in Cairo. Amsterdam.

van den Brink, E.C.M. 1988b. 'The Amsterdam University Survey Expedition to the Northeastern Nile Delta (1984-1986)'; with a Contribution of W. van Zeist, in: van den Brink (ed.) 1988a: 65-114.

van den Brink, E.C.M. (ed.) 1992a. *The Nile Delta in Transition; 4th - 3rd millenium BC*. Proceedings of the Seminar held in Cairo, 21-24 October 1990, at the Netherlands Institute of Archaeology and Arabic Studies. Tel Aviv.

van den Brink, E.C.M. 1992b. 'Corpus and Numerical Evaluation of the "Thinite" Potmarks', in: Friedman & Adams (eds) 1992: 265-296.

van den Brink, E.C.M. 1992c. 'Preliminary Report on the Excavations at Tell Ibrahim Awad, Seasons 1988-1990', in: van den Brink (ed.) 1992a, 43-68.

van den Brink, E.C.M. 1996. 'The incised *Serekh*-Signs of Dynasties 0 and 1; Part I: The Complete Jars', this volume.

van den Brink, E.C.M. 'Another Record of Horus Crocodile ? A Brief Discussion of *MAO* T. 160.1'. forthcoming.

van den Brink, E.C.M. 'The *Serekh* Signs of Dynasties 0-1. Part II: Fragments' (in preparation).

van de Walle, B. 1940. 'Empreintes de sceaux archaiques', in: *Fouilles de Elkab, documents*: 91-8. Brussels.

Vandier, J. 1955. *Manuel d'archéologie égyptienne, II. Les Grandes époques, l'architecture religieuse et civile*. Paris.

Vermeersch, P.M., Paulissen, E., Huyge, D., Neumann, K., Van Neer, W. and Van Peer, P. 1992. 'Predynastic Hearths in Upper Egypt', in: Friedman & Adams, (eds) 1992: 163-172.

Vertesalji, P. 1988. 'Naqada Chronology Reconsidered', in Cherif, A. (ed.), *Résumes des Communications. Cinquième Congres International d'Egyptologie*: 278. Cairo.

von Deines, H., Grapow, H. & Westendorf, W. 1958. *Grundrisse der Medizin der alten Ägypter,* IV 1. Berlin.

von den Driesch, A. 1986. *Fische im Alten Ägypten, eine osteoarchäologische Studie, documenta naturae* 34. Munich.

Weigall, A.E.P. 1911.'Miscellaneous Notes', in: *ASAE* 11: 170-6.

Weill, R. 1912. 'Un temple de Noutirkha-Zosir à Heliopolis', in: *Sphinx* 15: 9-26.

Weill, R. 1961. *Recherches sur la Ier Dynastie et les Temps Prépharaoniques*. Cairo.

Wenke, R.J. et al. 1988. 'Kôm el-Hisn: Excavation of an Old Kingdom Settlement in the Egyptian Delta', in: *JARCE* 25: 5-34.

Westendorf, W. 1982. 'Palette, Schminck-', in: *LÄ* 4: 654-656.

White, R. 1990. 'Analysis of Resinous Materials', in: *'Atiqot* XIX: 81-88.

Whitehouse, H. 1992. 'The Hierakonpolis Ivories in Oxford. A Progress Report', in Friedman & Adams (eds) 1992: 77-82.

Wildung, D. 1981. *Ägypten vor den Pyramiden. Münchner Ausgrabungen in Ägypten*. Mainz.

Wilkinson, E.M. 1974. 'Techniques of Data Analysis: Seriation Theory', in: Technische und Naturwissenschaftliche Beiträge zur Feldarchaologie. *Archaeo-Physika* 5: 1-134. Köln.

Wilkinson, T.A.H. 1993a. *Egypt in Transition: Predynastic - Early Dynastic Chronology and the Effects of State Formation*. Cambridge (unpub. Ph.D. thesis).

Wilkinson, T.A.H. 1993b. 'The identification of Tomb B.1 at Abydos: refuting the existence of a king Ro/Iry-Hor', in: *JEA* 79: 241-3.

Williams, B.B. 1980. 'The Lost Pharaohs of Nubia', in: *Archaeology* 33: 18.

Williams, B.B. 1986. *Excavations between Abu Simbel and the Sudan Frontier, Keith C.Seele, Director*. Part 1: *The A-Group Royal Cemetery at Qustul: Cemetery L*. Chicago.

Williams, B.B. 1988. 'Narmer and the Coptos Colossi', in: *JARCE* 25: 35- 59.

Williams, B.B. & Logan, T. 1987. 'The Metropolitan Museum Knife Handle and Aspects of Pharaonic Imagery before Narmer', in: *JNES* 46: 245-285.

Wilson, J.A. 1951. *The Burden of Egypt*. Chicago.

Wilson, J.A. 1955. 'Buto and Hierakonpolis in the Geography of Egypt', in: *JNES* 14: 209-236.

Wilson, J.A. 1960. 'Egypt throughout the New Kingdom, Civilization without Cities', in: Kraeling, C.H. & Adams, R.M. (eds) *City Invincible*: 124-36. Chicago.

Winter, E. 1957. 'Zur Deutung der Sonnenheiligtümer der 5. Dyn.', in: *WZKM* 54: 222-33.

Wood, W. 1974. 'A Reconstruction of the Triads of King Mycerinus', in: *JEA* 60: 82-93.

Yacoub, F. 1981. 'The Archaic Tombs at Tura el-Asmant', in: *ASAE* 64: 159-61.

Yacoub, F. 1983. 'Excavations at Tura el-Asmant', in: *JSSEA* 13: 103-6.

Yukutieli, Y. 'An Imported Pot Redated', in: *Friends of the Petrie Museum Newsletter* 13 (in press).

Zaki, A. & Iskander, Z. 1942. 'Ancient Egyptian Cheese', in: *ASAE* 41: 295-313.

Ziegler, Ch. 1990. *Musée du Louvre, Catalogue des stèles, peintures et reliefs égyptiens de l'Ancien Empire et de la Première Période Intermédiaire*. Paris.

Ziermann, M. 1993. *Elephantine 16, Befestigungsanlagen und Stadtentwicklung in der Frühzeit und im frühen Alten Reich*. Mainz.

Zimmermann, A.S. 1974. 'Il cimitero protodinastico', in: *Antinoe (1965-1968). Missione Archaeologica in Egitto dell'Universita di Roma*: 23-31. Rome.

Zohary, M. 1962. *Plant Life of Palestine*. New York.

Zohary, M. 1966. *Flora Palaestina*, Part One, Text, Israel Academy of Sciences and Humanities, Jerusalem.

Zohary, M. 1972. *Flora Palaestina*, Part Two, Text, Israel Academy of Sciences and Humanities, Jerusalem.

Zohary, M. 1973. *Geobotanical Foundations of the Middle East*, vol II. Stuttgart.

Zohary, D. & Hopf, M. 1993. *Domestication of Plants in the Old World*. Oxford.

Abbreviations used in the above bibliography

AfO Archiv für Orientforschung. Berlin.

ASAE Annales du Service des Antiquités de l'Égypte. Cairo.

BIFAO Bulletin de l'Institut français d'Archeologie Orientale. Cairo.

Bi. Or. Bibliotheca Orientalis. Leiden.

BMMA Bulletin of the Metropolitan Museum of Art. New York.

BMFA Bulletin of the Museum of Fine Arts. Boston.

BMRAH Bulletin des musées Royaux d'art et d'histoire. Brussels.

CdE Chronique d'Égypte.

CRAIBL Comptes-rendus des séances de l'Academie des Inscriptions et Belles-Lettres. Paris.

GM Gottinger Mizsellen. Göttingen.

IEJ Israel Exploration Journal. Jerusalem.

JARCE Journal of the American Research Center in Egypt. New York.

JEA Journal of Egyptian Archaeology. London.

JNES Journal of Near Eastern Studies. Chicago.

JRAI Journal of the Royal Anthropological Institute of Great Britian and Ireland. London.

JSSEA Journal of the Society for the Study of Egyptian Antiquities. Toronto.

LÄ Lexikon der Ägyptologie. Wiesbaden.

MDAIK Mitteilungen des Deutschen Archaölogischen Instituts Abteilung Kairo. Wiesbaden.

NARCE Newsletter of the American Research Center in Egypt.

OMRO Oudheidkundige Mededelingen uit het Rijksmuseum van Oudheden te Leiden. Leiden.

PSBA Proceedings of the Society of Biblical Archaeology. London.

RdE Revue d'Égyptologie. Paris.

SASAE Supplément aux Annales du Service des Antiquités de l'Égypte. Cairo.

VA Varia Aegyptiaca. San Antonio.

WZKM Wiener Zeitschrift für die Kunde des Morgenlandes. Vienna.

ZÄS Zeitschrift für Ägyptische Sprache und Altertumskunde. Leipzig/Berlin.

THE PLATES

Plate 1 (Adams)

a. Tomb 10 after excavation looking east.
   (*right*)

b. Tomb 11 after excavation looking north.
   (*below*)

Plate 2 (Friedman)

a. View along the north side of the complex at HK29A facing east towards the curved
end of the courtyard. Wall trench 1 dominates the scene. Remnants of the mud-brick
Wall 1 run parallel to the wall trench to the south. The raised mound of debris running
perpendicular to the trench is a baulk. Smaller trenches which outline the ancilliary
buildings along the northern perimeter are visible to the east of the baulk.
(Photo: M.A. Hoffman)

b. View along the south side of the complex at HK29A facing east. Three of the four
large post-holes which compose the façade of Structure III are visible along the
southern side of the courtyard. The raised area in the centre of the court is the
unexcavated sand which originally covered the entire paved area. (Photo: R. Friedman)

Plate 3 (Midant-Reynes)

a. Settlement. Surface: Amratian sherd.
   (Photo: A. Lecler, IFAO)

b. Settlement. Surface: clay seal showing
   horned animals (antelopes or gazelles)
   under an enigmatic motif.
   (Photo: A. Lecler, IFAO)

c. Settlement. Surface: Gerzean sherds.
   (Photo: A. Lecler, IFAO)

d. Settlement. Surface: incised sherd.
   (Photo: A. Lecler, IFAO)

e. Settlement. Surface: plane (h = 95mm)
   (Photo: A. Lecler, IFAO)

f. Settlement. Surface: heat-treated blade-
   core (h = 30mm). (Photo: A. Lecler, IFAO)

Plate 4 (Midant-Reynes)

a. Simple burial without grave-goods and without the head. (Photo: E. Crubezy – T. Janin) (*left*)

b. Settlement: living-floor. Human face in the middle of the photograph. (Photo: B. Midant-Reynes) (*below*)

Plate 5 (Adams, Friedman)

a. The 'Tomb 4' burial.

b. Detail of a large post-hole of Structure III. On the left are the remnants of floor 'e', a localised plastering, and the bricks of Wall 4, which may have served as a threshold for the structure's entrance. Behind the post-hole is Wall trench 2 outlining the internal divisions within this major building. The small post-holes to the right are of unclear function.

Plate 6 (Kroeper)

a. Grave 63

b. Grave 305

c. Grave 816

d. Grave 1340

Plate 7 (Kroeper)

a. Grave 160

b. Grave 400

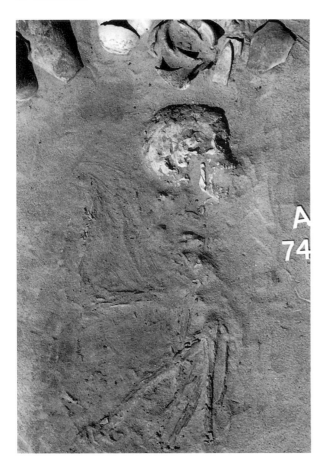

c. Grave 741

d. Grave 758

Plate 8 (Kroeper)

a. Grave 862

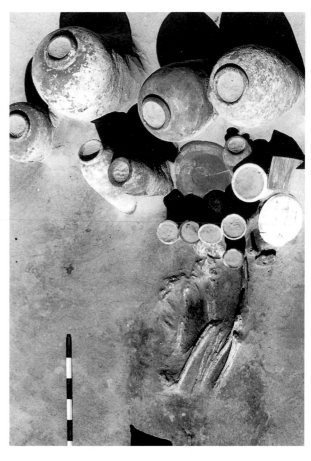

b. Grave 1050

c. Grave 1287

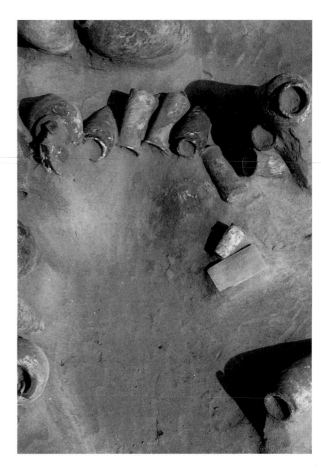

d. Grave 1295

Plate 9 (Kroeper)

a. Grave 1666

b. Grave 2200

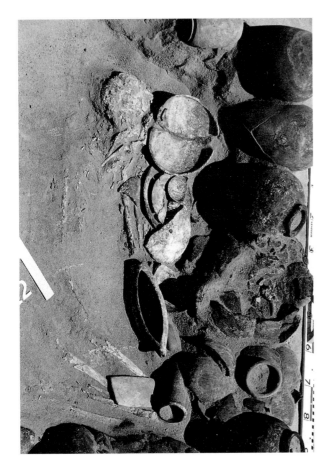

c. Grave 322

A
1147

d. Grave 1147

Plate 10 (Kroeper)

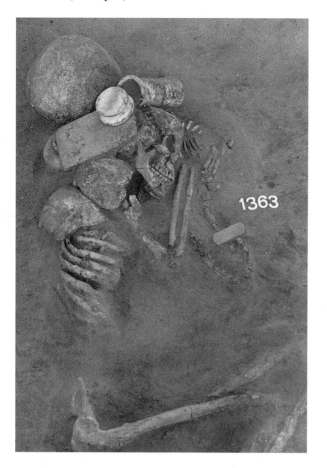

a. Grave 1363

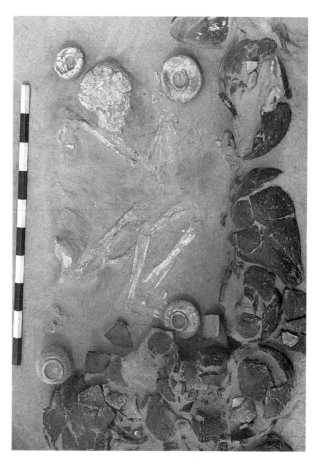

b. Grave 1430

c. Grave 1030

d. Grave 1150

Plate 11 (Kroeper)

a. Grave 305

b. Grave 816

c. Grave 400

d. Grave 434

e. Grave 1295

f. Grave 50

g. Grave 2200

h. Grave 1363

i. Grave 1150

All approx. 1:3

Plate 12 (Midant-Reynes)

a. View of the settlement along the cultivated land. (Photo: B. Midant-Reynes)

b. Ens.1002: trenches and mudholes. (Photo: T. Anderson)

Plate 13 (Midant-Reynes)

a. Ens.1002: possible post-hole with an elongated rod-shaped hammerstone as a wedging-stone. (Photo: T. Anderson)

b. Ens.1002: small basin smeared with mud. (Photo: T. Anderson)

Plate 14 (Midant-Reynes)

a. Ens.1001: remains of a living floor consisting of consolidated sand. (Photo: A. Lecler, IFAO)

b. Ens.1001: the small wooden posts constitute an earlier level of occupation. (Photo: B. Midant-Reynes)

c. S.11: double burial (head to the south). (Photo: E. Crubezy – T. Janin)

Plate 15 (Midant-Reynes)

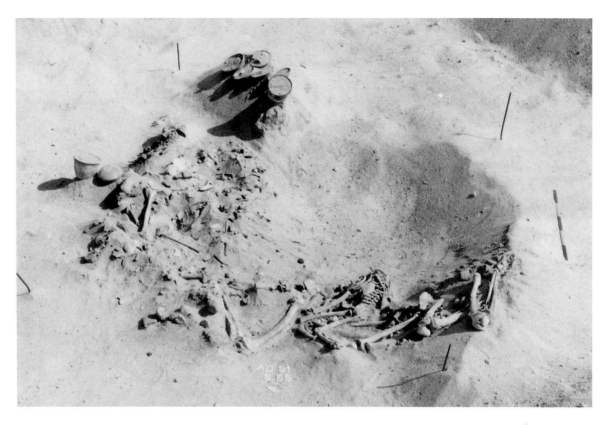

a. S55: five bodies associated with a big hearth. (Photo: E. Crubezy – T. Janin)

b. Pot-burial of a very young child and burial in a clay coffin. (Photo: L. Watrin)

Plate 16 (Adams and Porat)

a. UC.36617, Tomb Unknown
    (Group A)

b. UC.17387, ?Tomb of Djer (Group A)

c. UC.36616, UC.17407 and UC.36615, Tomb Unknown (Group A, A & B)

d. UC.36613 and UC.36614, Tomb Unknown (Group B & A)

Plate 17 (Adams and Porat)

a. UC.17390, ?Tomb of Djer (Group B)

b. UC.35785 and UC.36610, Tomb Unknown (Group B)

c. UC.36611 and UC.17437, ?Tomb of Djer (Group B)

d. UC.17427, Tomb Unknown
   (not analysed, probably Group B)

Plate 18 (Adams and Porat)

a. UC.17422, Tomb of Semerkhet (Group B)

b. UC.17429 and UC.17428, Tomb of Semerkhet (Group B)

c. UC.36609, Royal Tombs II, pl.LVB, 206 (Group B)

Plate 19 (Adams and Porat)

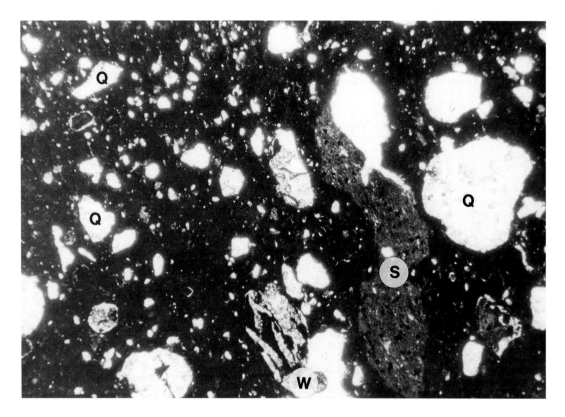

a. UC.17407, width of field 3.5 mm, plane-polarized light. Temper components in a typical Group A sample. Q-quartz; S-shale fragments (note minute particles of iron oxides); W-weathered basalt. Note grading of quartz (bright white grains) from sand to silt size.

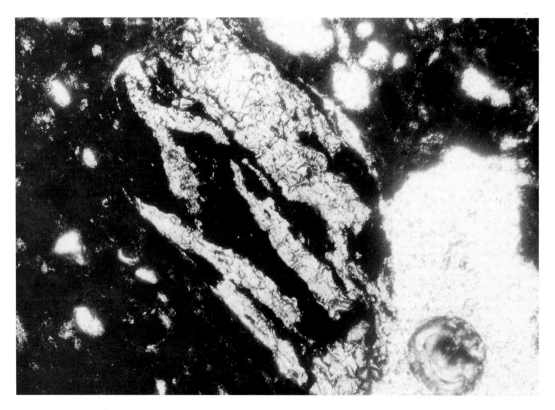

b. UC.17407, width of field 0.9 mm, plane-polarized light. A weathered basalt fragment. Two phases can be identified, dark and light.

Plate 20 (Adams and Porat)

a. BM.35569, width of field 3.5 mm, plane-polarized light. A single sand-size grain of quartz (bright white) within matrix rich in silty quartz.

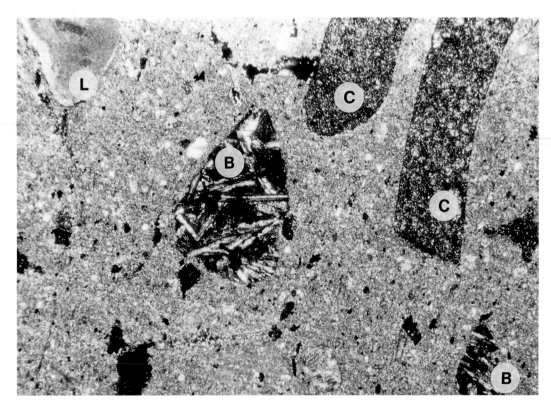

b. UC.17390, width of field 3.5 mm, crossed polarizers. Temper components in a typical Group B sample. B-basalt; C-chert; L-limestone. The matrix is rich in carbonate particles.

Plate 21 (Adams and Porat)

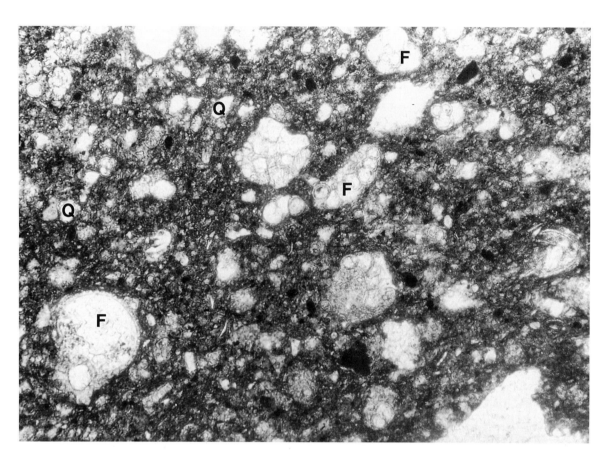

UC.36616, width of field 0.9 mm, plane-polarized light. Typical calcareous matrix of Group B. F-foraminifera; Q-quartz.

Plate 22 (Seidlmayer)

The Third-Dynasty administrative complex at Elephantine, seen from the west.

Plate 23 (Seidlmayer)

Seal-impression of king *Z3-nḫt* from Beit Khallaf (Liverpool University E5251) showing remains of a cartouche-sign.

Plate 24 (Brink)

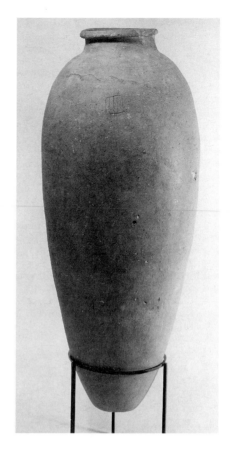

a. Type I, No. 1. Abusir el-Meleq
    Tomb 1021. Berlin 19330

b. Type I, No. 3. 'Rafiah'. Israel
    Museum 69. 31. 367

c. Type I, No. 3 (detail). Israel Museum 69.31.367

Plate 25 (Brink)

a. Type IIa, No. 5. el-Beda. Ismailia
   Museum, inv.nr. 1928

b. Type IIb, No. 7. Turah Tomb 16.
   g. 9. Kunsthistorisches Museum
   Wien, ÄS 6808

c. Type IIb, No. 7. Turah Tomb 16.
   g. 9. Kunsthistorisches Museum
   Wien, ÄS 6808

d. Type IIb, No. 7 (detail). Kunsthistorisches
   Museum Wien, ÄS 6808

Plate 26 (Brink)

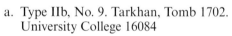

a. Type IIb, No. 9. Tarkhan, Tomb 1702.
   University College 16084

b. Type III, No. 11. Minshat Abu Omar,
   Tomb 1210. 21

Plate 27 (Brink)

a. Type III, No. 12. Minshat Abu Omar,
   Tomb 520. 3

b. Type III, No. 12 (detail). Minshat Abu Omar, Tomb 520. 3

Plate 28 (Brink)

a. Type III, No. 13. Minshat Abu Omar,
   Tomb 160. 1

b. Type III, No. 13 (detail). Minshat Abu Omar, Tomb 160. 1

Plate 29 (Brink)

a. Type III, No. 16a. Abydos, Tomb B 7/9

b. Type III, No. 16b. Abydos, Tomb B 19

Plate 30 (Brink)

a. Type III, No. 17. Eastern Nile Delta.
Metropolitan Museum of Art 61. 122

b. Type III, No. 20. Minshat Abu
Omar, Tomb 44. 3

c. Type III, No. 20 (detail). Minshat Abu Omar,
Tomb 44. 3

Plate 31 (Brink)

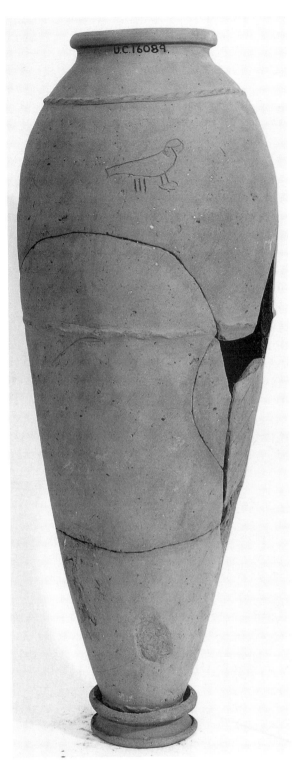

a. Type IVa, No. 22. Abydos, Tomb B1.
   University College 16089

b. Type IVa, No. 22 (detail). Abydos, Tomb B1.
University College 16089

Plate 32 (Brink)

a. Type IVa, No. 23. Tarkhan, Tomb 414.
University College 16083

b. Type IVa, No. 23 (detail). Tarkhan, Tomb 414.
University College 16083